The Thinking Dog

Crossover to Clicker Training

Gail Tamases Fisher

Dogwise™ Publishing

Wenatchee, Washington U.S.A.

The Thinking Dog
Crossover to Clicker Training
Gail Tamases Fisher

Dogwise Publishing
A Division of Direct Book Service, Inc.
403 South Mission Street, Wenatchee, Washington 98801
509-663-9115, 1-800-776-2665
www.dogwisepublishing.com / info@dogwisepublishing.com
© 2009 Gail Tamases Fisher

Illustrations: Verne Foster
Photos: Karen Hocker
Graphic Design: Lindsay Peternell

Library of Congress Cataloging-in-Publication Data:
  Fisher, Gail Tamases.
    The thinking dog : crossover to clicker training / Gail Tamases Fisher.
        p. cm.
    Includes bibliographical references.
    ISBN 978-1-929242-62-7
    1. Dogs--Training. 2. Clicker training (Animal training) I. Title.
    SF431.F58 2009
    636.7'0887--dc22

                                    2008051809

ISBN13: 978-1-929242-62-7

Printed in the U.S.A.

To all my dogs who have taught me so much.

Luci, Loki, Wilhelmina, Tisza, Juno, Reveille,
Paprikash, Argus, Calisto, Adam, Apple, Solo,
Orion, Shura, Katie, Hobbes, and
Mayday, my crossover dog.

How I wish I knew then what I know now.

More praise for *The Thinking Dog*

I've never been interested in dog training books. They tend to be prescriptive and dull—"take your dog in your left hand and your 2 x 4 in your right..." I grew up in a generation which believed that there were just two ways to train dogs—the wrong way and my way. One of my old sled dog mentors taught me to "make them run and then make them like it." Back then the how to train your bird dog book would say, "...if you have a problem try plan A, or try plan B, and plan C... get another dog!" When I watch popular TV shows, visit a dog shelter, or evaluate some service dog training program, I think, "things haven't changed so much."

But I was fascinated by this book. I followed Gail Fisher's thoughts through her transformation from an old-timer to somebody who could see how the advances in learning theory applied to dog training. Her historical analysis of "what happened?" and her generosity to the individuals who facilitated those happenings become a powerful teaching tool in Fisher's hands. She is very clear, with an interesting teaching technique which bridges the theoretical with the applied. At last I could see the connection between learning theory and dog training in a way I never have before. I now feel so sorry for all those dogs I trained!

Ray Coppinger, co-author of *Dogs: A New Understanding of Canine Origin, Behavior and Evolution*

Gail understands the questions and concerns of a crossover trainer because that is what she is. She was a successful and well known trainer who "crossed over" into clicker training. Her book presents a clear, easy-to-follow process for making the transition. Gail's book will make a great addition to the clicker library, easing crossover trainers through the process of becoming thinking trainers.

Alexandra Kurland, author of *Clicker Training for Horses*

TABLE OF CONTENTS

Acknowledgments vii
Preface..ix
Introduction.. 1

PART I: Putting it in Perspective: Past and Present **5**
1. Crossing Over 6
2. Learning and Training Fundamentals 15
3. Clicker Training Basics 36
4. Pitfalls and Payoffs to Crossing Over 48

PART II: Crossing Over...Just Do It!.. **59**
5. Build Your Clicker Skills... 60
6. Getting Behaviors... 81
7. The Joy of Shaping 109
8. Building Behavior 128
9. Building Reliability, Precision, and Speed...................................... 166

PART III: Brass Tacks **183**
10. Punishment, Corrections, and the Crossover Trainer 184
11. Engaging Your Dog 219
12. Putting It All Together.. 233

Afterword... 290
Appendix A. Cornerstones and Charts 291
Appendix B. Developing your skills.. 293
Appendix C. They're all tricks to your dog....................................... 296
Appendix D. Farm Life: A program of polite living for thinking dogs 300
Sources and Resources... 303
Bibliography.. 306
Index... 307
About the Author.. 317

ACKNOWLEDGMENTS

I have the most wonderful staff in the world. A more dedicated, principled, compassionate group of people cannot be found. Topping the list is Myrian Bergeron, my right hand for the past 15 years, and several incarnations prior to that. Wendy Bergeron and Shari Sarris whose training wisdom, kindness, counsel, advice, and philosophical synchronicity keep me focused. Donna Jones, Pam Stafford, Rachael Cody, Jean MacKenzie, and Ann Jowdy whose dedication to doing the right thing for the pets in our care and the clients they deal with daily allows me to sleep at night, and gave me the freedom to write this book. The instructors who shared the crossover experience, pitfalls, and joys with me, Judy Pollard, LynnMarie Millette, MaryBeth Tessier, Stacy Allard, Wendy, DJ, and Jean, and the other instructors, trainers, and staff at All Dogs Gym®, too numerous to name (and terrified I'll forget someone). Thank you all.

It is said, "When the student is ready, the teacher will appear." Nothing could be truer for my life, education, and evolvement in dogs. I have had the good fortune to have been mentored by some of the most wonderfully generous teachers, trainers, and friends throughout my career—in each training incarnation, each important in my journey prior to and in crossing over.

Susan Mayer, my first dog training instructor who put up with my incessant questions, recommended books, and convinced me I could teach. The late Olive Point, whose focus on teaching *people* was instrumental to my growth and who convinced me to teach a university course for dog trainers and instructors—leading to the greatest educational experience of my life. Jack Volhard, responsible for my first training epiphany, who put me in the front of the room, helped hone my public speaking skills, and whose collaboration and camaraderie I enjoyed in the many camps, seminars, and the two books we wrote together. Karen Pryor, whose books headed me toward the principles of clicker training long before I had the good fortune to meet her. My crossover odyssey was precipitated and guided by Gary Wilkes who challenged long-held beliefs, and whose countless hours talking to me on the phone often confused me as much as answered my questions—but in my confusion, I got it.

For this book itself, I am grateful to so many: Verne Foster and Karen Hocker, illustrator and photographer extraordinaire. The students, trainers, and dogs who helped demonstrate my words: Wendy Bergeron, Rachael Cody and Gabe, Kris DiBurro and Vision, Beth Gutteridge and Cami, Michelle and Bruce Kenney and Cody, Denise

Lind and Duke, LynnMarie Millette and Becke, Shari Sarris and Logan and Mazzie, MaryBeth Tessier and Finlay, Stella and Dharma, Carolyn VanderHorst and Kaylee, and Julie Wolf and Ryder. And our clients and students who loaned us their dogs for photographs: Darby, Dax, Journey, Kochi, Rosie, and Siku.

Elizabeth Kershaw and Corally Burmaster provided incalculable help advising, critiquing and encouraging me, not just for this book—which has been invaluable!—but with training, learning, growing, developing, progressing, and continuing this wonderful crossover journey. Chase Binder who helped early on. And the wonderful folks at Dogwise Publishing, most ably led by Charlene, Larry, and Nathan Woodward. And Lindsay Peternell for putting it all together, never losing patience with my nitpicking, and working just as late into the night as I did.

And finally, Skip Ashooh. Words cannot express, and really aren't necessary, to describe your profound contribution. Just as importantly, you wouldn't want me to.

PREFACE

The title of a book matters. It can profoundly affect the book's impact and influence. Consider if the first edition of *Don't Shoot the Dog!* had instead been called *Practical Use of Positive Reinforcement in Human Behavioral Interaction*. Such a title is unlikely to have sparked a sea of change in the world of dog training. While every dog book author certainly hopes their book will have such far-reaching impact as *Don't Shoot the Dog!* has had, I am not so arrogant as to imply this one will (though I can dream …can't I?). Nonetheless, a title is important.

I advocated for the title *The Thinking Dog* despite some expressed concern that its meaning isn't inherently clear to those unfamiliar with how clicker training works, or that some dog owners might fear training a dog that thinks rather than one that simply "obeys." But this book is about training that inspires your dog—that ignites your dog's mind. So let me start by allaying such fears and describe what I mean by a thinking dog.

A thinking dog works in partnership with the trainer, offering behaviors for the trainer to pursue, to guide, and shape the dog's actions. Once trained, a thinking dog makes choices—the right choices…for us, and for the dog. A thinking dog chooses to leave untouched the food on the table; chooses to greet the visitor at the door with all four feet on the floor; chooses to chew the toy lying next to the expensive shoe rather than vice versa.

A trained dog will "obey," but a thinking dog goes far beyond obeying commands. It goes beyond training your dog to sit, lie down, and come when called. While teaching responsiveness to commands is a component of any training, achieving *voluntary* good behavior—what most of us want from our dogs—is about so much more. It's about when a dog is faced with options, he considers them and chooses the right one—the good behavior. A thinking dog *chooses* to behave the way you want him to behave, not because you gave him a command, not because you manage or supervise her, but because you've taught your dog that the right choice for her is the choice that's right for you, too.

Some might be frightened at the idea of having a thinking dog—might the dog be too clever? Too creative or resourceful? Is a thinking dog more difficult to control, more challenging, harder to live with? The answer is, "No." A thinking dog is the greatest joy, the greatest dog partner imaginable, behaving in ways that make both of us happy.

There was a time in my 30 plus years as a professional dog trainer when I could not have envisioned recommending to my clients and students that they encourage their dogs to think, a time when I could not imagine encouraging a dog's individual initiative. In my "prior training life," a clever, enterprising dog was a greater challenge, requiring more management, more control, more domination, more correction. In my former methods a bright, thinking dog caused frustration for most owners, exasperating their patience, often leading to anger and other relationship-damaging reactions.

Far from fearing cleverness, I now appreciate and delight in watching a dog's mind turn on—seeing the wheels begin to turn, seeing the dog start to use his initiative—to think. As you will see, this about-face, this complete change of attitude happened when I became a crossover trainer. I hope this book sparks the same epiphany for you and your dog—delighting in and relishing your training collaboration—training your *thinking* dog. After all, a dog's mind is a terrible thing to waste.

INTRODUCTION

I attended my first clicker training seminar in 1996. Little did I know at the time that this event would be life-changing, sparking a total transformation in both how I train dogs and teach people. Clicker training was to become the third incarnation in my career as a professional dog trainer. I was about to become a "**crossover**" trainer—a trainer with experience in another method who "crosses over" to clicker training.

Virtually every dog owner has opinions and beliefs about training a dog—some degree of "crossover" thinking. Regardless of your training background and experience, chances are you have ideas about how to train a dog, and you've had some success. You may be curious about clicker training, but you like what you've been doing. Or you think there may be something better, but you aren't convinced that your "old" approach isn't the best. Or you're trying to be a clicker trainer, but your prior method creeps in, perhaps without your even being aware. Or maybe you, like so many others, have had some exposure to something called "clicker training," which has resulted in basic misconceptions about just what clicker training really is.

Changing from one approach to another is not easy. I don't mean refining a technique, finding an easier way to train "down," a better way to teach a retrieve, or a more elegant approach for training heelwork. I mean a total change in philosophy: examining, assessing, and discarding past practices. Each of my training conversions followed an epiphany—an awakening replete with self-examination, confusion, uncertainty, apprehension, and even depression—sadness about how much better it would have been for previous dogs I trained had I only known then what I know now. As I have learned, grown, changed, and learned still more, my new knowledge is enhanced and strengthened by my past. I have not so much abandoned what I had previously done, as much as put it in perspective, moved on, filing it in the recesses of my memory to examine from time-to-time, and possibly even use, if circumstances dictate.

My training career started with the "Koehler Method," an approach that is commonly referred to as "traditional" or "correction" training. Such training uses physical manipulation along with the discomfort of collar pressure to communicate to a dog, "Avoid doing that."

A few years into my profession, I was introduced to the "Motivational Method," an approach using a combination of physical placement, luring with food, and collar checks. This led to my collaboration with Jack Volhard with whom I wrote two books:

1

Training Your Dog followed by *Teaching Dog Obedience Classes.* The teaching manual was conceived and written as the text for the two-year certificate program I was then teaching at the University of New Hampshire, entitled "Instructor Training for Teaching Dog Obedience."

Despite no longer using these training techniques, I am proud of these books, especially *Training Your Dog*, which won a prestigious award from the Dog Writers Association of America as the Best Care and Training Book of 1983. This book filled a critical niche at the time—not just for my university students, but for dog owners looking for a kinder, gentler method to supplant the "traditional" approach.

While the method in *Training Your Dog* was different from anything else at the time, there are specific similarities in virtually all non-clicker training approaches. Pick up any of the hundreds of dog training books in publication (and countless others no longer in print), and the focus is on two things: the mechanics (physical procedures for the trainer to follow) and the exercises (specific behaviors such as sit, lie down, and heel, for example).

A training "method" puts mechanics together with exercises. For example, this is the procedure for teaching (fill in the blank) using a food lure to entice the dog into position. Or this is how to train it with physical placement. Or this is what you do to get a behavior using some mixture, a combination of approaches called "The (fill-in-the-blank) Method of Dog Training."

The specific exercises you train depend on your goals, such as to enjoy a well-mannered family pet, to train an agility wiz, develop an obedience trial champion, a hunting buddy, search and rescue partner, or to participate in any of the many dog sports, activities, and occupations available to our canine partners and to us. Look through the book and DVD listings on Dogwise.com—a site devoted to dogs, dog training, sports, and pursuits—and you'll find books on virtually every imaginable activity you can do with your dog, each with the author's instructions: *the recipe to train the exercises for that endeavor.*

Both of my prior methods were mechanics and exercise-based. Instructions explained the procedures for teaching the first exercise, then another, and another, and so on. With a structured approach, after you learned how to train the foundation exercises, you moved on to the intermediate level, where you then learned how to train several new behaviors. Want more advanced training? Sign up for class or get the next book that covers those procedures and exercises.

I was happy with how I trained for the 20 plus years that I used and taught this approach, believing it was by far the best way to train for both dogs and people. Then, nearly ten years after the publication of the teaching text, I tried clicker training. Despite the ties to my two training books and the method they espouse, I could not deny clicker training's pre-eminence.

When I began my crossover odyssey, first training my own dog and then introducing it to my students and clients, I hosted several seminars at All Dogs Gym®, my training business. At one of these early presentations a participant who used my training books and had been to several of my seminars and training camps, told me she was there to learn about clicker training, having heard a rumor that I had changed to it.

Almost secretively, in a grave and serious tone, she said, "I know going public couldn't have been easy for you." I had to laugh. I'd been outed: *"Ohmygosh, Gail Fisher's...a clicker trainer!"*

At first, it seemed like a daily occurrence that someone would say, *"You're* switching to clicker?! What about your writings, teaching and seminars—the years you've devoted to espousing your training method? How can you chuck it all?" My response was simply, "I have no choice." Seeing how well clicker training works, I couldn't *not* change. Nor have I ever, even for one moment, regretted doing so.

What is it that makes clicker training different from methods that rely on either luring or physically placing a dog into position? Clicker training is based on the laws of learning (operant conditioning in this case), but then so are other methods. It is based primarily on using positive reinforcement, but so are other methods.

What makes clicker training different is that it is uniquely principle-based, not exercise-based. Rather than learning how to teach your dog specific *exercises*, the clicker trainer understands how to apply concepts rather than procedures, using the immutable principles of how learning happens rather than following a recipe. Understand the concepts and principles, and you're good-to-go to *fully* enjoy your dog. Not just to teach exercises, but to understand and influence how your dog learns *anything*—limited not just to "training," but how every-day interactions can result in having the dog of your dreams.

But wait. There are already books about clicker training. Why write another? Because this book isn't just about clicker training. It's about *all* training—what you know, what you've heard; what you've done; even what you've rejected. It's also about helping you make the *transition* from whatever method you use now to clicker training. It's about how to understand and contrast differences between methods, the pros and cons of each, difficulties and obstacles, as well as advantages and benefits.

I often meet crossover and potential crossover trainers, who say they have "tried clicker training...but...." The very word "try" implies a built-in safety valve, a safe implication of regret: "I'll try...but if I don't like it, you can't blame me. At least I *tried*." In the immortal words of Yoda the Jedi Master, "Try not. Do...or do not. There is no try." Trying clicker training, learning the basics is easy. Learning the ins and outs, the whole picture—not so easy. Yet going beyond "trying it" is *so* well worth the effort.

Nothing in this book is intended to denigrate any approach or diminish your prior successes with whatever training method you have used. My goal is to look at different methods of training, compare and contrast them, while examining how they affect how a dog learns. Also how you, as a trainer, react to them, and how these methods differ from clicker training.

It is not my goal to convince you that "my way" is best. This isn't about personal opinions or preferences. Rather, it is about what happens in your dog's head. It is about how your dog thinks and how your dog reacts to training. While another method might work (they all do, at least to some extent!), clicker training makes learning easier for your dog, and ultimately easier for you. Crossing over isn't about what you've done previously—it's about what you do from now on.

I dislike using clichés, but there is a perfect adage that applies to clicker training: "Give a man a fish, you feed him for a day; teach a man to fish, you feed him for a lifetime." Better still, when a man understands the fish, he can feed the village and eat like a king. *Clicker training provides more than a trained dog, it teaches us how to achieve dog behavior.* Not by exercises, but by principles and philosophy.

Had I not already been a believer in clicker training, I would have become a devoted advocate the day I got the following note from one of the crossover students in the very first intermediate (Level 2) clicker class I taught. As a new crossover trainer myself, this student had severely tested my new-found, burgeoning, fragile, clicker-training knowledge. Dubious about this "new fangled" training, she had openly challenged me several times when her small, blond, Sheltie mix was non-responsive and noisy. Several weeks after her class ended, I got a letter from her that could not have expressed any better the relevance of the fishing adage, and the profound power and implications of learning clicker training. She wrote:

> *Dear Gail:*
>
> *Skeptical as I was in class, I have to relate a "clicker" experience I had last night with Maddy. We wanted to teach her to retrieve a Frisbee, and she's not a retriever by nature. If we throw a ball, stick, whatever, she might chase it once, never brings it back, and usually looks at us as if to say, "Hey, that's a good toy, why'd you throw it way the heck out there?!" Then she trots off to sniff the bushes. So last night I decided to try to use the clicker (and treats of course!) and teach her to get the Frisbee (one of those cloth ones.). Honest to God, in 15 minutes she was chasing it across the living room, bringing it back, and dropping it at my feet. Now you know Maddy, so she was pretty vocal when she would get confused. But I'd just go back to the step she understood and take it from there. The progression was: 1. Touch the Frisbee next to me in my hand. 2. Touch the Frisbee next to me on the floor. 3. Touch it after I threw it across the room. 4. Bring it back to me (then we had to get her to not want to play tug-o-war with it, so I had to do "give" a few times.) 5. She got it!*
>
> *I know we may have to back track a little tonight and when we move to outdoors, but she did it! I'm a believer! Thanks!*

Gaining an understanding of how to teach your dog anything you want does not mean abandoning what you already know. Just as I have the knowledge gained from my experience with prior methods, you, too, likely have previous learning. There may come a time when a former technique is not only useful, but is appropriate. Armed with a new perspective based on objective information and knowledge, you will not only know how to use it, you'll understand why it works, why it might be the technique of choice, and be able to evaluate how it will affect your dog, your dog's learning, and most importantly, your relationship.

You are embarking on an adventure. As with any major change, it may be rife with frustrations, uncertainties, and confusion—and trust me, as a crossover trainer, you'll feel all that and more—but the result will be a profound respect for your thinking dog's mind, and a deeper, more fulfilling relationship than you ever imagined possible, for you and for your dog. Let the adventure begin.

I

Putting it in Perspective:
Past and Present

"Those who cannot remember the past are condemned to repeat it."

—George Santayana

Overview

When I see a new training book by the latest "designer trainer," or a TV program with the telegenic "trainer to the stars" du jour, I think we are condemned to repeat the past. Dog training and our knowledge of dog behavior has come a long way over the past 100 years, but little (if anything) is "new." As you'll see in Part I, virtually every method falls into one of three discernable categories.

To put dog training in perspective, in this section I review and evaluate training methods using our knowledge of the past—where modern dog training started; what has happened over the past hundred plus years; and where we are now. As dog trainers have become better informed about how dogs learn, there has been greater evaluation of training methods from the dog's perspective, using our improved recognition of dog body language and communication for insights into what our dogs are thinking and feeling. With this as a sound foundation, we are not condemned to repeat the past. Dogs are certainly the better for that!

Chapter 1
CROSSING OVER

My Crossover Journal
I was frustrated, disappointed, and, truth be told, embarrassed
when I first tried clicker training with my four-year-old Bearded
Collie, Mayday. Enrolled in a clicker training seminar with Karen Pryor and
Gary Wilkes, I was not just a participant, I was the host—and an experienced,
successful dog trainer. Given instructions to shape a behavior, we participants
spread out to train our dogs. All around me I heard click, click, click as others
successfully shaped behaviors. I stood silent. Well-trained and extremely "obe-
dient," Mayday looked at me, patiently waiting to be told what to do, offering
nothing to click. Why wouldn't my dog cooperate?! Move! Offer me something!
But Mayday's extensive training history said not to, and I couldn't make him.
I had to allow him. A new approach to me and foreign to my dog, it would be
two months before Mayday stopped waiting for a directive. We were, the two of
us, quintessential "crossovers."

As you embark on this training adventure, you may not experience the same level of
frustration as I did when Mayday and I first tried clicker training. You may not even
consider yourself a crossover trainer, but the chances are good that you are.

The term "crossover" was coined by Corally Burmaster, founding editor of *The Clicker
Journal*, to refer to those of us who have some training experience and have decided
to "crossover" to clicker training. Whether or not you have a great deal of previous
experience, it is rare for someone to know absolutely nothing about training a dog and
have no preconceptions.

Almost everyone's a "crossover" trainer

Dog owners get information and impressions from many sources that may include
training on your own, taking a training class, reading a book, or training instinctively—doing what "feels right." We get ideas from watching dog trainers on TV, and
even from friends and co-workers with (or even without) dogs.

Sit in a restaurant and tune in to snippets of conversation from a nearby table. Chances
are you'll hear the word "dog." Often the topic is a behavior issue, complete with a
layperson's advice and counsel. Anecdotal information and opinions about dealing

with dogs are easy to come by and they influence dog owners both subtly and explicitly. Even people who have never actually trained a dog have preconceptions and ideas about training, making everyone a potential "crossover" trainer.

Backgrounds vary, but as their dogs' trainers, all owners, fall into one of the following. You may be:

- A trainer with knowledge (from a little to a lot) of clicker training.
- A crossover trainer with a crossover dog (one that has had some prior training by another method).
- A crossover trainer starting fresh with an untrained dog.
- Or one of the fortunate few—a dog owner with no prior training experience—nothing to unlearn—starting fresh with an untrained dog who also has nothing to unlearn.

Regardless of your background or experience, before learning about clicker training, it is helpful to understand what has gone before as training methods have developed over time.

A brief history

Dog training has been around as long as we've had relationships with dogs, but "modern" dog training is only about 100 years old. Over the past century, many dog training techniques and methods have developed, evolved, come, and gone.

How it started

Col. Konrad Most, arguably the father of modern dog training, trained military and service dogs in Germany at the turn of the 20th century. Most wrote the first comprehensive "how-to" book, *Training Dogs, a Manual*, published in Germany in 1910, and then translated into English in 1954, the year of his death.

Training resilient dogs with strong temperaments, Most's techniques relied on collar corrections and punishment, an approach viewed as heavy-handed by the majority of pet dog trainers today. While now considered harsh, Most's training followed the principles of **operant learning** (which is how dogs learn to offer voluntary behaviors), effectively using consequences (corrections and praise) to reward or punish a dog's behavior. By and large, his techniques were successful, especially with the working dogs Most and his disciples trained.

Most's compulsion-praise training techniques spread throughout the world as his students and disciples emigrated to other countries. His structured approach to training was adopted as the model for military training throughout Europe and North America, and his methods are still used today in many military, police, and service dog training programs.

Three trainers helped spread Most's training philosophy to America. They were Carl Spitz (*Training Your Dog*, 1938), Josef Weber (*The Dog in Training*, 1939), and Hans Tosutti (*Companion Dog Training*, 1942).

Spitz lived in California where he trained dogs for the movies (Toto in the *Wizard of Oz* and Buck in *Call of the Wild* among others). He is credited with devising a system of silent hand signals by which to control his dogs at a distance. Significantly, it was Carl Spitz who developed the American war dog training program in World War II, training Doberman Pinschers for the Marines at Camp Pendleton.

Hans Tosutti immigrated to Boston, where, in 1936, he founded the New England Dog Training Club, the oldest existing AKC member obedience training club in the country. Josef Weber lived in Philadelphia, and it is through his students that this method of training was spread even further.

One of Weber's students was Blanche Saunders (*The Complete Book of Dog Obedience*, 1954 and *The Story of Dog Obedience*, 1974) who, with Helene Whitehouse Walker, originated AKC Obedience trials, traveling around the country spreading the concept of companion dog training to the general public. Among Saunders' students and followers were many of the well-known trainers of the 1950's and 60's, including Winifred Strickland (*Expert Obedience Training for Dogs*, 1965) whose book, *Obedience Class Instruction for Dogs*, published in 1971, was the first publication targeting group class instructors—those who taught others how to train, rather than trainers who worked one-on-one with a dog.

The "Koehler" era

It was the advent of World War II that solidified the military training approach as the model for pet dog training. At the end of the war, many soldiers came home with a skill: training dogs using the methods developed by Konrad Most fifty years earlier. In the U.S., the most famous of these dog-training veterans was William Koehler, whose book *The Koehler Method of Dog Training* (1962) was, and may still be, the all-time best-selling dog training manual.

With relatively few training books to compete with it, and unabashedly self-promoting, Koehler's manual became a reference for virtually every dog owner and dog trainer for the next two decades. While it requires a trainer to have good timing and coordination, the "Koehler Method" can result in successfully trained dogs. It offers clear instructions and effective techniques for trainers able to employ them, at least with dogs that are able to handle "corrections." Using the consequences of punishment and praise as Konrad Most before him, Koehler's book profoundly influenced dog training throughout the U.S.

Adding to the popularization of dog training were the movie (and later TV) dogs, Rin Tin Tin (trained by Corp. Lee Duncan, who learned from a Most-trained German Kennel Master who was held in an American prison camp in World War I), and Lassie (trained by Rudd Weatherwax, whose brother Jack worked for Carl Spitz). So it was that the two world wars laid the foundation for the German military dog training method that spanned the next 80 plus years.

This history puts in perspective the global nature of "traditional," compulsion-praise training, based on the teachings of Konrad Most, down to William Koehler who made an indelible mark on dog training in America, and whose method is still followed by many today.

The dawn of "dog-friendly" training

Other training methods also began to evolve during this same time. *Patient Like the Chipmunks*, a video by Bob and Marion Bailey, presented an overview of operant conditioning as a method of training animals. Marian Breland Bailey and her late husband, Keller Breland, were graduate students of behavioral psychologist B.F. Skinner, who wrote about operant learning in his book *Behavior of Organisms* (1938). Leaving graduate school in the early 1940's, the Brelands founded a business devoted to training and providing many different animal species for commercial and government enterprises. Unlike Most and Koehler, their training focused primarily on positive reinforcement rather than relying on "corrections" or punishment.

Keller Breland was the first to use a clicker in training a dog—a tin cricket he used to train field dogs and herding dogs to work away from the handler. Calling the sound a "bridging stimulus," Breland marked the behavior with a clicker, as Marian told it to me, "to **bridge** the time between the behavior and the delivery of the reinforcer."

Breland's training with a marker might have spread beyond his own business were it not for the returning soldiers infused with compulsion training ideas and the fact that the Brelands' focus was not on pet dog training. Keller Breland used his techniques with other species, notably in the 1950's developing the training program for marine mammals that is still in use today. The Brelands worked with trainers and associates in many locations, including Sea Life Park, then owned by Karen Pryor and her husband.

In the 1970's and 1980's the dog training world saw a growing movement away from correction-based training. Milo and Margaret Pearsall (*The Pearsall Guide to Successful Dog Training—Obedience From the Dog's Point of View*, 1973) introduced the concept of Puppy Kindergarten classes for puppies as young as eight weeks. A radical departure from the "rule" of waiting until a dog was six months old, Pearsall used gentle placement rather than the collar corrections and force that precluded obedience training for such young puppies.

Jack Volhard and I took it a step further (*Training Your Dog—The Step-by-Step Manual*, 1983), introducing a food lure with the "Motivational Method." Around the same time, Ian Dunbar introduced lure-reward training to the general public with his ground-breaking dog training video, *Sirius Puppy Training*.

> ## Enough training books!
> In the early 1980's, when Jack Volhard and I first approached publisher Howell Book House, known for their quality dog publications, they were reluctant to publish "yet another" dog training book. Having previously rejected many manuscripts, they believed there were already enough training books on the shelves. We convinced them to take a chance on *Training Your Dog*. When the critical acclaim and popularity of our book clearly demonstrated that the dog-owning public likes training books, Howell pulled out the stops. *Training Your Dog* opened the door to the new generation of dog training books that pack the shelves you find in bookstores today.

Karen Pryor's impact

At about the same time, a book that had nothing to do with dog training would nonetheless profoundly impact it, changing its face forever. In 1984 Simon and Schuster published Karen Pryor's guide to *human* interpersonal relations, which they titled *Don't Shoot the Dog!* The serendipitous selection of this title brought Pryor to the attention of dog trainers, setting in motion a convergence between Keller Breland's approach to animal training and the dog training community.

In the early 1990's, Pryor teamed up with Gary Wilkes, a professional dog trainer and the first since Keller Breland to use clicker training with dogs. Through their articles and seminars, the collaboration of Pryor and Wilkes cast the die to spread the word of clicker training.

To meet the needs of a growing community of clicker trainers, Corally Burmaster founded and published the quarterly *The Clicker Journal.* Coining the word "crossover," Burmaster gave a name to the hundreds, soon thousands of dog owners and trainers from a variety of backgrounds, who were discovering, learning about, and embracing clicker training.

Through the wonders of the Internet, clicker training for dogs has spread across the world in a few short years. But as this brief history demonstrates, the principles of clicker training have been around for over 70 years. It is not a New Age, touchy-feely gimmick, as those who try to marginalize it may claim. It has just taken this long for the dog training community to catch up, with crossover trainers leading the parade.

"Natural" or "Pack Mentality" methods

Recently there has been a surge of interest in training methods claiming to be based on "pack mentality." Rooted in common (and often mistaken) beliefs about how dogs (and wolves) interact with each other and maintain pack order, the focus is on the trainer replicating the way a "dominant" dog supposedly disciplines lower ranking members of the pack. This approach is personified by Cesar Millan, a charismatic TV personality who, in an online interview for National Geographic News, erroneously claims: "If you study a pack of dogs, the first authority figure is the mom, and the mom does pin the puppies down. It's an instinctual relationship that I have to establish with them...Domination, dominating, and the alpha roll exist, and will exist, until we get rid of the species of dog."

While the concept of training dogs the "natural way" has some intellectual appeal, unfortunately much of what Millan and others claim is based on faulty research. For example, the "alpha roll" does not exist, and the mom does not pin puppies down. (For the real skinny on what mom does and what her lesson is, see "Life Lessons" in Chapter 10.) The dominant dog does not roll the subordinate; the subordinate dog falls over onto his back, "rolling" himself. When a more assertive being (dog or person) rolls a dog, it is an *attack*!

The second fallacy is the idea that dogs view us through the same lens as they view each other. While hierarchies may exist within an intra-dog pack, that differs from our inter-species relationship. People are not dogs, and dogs aren't fooled when a human attempts to "act like a dog." To try to act like a dog demeans a dog's intelligence, awareness, insight, and perceptions. Just as we must not be anthropomorphic—viewing dogs as "furry people with four legs"—we must not presume that dogs suffer from "caninepomorphism," viewing humans as "two-legged, sparsely-haired dogs with inferior biting ability."

Happily, this dominance model appeared to be dying out with a number of leading trainers like Pat Miller and Jean Donaldson pointing out the many fallacies of this approach. Sadly, it makes for exciting television, leading to a popular revival of this erroneous "natural" approach, that undermines our bond of trust, is unkind to dogs, and damages our relationship with them, often irreparably.

Why I crossed over to clicker training

Throughout my career as a dog trainer, I've been open to finding something better than what I already know. As I learned different ways to get a dog to "obey," it became clear that virtually every approach I tried, read about, heard about, or observed "worked"—that is, they all achieve some level of dog compliance (potential downsides or side effects notwithstanding). Since so many training methods "work," at least with some dogs some of the time, how does one discover or choose which method is "best?"

As I've studied dog training and instructing (teaching others to train their own dogs) and learned about learning theory and dog behavior, I've solidified my principles into a philosophy that seeks and uses training techniques that meet the following criteria:

1. A technique must "work"—the dog can learn how to perform the desired behavior.

2. It must be fair to the dog and do no harm to either the dog or the relationship between the dog and owner.

3. The average dog owner, including children, must be able to do it. That is, it cannot rely on exceptional talent, innate dog-handling skills, or dominating the dog.

4. The average owner must be willing to perform the training technique. That is, a method must not require owners to do something to their dogs that they find too challenging or objectionable.

My "old" approach to training, based on the method in my two books with Jack Volhard, met these criteria. But in terms of #1—that it works—clicker training blows everything else out of the water, while being in harmony with the rest of my philosophy. I simply could not ignore this "new" training.

As I've learned clicker training, using it to train dogs and teaching it to others, I have become more and more convinced that clicker training communicates information to and with dogs as it should be. But it was a tenacious little dog that changed my training approach forever.

Maggie the Pug

My staff and I first saw clicker training in action when we hosted a seminar with Karen Pryor and Gary Wilkes. The effect was monumental, with every one of our trainers agreeing that we wanted to learn more. I was not about to blithely toss out the method that had served us well for over 20 years of training people and their dogs, but we all wanted to experiment and learn more about clicker training. It wasn't long however, before clicker training was put to the test.

About a week after the seminar, Laura, our head trainer, came to me with a problem. She had been training Maggie, a five-year old rescue Pug who had recently been adopted by two of our doggy daycare "parents." Maggie had been coming to daycare-training for three weeks and was doing well in everything except lying down. Clearly having had some prior training with a method that had created an aversion, this otherwise sweet, loving Pug became a Tasmanian devil, viciously biting at any attempt to get her to lie down.

Laura had tried everything she could think of—luring with food didn't work, and gently placing her in a down was out of the question. Even after three weeks of desensitization, Laura could not touch her if Maggie thought lying down was in the offing. And the pressure was on: We had just learned that Maggie's family was moving to California. Training Maggie to lie down before she left had become a mission…and we had just three days to do it.

With other options exhausted, we had nothing to lose: Let's try clicker training—our first "professional" foray. Armed with a clicker and a bowl of cut-up hot dogs, Laura, Maggie, and I got started. I began by clicking and giving her a treat. Maggie got right into this neat, new game: "You make a funny noise and throw me a hot dog? Awright!!!"

Next, I started clicking for different behaviors—whatever she did. She sat—I clicked and tossed her a treat. Stand up—click and treat. Walk toward me—click and treat. Eye contact—click and treat. I didn't say anything; no commands, no cues, just a click followed by a hot dog.

A Pug's face, with its wide, alert eyes, smiling mouth, and open, honest expression is really easy to read. We could tell that Maggie was having a good time, when suddenly her expression changed from enjoyment to pensive. In a moment of clarity Maggie realized that I was clicking *her*—that I clicked when *she* did something. She paused. Her eyes got even wider, and in a moment of pure communication, she tested me. Looking directly into my eyes, she sat—click and treat. It was instantly clear to us that Maggie got what the click meant: *She* could make me click.

With Maggie now playing the game, I began to use **selective clicking** to shape the behavior we wanted. I clicked anything that led toward lying down. If she lowered her head, dipped her body, sat and put a foot forward, anything that approximated starting to lie down, I clicked and treated. This meant that she was no longer clicked for everything she did. Maggie didn't like this rule change. She got mad. Looking right at me, she started swearing—barking, spitting, sputtering, growling—language that would embarrass a longshoreman. Suddenly, in a fit of temper, Maggie threw herself down! Click.

Silence. No one moved. Maggie stopped dead. Clearly, her brain was working overtime as she pondered this new development. Then she erupted in furious barking…and threw herself down again. Click and treat. She ate and immediately began barking again as she quickly lay down once more. Click.

Maggie threw herself into a down, hollering and swearing at the top of her lungs.

At that point, I began to wait for her to lie down without barking or we would have achieved our mission of getting Maggie to lie down, but only accompanied by furious noise! Waiting for quiet took a while as Maggie continued loudly barking, repeatedly throwing herself to the ground. And then she took a breath as she lay down. An accidental moment of quiet—I'll take it! Click and treat. She went through another spate of barking, then quiet with another down. I waited until I had marked and rewarded two more quiet ones, then we took a break.

I looked at the clock. From start to finish, from the first click to the third quiet down in a row, had taken …What?!…Could it be? No…This isn't possible!

Just *eight* minutes?! I was flabbergasted. There was something really powerful here. In eight minutes we had accomplished more than we had been able to in literally weeks of training and desensitization.

Over the next two days, Maggie continued to improve. On her last day with us, after just three days of clicker training, we were able to show her Mom that Maggie would lie down on cue. She performed beautifully. And we were hooked!

The "Aha!" Moment
Actually, I was hooked before Maggie's final "go home" performance. Unquestionably the most exciting moment for the clicker trainer is when your dog "gets it"—that "Aha! moment" when it "clicks" for your dog…when you can see your dog's mental wheels start to turn. I was hooked the moment Maggie figured out that it was her behavior that got me to click and toss her a treat. I didn't know it at the time, but in retrospect, this was a momentous event. By giving Maggie—and every dog I train—volitional control of her own behavior, I was for the first time, working in partnership with a "Thinking Dog."

I get an adrenaline rush whenever I work a new dog through a behavior, especially the moment the dog unhesitatingly and proudly performs the behavior I'm looking for. I particularly love that moment at a training seminar when participants can see the dog thinking it through, testing the behavior, working out what he needs to do to get me to make that noise and reward him—and then finally, he's got it!

My Crossover Journal
At a seminar in California, I was demonstrating shaping a Papillon to "settle" (go to the blanket, lie down, and stay there). Because I was looking for feet on the mat, not how the dog got onto it, I happened to click him several times when he moved onto it backwards. After just two or three repetitions, this wonderfully bright boy was literally leaping backwards onto the mat. After the click, I'd toss the treat away from the mat. He'd eat, and then cavort over to the mat, turn his back, pop up into the air, and land backwards, much to everyone's delight.

Delighting the audience with his antics, it didn't matter how the Papillon got there. It is being on the mat that gets a click.

An "Aha! moment" doesn't happen just once. Thrillingly for the trainer, it happens over and over. Seeing a dog start to think, offering you behaviors as your true partner-in-training: "Watch this! Did you like that? How about *this*?!" Having your dog become an active participant—helping drive the bus, not just along for the ride—makes for the most exciting human/dog partnership, the most wonderful human/dog relationship imaginable. This is what training a thinking dog is all about!

Clicker training is fun; it's exhilarating; it's rewarding, joyous, and exciting. I can't promise that you won't have moments of frustration. In fact, I guarantee you will! The information in this book is for you, the crossover trainer, to prepare you for some of what you'll likely encounter so you and your dog can experience that thrilling "Aha! Moment" many times over the years to come.

Chapter 2

LEARNING AND TRAINING FUNDAMENTALS

My Crossover Journal
I was presenting an evening program in England. In the audience
was the late John Holmes, whose early dog training books profoundly
influenced my training philosophy. Speaking about the constructive movement
away from physically harsh training methods, I referred to an unintended and
undesirable consequence of this shift: that many dog owners and trainers equate
"positive" with "permissive." I saw John nodding his head in agreement when I
mentioned the growing reluctance to say or mean "no," the apparent aversion to
discipline, and the increasing tolerance of undesirable, even unacceptable behav-
ior. In his no-nonsense, candid manner, John agreed, saying, "It used to be if a
dog grumbled at being told to get off the bed, the owner would just take him off
the bed. Now, if a dog grumbles at being asked to move, the owner sleeps on the
couch and calls a behaviorist in the morning."

"These days, if a dog grumbles at being asked to move, the owner sleeps on the
couch and calls a behaviorist in the morning."

Everyone who trains a dog wants to use a method that gets results as quickly, efficiently, and successfully as possible. By understanding how learning happens—be it dogs, people, horses, cows, cats—trainers are able to make well-reasoned, informed decisions in selecting a fair, effective approach.

Three basic "methods"

Despite the impression created by the hundreds of dog training books, all dog training fits into one or more of three basic methodologies: compulsion-praise training (C-P), lure-reward training (L-R), and clicker training (CT). (I use the term clicker training here, but one could call this behavior-marker training.) L-R training utilizes a food treat or other object to entice the dog into position. With C-P training the trainer places the dog in position followed by verbal praise or a food reward. In addition to physical placement, C-P training may also include using a collar correction for non-compliance. Clicker training uses a sound to mark a behavior which is then reinforced. You'll find a more detailed description of each methodology in Chapter 4.

Putting clicker training aside for the moment, every other training "method" uses the mechanics, exercises, and fundamentals of lure-reward and compulsion-praise methods, or a mixture and combination of the two. For example, a method might start with luring to lay the training foundation, then utilize a collar correction, for non-compliance. Or a method might use physical placement for some behaviors, and luring for others.

No matter what training method you use, your dog's learning follows "laws"—principles that influence learned behavior. Over the last decade there has been a sea change in the dog-training community resulting from a growing awareness of and attention to these laws. By understanding how dogs learn, a trainer can objectively consider different approaches that might improve upon, and may be "nicer" than previous methods. Such was my epiphany in each of my training incarnations: from Koehler, to "Motivational," to clicker training (see Introduction).

Regardless of your training history, it is helpful to understand the laws of learning, and how they apply both to your previous method(s) and to clicker training. Armed with this knowledge, crossover trainers are able to make intelligent, objective decisions about their dogs' training. So let's briefly examine the science of learning, the basis of all methods of training. (See Resources for references to a more in-depth exploration.)

How dogs learn

When your dog grumbles at you and you end up sleeping on the couch, as John Holmes referred to, is your dog learning something? Of course he is. He's learning that you move away when he grumbles. Moving away reinforced grumbling: cause and effect; behavior and consequence.

The axiom of learning theory is Edward Thorndike's Law of Effect (published in 1911), which says *behaviors just prior to a pleasant event are more likely to be repeated; behaviors just prior to unpleasant events are more likely to diminish.* Put another way:

- Behaviors that have pleasurable consequences tend to strengthen.

- Behaviors resulting in undesirable consequences tend to weaken.

More than just being about your dog's present behavior, the consequences of *this moment* are about her future behavior. Any one training session, any one interaction, any one reward you provide or punishment you invoke is less about this moment than it is about the future—how that consequence will affect your dog's behavior moving forward.

Terminology Issues

Psychologist B.F. Skinner's work with **incentives** (motivation) and **behaviors** (outcomes) took Thorndike's axiom to the next level, that the consequences of behavior are what learning is all about.

While Skinner, Thorndike, and the other early behavioral psychologists classified how operant learning takes place, they did no one any favors in selecting terminology. They chose familiar words in common usage that have other, unrelated meanings outside the "ivory towers" of academia. Their choices have led to confusion and misunderstanding.

They used the symbols + and − to mean add and remove. That's fine, but rather than calling them "add" and "subtract", they called them **positive** and **negative**. To most of the world positive and negative mean good and bad. Not so in "their" world. Thinking of them as "add" and "subtract" or, "provide" and "remove" makes the consequences easier to understand and apply.

Next are the consequences themselves. **Reinforcement** offers no problem—after all, reinforcement strengthens, even in "our" world. The problem is with the word **punishment**. In behavioral terms, punishment is not reprisal, payback, or vengeance, as it so frequently means to us. Rather, punishment is defined retroactively by its effect on behavior. If the behavior decreases, the consequence was punishment. With this terminology in mind, let's investigate the four possible results.

The four consequences

There are four possible ways that a behavior can be either strengthened or weakened, called **behavior effectors**. Let's look at each from the perspective of the trainer's action and the dog's perception.

Reinforce = strengthen behavior

There are two ways that reinforcement increases the likelihood of a behavior being repeated—positive and negative reinforcement:

- **Positive Reinforcement (R+)**. The trainer *provides (adds) something desirable to the dog* to strengthen a behavior. The dog perceives that his behavior results in *good things*. Examples are rewarding a behavior with a food treat, verbal praise, playing with the dog, or giving him permission to chase a squirrel.

- **Negative Reinforcement (R−)**. The trainer's goal is to strengthen a behavior by *removing (subtracting) something the dog perceives as undesirable*. From the dog's perspective *bad things stop* when he performs the behavior. For example, collar pressure is released when the dog sits, reinforcing sit. An electronic stimulation ends when the dog moves away from the invisible fence boundary, reinforcing boundary training. When the dog stops pulling, pressure on the nose loop of the head halter is relieved, reinforcing loose-leash walking.

Punish = weaken behavior

Punishment involves two possible outcomes that decrease the likelihood of the behavior being repeated: positive and negative punishment:

- **Positive Punishment (P+).** The trainer *provides (adds) something undesirable* to diminish or weaken a behavior. From the dog's perspective, *bad things result.* Some examples are a leash pop for pulling, a squirt of water for barking, or the zap of an invisible fence collar for straying over the boundary line.

- **Negative Punishment (P-).** The trainer *takes away (subtracts) something desirable* for the purpose of weakening or eliminating a behavior. From the dog's perspective, *good things stop.* Examples are a time-out (removing the dog) or leaving the room (removing your attention) to punish attention-seeking behavior; punishing non-compliance to a cue by eating the treat yourself or giving it to another dog.

By turning her back to him, Shari's removal of her attention is negative punishment for Siku.

My Crossover Journal
"Delimishment"

On a long car ride across England, Elizabeth Kershaw, a wonderful British dog trainer and behaviorist, and I were lamenting the problems caused by the word "punishment." If only the early behavioral scientists had used a different term, there would not be such a hue and cry about employing punishing consequences. After all, punishment per se is not bad. Abuse and mistreatment are, but that's not what punishment means. Defined by results, punishment doesn't have to hurt to affect behavior. If the behavior decreases, the consequence was "punishment." We thought if it were a different word, dog trainers would not be so reluctant to talk about it. We came up with the word "delimish": a combination of decrease, diminish, limit and eliminate. Delimish is a silly word; it made us laugh—the antithesis of the effect of *"punish." Since delimishers don't need to be painful to be effective, nor do they need to be profoundly memorable (eye contact can delimish behavior), we like having a nonsense word to replace the often misused and misunderstood word "punish."*

It sometimes seems as if the problem isn't so much the technique as it is the word. Perhaps trainers can discuss delimishing behavior with greater civility than when talking about "punishment." If we could discuss delimishing consequences unemotionally, maybe it would put an end to delimishing trainers who admit to using delimishment. The result would be a better understanding of employing such consequences—or choosing not to.

The behavioral circle

Figure 2-1 is a graphic representation of the four behavioral effectors as equal quadrants. Every method of training uses each consequence to a greater or lesser degree. What differs from method to method, and even from dog to dog within a method, is the emphasis; the use of procedures within each sector. Figures 2-2, 2-3, and 2-4 are representations of how each training method—compulsion-praise, lure-reward, and clicker training—generally employ consequences. Regardless of the overall approach, trainers make choices all the time. No method is absolute.

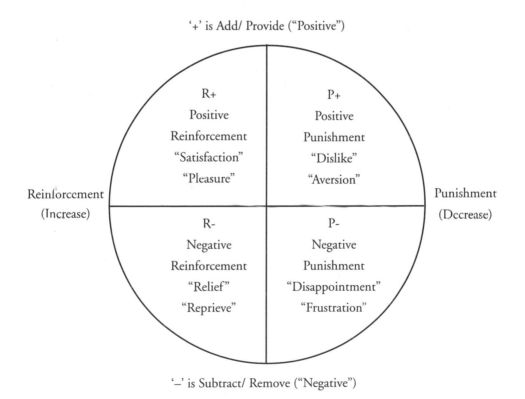

'+' is Add/ Provide ("Positive")

R+
Positive
Reinforcement
"Satisfaction"
"Pleasure"

P+
Positive
Punishment
"Dislike"
"Aversion"

Reinforcement
(Increase)

Punishment
(Decrease)

R-
Negative
Reinforcement
"Relief"
"Reprieve"

P-
Negative
Punishment
"Disappointment"
"Frustration"

'−' is Subtract/ Remove ("Negative")

Figure 2-1. This circle represents the four behavioral effectors, called the four "quadrants."

Compulsion-praise training

This method comes closest to applying equal weight to each quadrant. The Koehler Method, for example employs verbal praise (R+) to reward behavior, while verbal reprimands and/or collar "corrections" (P+) punish non-compliance. The ear pinch (R-) is an example of using negative reinforcement in training a dog to retrieve—ear pressure is released the moment the dog opens his mouth to take the dumbbell. Figure 2-2 illustrates the approximate weight of each sector in C-P training.

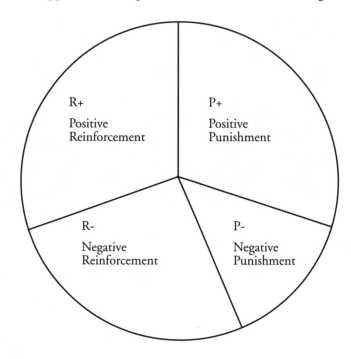

Figure 2-2. Compulsion-praise training: Close to equal quadrants, with approximately equal weight to positive reinforcement and positive punishment, and less emphasis on the removal of rewards (negative punishment).

Lure-reward training

Lure-reward training as described by Ian Dunbar who popularized the method, emphasizes positive reinforcement (R+) for desirable behaviors and negative reinforcement (R-) (what Dunbar calls "instructive reprimands") to correct errors. For example, as Dunbar described in a Town Hall Meeting teleconference, if the dog fails to lie down on command, the handler calmly repeats the command without threat until the dog complies. The message is that the trainer won't stop until the dog responds. Cessation of nagging reinforces the dog's ultimate response (R-). Lure-reward trainers use some negative punishment and little positive punishment.

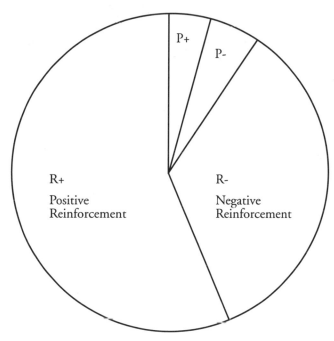

Figure 2-3. Lure-reward training. This method is heavily weighted toward positive reinforcement. Non-compliance is generally handled with an "instructive reprimand" (R-) that ends when the dog complies.

Clicker training

Clicker training, too, is heavily weighted in the positive reinforcement (R+) sector: rewarding desired behavior. For non-compliance or to reduce or eliminate undesirable behavior, the clicker trainer often uses negative punishment (P-), removing or withholding something the dog wants, or removing the dog from something desirable. The clicker trainer rarely uses positive punishment (P+) or negative reinforcement (R-). For most clicker trainers, the harshest positive punishment would be a verbal reprimand "Ah!", or perhaps a squirt of water, rarely using a more aversive consequence (see Chapter 10). On the negative reinforcement side, the clicker trainer may use a head halter for pulling on leash, rewarding a slack leash with relieved pressure on the nose loop and moving forward.

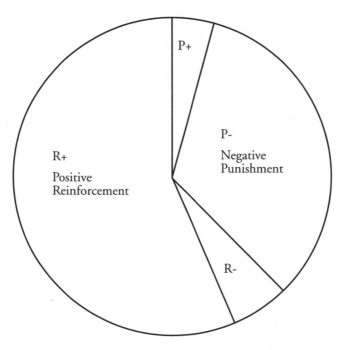

Figure 2-4. Clicker Training. Clicker training is heavily weighted toward positive reinforcement—getting the dog to offer desirable behaviors, and providing rewarding consequences. Non-compliance is generally handled by the removal of something desirable (P-).

Interconnected quadrants: Punishment and reinforcement

Astute trainers will recognize that it is not possible to employ reinforcement (or punishment) without enlisting the opposite punishment (or reinforcement): one positive the other negative. Take, for example, the strategy called 'be a tree' to train loose leash walking: As soon as the dog pulls on the leash, the trainer stops and stands still to prevent the dog moving forward to sniff something such as a hydrant. When the dog stops pulling, the trainer moves forward again. There are two ways to interpret how this strategy affects pulling behavior:

When the trainer stops walking forward, she is employing negative punishment for pulling, preventing access to sniffing the hydrant. Moving forward so the dog gets to the hydrant is positive reinforcement for the cessation of pulling, rewarding the loose leash. Two quadrants: P-/R+.

Another way to view this is that the trainer maintains pressure on the leash until the dog stops pulling. The relief the dog feels when the leash goes slack is negative reinforcement for his having stopped pulling. But in order to stop pulling, the leash had to tighten up first. Straining against the collar is an aversive that constitutes positive punishment. Two quadrants: P+/R-.

What motivates your dog?

Dog training is all about the effective use of consequences (providing motivation), along with an efficient communication system (providing information).

As the behavior effectors demonstrate, there are two sides to the motivational coin—things your dog wants (reinforcers), and things your dog doesn't want (punishers). The use of punishment is described in Chapter 10, so let's start with the upside of the coin, the payoffs that reward and reinforce behavior.

Consider what your dog will find rewarding for a job well done. Payoffs, rewards, reinforcement—whatever you call them—these are what motivate your dog. Higher value rewards are more motivational, making training easier and learning faster. Dogs will work for "minimum wage," but the idea is to inspire your dog to *readily* and *eagerly* perform a behavior.

There is a virtually endless list of potential items, activities, and opportunities that motivate dogs—and a bunch of things that we may think are motivating, but often aren't. Virtually anything your dog likes and wants can be used as a reward, falling into six general categories:

- Food
- Human companionship/interaction
- Games and play
- Toys and resources (not food)
- Expression of instinctive behavior (like allowing the dog to chase something or dig)
- Freedom

Food

Food treats top the list of payoffs because food is required for life itself. Dogs work for food much as we work for money—for what money can provide. Even if you love your job and find the work itself rewarding, there's still the issue of "gotta eat." So it is for dogs, placing food at or near the top of the list of rewards for most dogs.

While a dog's sense of taste is not as highly developed as ours, he still has culinary likes and dislikes. The better the taste, the higher its value. Not all dogs like the same things— some love bananas, others won't touch them. Food treats range from just this side of boring to Wahoo! *Your* opinion about your dog's likes and dislikes is immaterial—it's up to your dog.

Test your dog's preference

Often a student will tell me how much their dog loves vegetables. I believe them, but is a carrot the most motivating treat you can use? Test your opinion about what your dog likes against your dog's opinion. Take two different treats and hold one in each hand. With your hands close together, show your dog both treats and close your fists around them. Move your hands away from each other until they're about 12 inches apart, and see which hand your dog follows. If the dog is consistent in his choice, then that's probably the one your dog prefers. Remember, a higher value treat is more motivating than one that is "better-than-nothing."

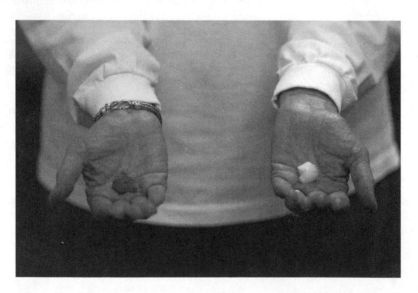

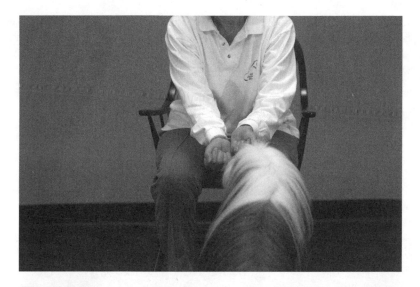

Showing him a dog biscuit in one fist and cheese in the other, Cannon makes his choice. No surprise…cheese wins.

Bribe versus reward

If you have never used food rewards for training, you may be thinking, "Food is bribery, and I won't bribe my dog." But there's a difference between a bribe and a reward. A bribe is presented *before* the behavior as inducement for the dog to perform. In its absence, there is no performance. A reward comes *after* the behavior, reinforcing what the dog just did. It is the possibility of a reward, based on past experience (Thorndike's Law), that motivates the dog to perform the behavior. Unlike a bribe, a reward does not have to be present to trigger a behavior. Here are examples of the difference:

Bribe: Sue went out to the yard to call Argus. When he didn't come, she called again with no results. Sue went inside and got a treat. Returning to the yard, she held the treat out for Argus to see, and called him once more. Seeing the bribe, Argus came running.

Reward: Argus was trained that touching his nose to Sue's palm in response to the cue "Here!" earned a reward. Sue called "Here!" and held out her hand. Argus came running, knowing that when he touched her hand, he'd likely get a treat. When he complied, Sue gave him a reward.

People food? Not for my dog!

So you're willing to use food treats, but (darn it!) not "people" food! Trainers reluctant to give their dogs people food fear it will unleash a monster—begging. If that's your concern, worry not. It isn't *what* you feed, it's *how, when,* and *where* you feed that creates begging. Feed dog food from the dinner table while you're eating dinner, and your dog will beg at the table. Feed him the tastiest leftovers scraped into his dish, fed apart from your meal, and he won't associate leftovers with begging at the table.

But "it" has always worked for me…

Some crossover trainers resistant to using food treats may be thinking, "So *you* say… but I've trained lots of dogs using praise without food rewards, and I don't want to start using food now!" Fine. You don't have to. Clearly it is possible to train without food treats. You've done it before. But consider how *your* performance changes depending on your motivation. Say you've just finished a difficult project, and your boss says, "Good job!" That's nice. But what if in addition, your boss said, "Here's a bonus of a month's pay!" Do you think your future performance might be impacted more by the higher value reward?

You may think praise has a high value to your dog, but for most dogs, really it doesn't. It isn't that praise isn't rewarding—it's about the relative value of praise versus food. Even when we love our jobs (and I do!) and find the work itself rewarding, we still have to put food on the table. So it is for dogs. They need food to live. You can choose not to use it, but using food will speed your training.

What about making him fat?

Dogs are overweight for precisely the same reasons as humans—more calories consumed than burned. If you're giving your dog a lot of treats, cut back on his regular meal a bit, or use some of his dog food with tasty goodies and give a portion of his meal as training rewards.

Human interaction/companionship

This category of rewards includes physical and spoken praise, petting, companionship, and attention. The first method of dog training I learned, the Koehler Method, used verbal praise, attention, and companionship as rewards. Affection and human interaction are reinforcing for most dogs. Petting, ear scratches, belly rubs, and sweet talk are payoffs, but are usually context-related. If you're lying on the couch watching TV, a companionable massage ranks high on the list of desirable things. But if you're out for a walk in the woods, and you call your dog away from a wonderful smell, you'd better have something better to offer than a scratch behind the ears or your dog won't be so quick to come next time.

My Crossover Journal

Believe it or not, not all dogs love food treats. Mayday, my Bearded Collie, was disinterested in food treats—even roast beef. A courteous fellow, he would politely take whatever was offered and quietly deposit it on the floor. At the office one day, he was sitting by Myrian's chair as she ate a hamburger and fries. She offered Mayday a french fry, which he took. A few minutes later, she gave him another. Then another. When she got up at the end of her meal, she looked down to find a small pile of french fries by her chair. What motivated Mayday to stay by her side? It wasn't the promise of food. It was companionship.

Mayday politely took the french fries, and dropped them into a pile on the floor.

What about verbal praise?

The good news about praise is that it is something you always have available, even if you don't have food treats. But be aware that praise is not something innately reinforcing to dogs. They have to learn its value as positive reinforcement. We automatically and unconsciously create this association by praising as we give the dog a treat, but even when the association is made, the value of praise will not be as high as food treats for most dogs, making it less motivational to use for "formal" training sessions.

In addition to praise having a lower value than food to most dogs, some dogs are completely unmoved by it—they simply don't care about or respond to praise. Unmotivated by praise and affection, these dogs are often thought of as "stubborn." They're not. They're simply unmotivated.

Laugh and your dog laughs with you

Laughter is highly reinforcing for many dogs, often a more powerful reward than petting. Not all dogs have a sense of humor, but for those that do, laughter is highly rewarding. The good news is that clicker training can be so much fun that you may laugh a lot. The not-so-good-news (it's really not *bad news*, just something to be aware of), is that your laughter can reinforce something you don't intend to reward.

Many trainers who compete in dog sports have experienced the pain of their dog making an entertaining error in the ring. The spectators laugh at the dog's antics, possibly unaware that their enjoyment encourages the dog to repeat the same error time and again. After all, the crowd loved it even if his handler didn't.

So when your dog's antics make you laugh, consider that your laughter may be all your dog needs to reward that behavior, encouraging him to do it again…and again… and….

Sociability

Because dogs are social animals, for most dogs companionship with people is a reward—but again, not for all. There are breeds of dogs that have been selectively bred for independence and disinterest in affection. Such genetic independence means these dogs are not motivated by demonstrations of affection or by companionship. If this is your dog's background, just as with praise, this category of payoffs is probably low on the list of motivational consequences.

> ## Are dogs motivated by love?
>
> At the Introductory Workshop to our classes, we ask students to list things they think motivate their dogs. Almost invariably, someone says, "love." Whether or not my dogs "love" me (personally, I believe they do), the fact remains that we can't control a dog's "feelings." More importantly, we can't use emotions as a payoff to motivate our dogs' behavior. It wouldn't work, for example, to say, "If you really truly love me, you'll stop pulling on the leash." Or, "If you stop pulling on the leash, I will love you even more than I do now."

Games and play

The elements of this category are interactive, that is, the dog plays with other dogs or with people. Most dogs are highly motivated by games. Some even prefer chasing and retrieving over a food treat. Play can build enthusiasm in a low-drive, sluggish dog. Games are a great way to turn on the crossover dog, making training sessions an active, fun time rather than a repetitive practice session.

The list of games most dogs love includes chase, hide and seek, retrieve, search and find things, and tug o'war. This category also includes games the dog invents, often frustrating the owner. For example, a dog that grabs a child's mitten and runs is initiating a chase game—great fun and highly reinforcing—for the dog. Remember, reinforcement is from the dog's perspective, not ours.

"Let the games begin!"

Toys and resources

This category covers items your dog enjoys by himself—things he can enjoy on his own such as chew toys, squeaky toys, balls, bones, treat-filled toys, and the like.

These items don't work well for an interactive training session since they are solitary endeavors, but there are times these payoffs can be helpful. For example, you might give your dog a treat-filled Kong® when you go out leaving the dog at home, thereby providing a rewarding activity in your absence.

Expressions of instinctive (innate) behavior

The opportunity to be a "normal" dog is powerfully rewarding. This category of rewards covers everything that is hard-wired in the species such as chasing a squirrel, sniffing the ground, and playing with other dogs—all normal instincts. It also includes instincts specific to and typical of your dog's breed or mixture of breeds—intrinsic behaviors like digging (terriers), scenting birds (sporting dogs), barking (scent hounds and herding dogs) and chasing (terriers, hounds, and herding dogs).

Engaging in instinctive behavior is tremendously rewarding. Terriers dig!

When your dog engages in something instinctive, whatever he did to gain that opportunity is reinforced. This means, if you call your dog and he ignores you to chase a rabbit, his non-compliance was reinforced by the joy of the chase. On the flip side, giving your dog the opportunity to express an instinct can be used as a powerful reward. (See the Premack Principle below.)

Your dog's breed or combination of breeds shapes his genetically programmed, instinctive behaviors. The history of the breed, including what other breeds (and their behaviors) are included in the mix, will tell you the function and behavior characteristics for which his breed was originally selected. This information is helpful for ideas and opportunities to provide the best possible rewards for your dog—and to better understand his behavior.

You don't have to keep sheep

It isn't necessary to keep sheep as a reward mechanism for your herding dog, or to let your terrier dig up your lawn, or go hunting with your hound, pointer, or retriever. While dogs might think it's wonderful to engage in the activity for which they were bred, doing so is both unrealistic, impossible to control as a regular reward for behavior, and unnecessary.

Consider your dog's instincts as *energies* that need a healthy outlet. The expression of the instincts shared in common by all dogs can serve both as an outlet for such energies, as well as to reinforce behaviors. The expression of instincts can be well-served through outlets such as going for a walk and exploring, using his nose (tracking, searching for, and finding objects), through physical exercise, performing tricks, and through training—providing a healthy outlet for your dog's mental energies.

Freedom

Freedom provides your dog with the opportunity to be a dog—to enjoy the great outdoors, to sniff and explore, take a walk, romp through the woods or run on the beach. Freedom is one of the most powerful rewards for your dog.

It isn't just the great outdoors that is reinforcing to dogs. Freedom includes getting let out of a crate. You've likely heard that you shouldn't let a barking dog out of the crate. Good advice! Here's why: Freedom reinforces barking, making it highly probable that next time he wants out, the dog will bark louder and longer. By waiting for quiet, then releasing the dog, you reward the absence of barking. (Chapter 10 includes information on reversing this, if you've already got it.)

Will reward-based training undermine my relationship with my dog?

Some crossover trainers come from methods that disdain food rewards under the presumption that dogs respond best to a dominant pack leader, or that the dog needs to learn to be responsive out of "respect" for the trainer. Let's explore these concepts for motivating a dog to learn.

Dominance as motivation?

Some methods characterize dog motivation as dominance-driven. In fact, I used to believe (and teach) this. While a social hierarchy can exist and influence behavior between dogs, such a hierarchical relationship is not relevant to our interaction with our dogs. Dogs don't think we're funny-shaped dogs, and they're not in competition with us.

When you get right down to it, the concept of dominance—of a dog vying for power and control over a human—doesn't really make sense. What would a dog gain from dominating us that he doesn't already have? We feed, shelter, and care for our dogs. We take them places and provide for all their needs. We walk them and pet them for both our pleasure and theirs. What's missing? Does your dog want to bring home the bison? Does he care what you wear, what you drive, where you work, your friends, or your politics? Of course not. The issues that come into play in human domination and control are irrelevant to our relationship with dogs.

What is mistakenly interpreted as "dominance" is simply reinforced behavior. If assertiveness works, that is, if pushy behavior is reinforced by the dog getting something out of it, pushy behavior is strengthened. The apparent dominant behavior of a dog toward a human is simply pushiness that earned a reward. A dominance hierarchy may exist in a multi-dog pack, but inter-species dominance does not. Reinforcement, not social status, is what motivates our dogs' behavior with us.

It's important to recognize the fallacy of dominance between our species because many crossover trainers either come from or are familiar with approaches that embrace the idea that dog behavior is ruled by attempting to take control, to win out over us. If you accept that concept, the antidote is to fight fire with fire—to out-dominate the dog. Since training through domination undermines your dog's willingness to think, it's important to understand why domination-based training is not the best way to achieve better behavior.

It's not that dominance-based training doesn't work sometimes—remember, all approaches to training can be successful at least some of the time. Rather it's a question of whether or not it's necessary or even helpful. It is not. Just as importantly, it's a question of what kind of trainer you want to be—what kind of relationship you want with your dog, how you want your dog to view you, and what you want the motivating factor to be that triggers your dog's behavior.

"R-E-S-P-E-C-T"

And then there's the fallacy of "respect." That a dog will perform because he "respects" the handler. In reality, in the dog world "respect" stems from fear. A dog "respects" another dog's space or another dog's possessions, not out of recognition of that dog's need for room or of his ownership, but rather that when he got too close or he tried to take the toy, he got a warning look, growl, or even a snap.

The bottom line to both dominance and respect as motivation for learning is that, while they work, they can be oppressive and result in undesirable fallout. Consider working for a domineering boss, feeling pressured to work overtime out of fear, or being asked to put in extra hours out of respect for your boss. Happy to do it? Probably not. Resentful? Perhaps. Looking for another job? Likely.

Make the most of your dog's rewards

Now that you understand the six major categories of rewards, make a list of four items in each of the above categories, and give each a ranking from one to ten, with one being "Ho hum...better than nothing," and ten being *"Whoa, Nellie!"* Consider the rewards your dog likes best. Keep in mind it's *your dog's opinion*, not *yours*. Would your dog rather have prime rib or enthusiastic praise? Would she be more motivated by an open door to freedom or a pat on the head? Would he rather have a carrot or chase a ball? Be honest, and don't take it personally. It's not about you. It's about what best pleases your dog.

Knowing what your dog likes enables you to choose the payoff that has the most appeal (the highest value) at the moment. The more motivated your dog, the easier training will be.

Eat your spinach—The Premack Principle

"Eat your spinach, and you can have dessert." Parents practice the **Premack Principle** even without studying Psychology 101. The Premack Principle asserts that the opportunity to engage in a desirable activity reinforces the less desirable behavior that earned that opportunity. But wait! There's more—the low probability behavior improves when it is reinforced by the high probability behavior. So "finish your homework" is more than merely reinforced by "then you can go out and play." "Finishing homework" behavior actually improves when it is rewarded with a more desirable behavior. What does this have to do with dog training? Plenty!

Use the opportunity to engage in something that the dog wants to reward a behavior that you want. For example, your dog wants to go out (engage in freedom) to explore in the yard (expression of instincts)—both highly desirable. Since you control your dog's access to the yard, use it. Ask for a learned behavior, mark it, and then open the door. No other reward is needed.

Some trainers call using Premack "nothing in life is free" or NILF—a bit of an over-statement since for most dogs *plenty* in life is free. We can only control what we actually have control over, everything else is "free." Premack provides an opportunity to practice a behavior in return for something you're going to give your dog anyway, so I call using Premack "earn life," that is, controlling and using access to an *activity* as a powerful payoff for good behavior. (For more on this, see Appendix D.)

My Crossover Journal
Donna was working on having her Border Collie, Hamish, stay at
the agility start line while she led out, moving away from him
toward the first obstacle. As her eager dog stared intently at the first jump, she
repeated, "Stay," and returned to Hamish to give him a treat for staying. A brief,
puzzled look passed over his face as he quickly snatched the treat from her hand,
and continued staring at the jump, his entire body quivering in anticipation.
Her instructor called, "Let him go! He doesn't want a treat; he wants to run!"
That's all the reward Hamish needed...or wanted.

Choices...and conflicts

When your dog is playing with his buddies, a carrot is not likely to be sufficient reward to cut short his fun. The environment in which you're trying to motivate your dog, the context, changes the value of a reward.

Picture yourself holding the best food treat you can think of, standing next to your front door, which is open a crack, just enough for your dog to nose his way out. Which do you think is the more powerful enticement, the treat or the door to freedom? For most dogs, it's freedom. Some clever dogs may snatch the treat as they rush by you out the door, but few dogs will ignore the open doorway and stop for the treat.

Choosing between good, better, and best may not always be what we think.

When faced with conflicting motivation, the dog will go for whatever has greater appeal *at the moment*. Keep this in mind as you build your dog's reliability. The more distracting the environment, the more attractive the distraction, the better your reward for compliance needs to be. Occasionally a student disregards this advice the first week of class, bringing a treat that works well at home, such as dry kibble. Unable to motivate the dog in such a stimulating environment, when we offer them some tasty treats and their dog starts performing, they get the point.

You *can* have too much of a good thing

As hard as it is to believe, it is possible to have too much chocolate. Not for dogs (chocolate is toxic to dogs), but for humans. Not only that, but if chocolate is the only reward you get for a job well-done, it loses its motivational value. Perhaps I'm being too personal. The point is, regardless of the value of a reward, if it never changes, it loses impact.

Don't use the same treat day after day. Mix them up. Vary both food treats and payoff categories: play tug or chase, release your dog to go outside, throw a ball. Be unpredictable, interesting, and fun!

Improving motivation

Some crossover dogs are not highly motivated until they learn the game. If your dog is unmotivated, mild deprivation may increase your dog's motivation. Here are some strategies to tip the scales in your favor:

- A hungry dog is more motivated by food. Try "resting from food" prior to training. Skip a meal or feed your dog after you train.

- A dog that's crated craves companionship. Try isolating your dog for an hour or so before you train.

Once your dog gets into clicker training, you may not need these strategies.

My Crossover Journal
When I first started clicker training, Mayday, my crossover dog, wasn't motivated by food treats. In training, he'd politely take the treat. He might eat it, but he wasn't turned on by food. The first behavior I clicker trained was to touch a target. Mayday's performance was lackadaisical. He'd saunter to the target, touch it, I'd click, he'd return, take the treat, and walk back to the target. Then, one day it changed in a flash. Mayday went to the target and touched it. I clicked. He paused, then he turned, ran to me, grabbed the treat, swallowed it and ran back to touch the target. From that moment, Mayday got into clicker training. In that instant, it "clicked"—he controlled the game and "the game" itself was rewarding. To play the game, he had to get the treat out of the way. And by the way, after that Mayday was motivated by food. Premack!

Motivation and information

Now that you've got a list of things that reinforce your dog's behavior, let's revisit Thorndike's Law. Since what follows a behavior (the consequence) is what motivates the dog to want to repeat that behavior, the faster the dog "gets" precisely what he did to earn the reward, the faster he will learn to purposely offer it.

Training is about providing useful information to your dog so he can perform the desired behavior on his own. The more clearly and effectively this information gets through, the better training will proceed. Good dog training is based on clear communication without gray areas, uncertainty, or ambivalence about what earned the reward.

The profound power of clicker training is based on this one element: communication. The click offers the clearest, most accurate, and unambiguous communication, telling the dog the precise behavior that earned the reward. At first, the dog doesn't consciously understand what he did to get clicked, but that will happen, often with explosive suddenness. When your dog understands what your click means, you are giving him the power to control what happens to him, something he hasn't had before. That "Aha! Moment" when your dog "gets it" is so powerfully reinforcing, not just for your dog, but for you, too. At that moment, you will have a thinking dog and all the joys this brings…to both of you!

information.
communication

Chapter 3
CLICKER TRAINING BASICS

My Crossover Journal
In the course of just a few days, I was approached by three people
who went out of their way to tell me how smart their current
dog is. Each said, "I've trained a lot of dogs, but this is the smartest dog I've
ever known." These students had each trained with different methods including
our former method, but the dogs they were bragging about were the first they
had clicker trained; the first dogs they had allowed and encouraged to think.
Regardless of your background, clicker training is about training the smartest
dog you've ever known.

In the Introductory Workshop for our beginner training classes, I ask our new students if they know anything about dog training—either from having trained a dog on their own, with a book, or in a training class, from watching a television program, talking to friends, or from anywhere else. Almost everyone raises a hand. Then I ask if they know anything about clicker training. Usually a few students will raise a hand in answer to this question. Everyone who answers yes to the first question is…you got it—a crossover trainer.

Acknowledging that my students have already-formed impressions about how to train a dog, I ask them to suspend their beliefs, to be open to new ideas that might seem odd, puzzling, or even counterintuitive. All crossover trainers are faced with this dilemma, challenging long-held ideas, exploring concepts that may seem foreign, and tactics that are contradictory to what they (you) know—to what has worked previously. That's what this chapter is about—shifting your focus. Let's start by addressing some of the more common erroneous beliefs about clicker training.

Misunderstandings and misconceptions

Many crossover trainers harbor a variety of misconceptions about clicker training, the first "new" training approach of the Internet era. Just as rapidly as information speeds through cyberspace, so does misinformation and misunderstanding. In part, confusion about clicker training is related to the use of the "gizmo," the clicker. So before tackling concepts, let's explore that little plastic box. Here are the common questions my trainers, students, and I asked when we first crossed over—questions I still get asked.

Common questions about the clicker and the click sound

What, exactly, is a clicker? The typical box clicker is a small, plastic noisemaker with a metal spring to push in and release. The in-out action of the spring makes a clear and precise sound called a "click." There are inexpensive box clickers and more costly digital clickers with adjustable sounds. There are clickers for people with large hands, and clickers you can put on the floor and operate with your foot.

From a plain box clicker to digital clickers to clickers on a stick, new types of clickers are entering the market all the time. If there's a need, someone will design a clicker to meet it.

So that's what a clicker *is*; but what, exactly, does the clicker *do*? The clicker is simply an implement that makes a noteworthy sound. The sound indicates or marks a precise event—the behavior occurring at that precise moment. As you'll soon see, other markers can be used in place of a clicker.

What does the click mean to the dog? The sound indicates that a payoff is forthcoming. It says, "That *precise behavior you just offered* is worthy of reinforcement." Using a sound to indicate the reward-worthy moment provides critical *information* to the dog, marking the specific behavior that earns a payoff. Providing this information means the trainer does not have to deliver the reinforcer simultaneously with the behavior. The click bridges the time gap between the moment of the behavior and the reward.

How does the dog know that a click means he's earned a reward? By giving a reward after every click, it takes very few repetitions for the dog to form the association that *click means a payoff is coming*. Chapter 6 has specific recommendations for teaching this to your dog.

Why mark a behavior? Can't I simply praise my dog? With most training methods, praise serves double-duty as both marker and reward, two distinctly different aspects of learning. The click provides information—it identifies the precise behavior earning the reward. Praise may be a reward if it motivates the dog to perform the behavior. Using praise as both information and motivation—the marker and the reward—works, but not as fast as separating the two.

Even more important, praise lacks clarity as a precise event marker like a click. The longer the trainer continues praising, the muddier the parameters of the behavior become. The dog sits: "Good boy! What a good dog!" continues long after the moment the dog sat, often even after the dog gets up again. Consider from the dog's perspective: For what is he being praised?

Do I have to use a clicker? Despite its name, clicker training does not require a clicker. If you choose not to use one, that's fine. Neither the tool nor the name makes the method. No matter what it's called, what makes this approach work is using a clear **behavior marker**. The power of marker training is in giving helpful information to the dog—*clearly marking the behavior* that has earned the reward.

If I don't use a clicker, what can I use as a marker? A marker can be virtually anything: a word, a light, a hand signal or a sound. A marker can be a buzzer, a whistle, the click of a ballpoint pen or Snapple® bottle top. A marker should be notable, recognizable, clear, distinctive, and unique. The best one, of course, is a clicker!

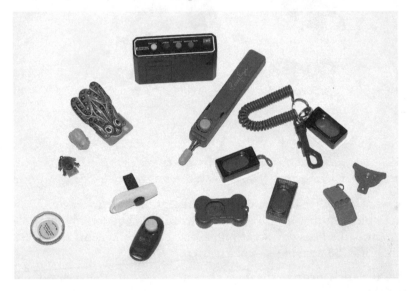

Some of the items you can use for a marker signal include a pen light, a ballpoint pen, a whistle, or the vacuum top from a drink bottle.

My Crossover Journal
A potential training client was looking for help training her Lhasa Apso show dog to stand confidently while the judge examined her. She emphatically told Wendy that she absolutely would not use "clicker training," saying if that's all we did, she'd look elsewhere. Wendy assured her that we could help her without using a clicker. After a few training sessions, her lovely dog finished her Championship, having been "marker trained" without a clicker.

Can I use more than one marker? Use as many as you like. There's no limit to the markers you can use as long as your dog understands that it's a behavior marker (see Chapter 6 for teaching your dog a marker). I use both a verbal marker and a clicker. There are specific instances when one serves better than the other.

- **When a click is best.** The click is an incisive sound that zeroes in on an instant of behavior. Because of this precision, the clicker is unparalleled for **shaping behavior**, that is, systematically guiding the dog step-by-step to perform the goal behavior (see Chapter 7). In the learning stages, using a precise sound marker (a click) is faster and more accurate than a vocal sound or word. The difference may be fractions of a second, but when shaping a behavior, fractions make a difference.

- **When a word will do just fine.** When there is no ambiguity as to what behavior you're marking, you don't need to click; a marker word can work just fine. Our word marker is "Yes" or "Yup." For example in training "stay," the dog either stays, or he doesn't. When the dog remains in position, "Yes" will do. With any behavior, once it is learned, a verbal marker is all you need. Chapter 12 has specific recommendations for using a click versus a word.

- **Other markers for special circumstances.** For specialized training and special needs, such as deaf dogs, other markers (like quick hand signals) work well. For example, I had a student who used a thumb up with a smile as a marker for her deaf Great Dane. The dog quickly learned that this particular silent marker meant a "reward is available for that behavior."

The bottom line is that you can achieve at least some of your goals using an alternative marker other than a clicker, but it's like flying versus traveling on the ground. Different modes of transportation will get you to your destination, but why take a slow one if a fast one is both available and better?

So you say, but I've trained a dog or two just using praise to "mark" the behavior and it worked just fine. Why should I change? Because as successful as you've been, you would have even greater success with clicker training. Here are just a few reasons that a marker, especially a clicker, is better than just praise, or praise with food treats.

- **A click sound is uniquely attached to the dog's successful performance**, giving the click great significance and impact. Think of it as the opposite of the dog in the "Far Side" cartoon ignoring his owner's "Blah, blah, blah Ginger."

- **The click is an "acoustic arrow" zeroing in on the precise moment of success.** Such precision and the clarity of the information it provides make clicker training far faster and clearer than not using a click. Not as sharp as a click, the voice blurs the edges of the behavior. Petting is even less exact.

- **The click is neutral.** When you're tired or stressed your voice changes. The click has no moods; it sounds the same regardless of your emotional state or attitude.

- **The click eliminates ambiguity.** Black/white; payoff/no payoff. Clarity makes learning quicker and easier. This is true with any marker, but a click is clearest.

The click is like an acoustic arrow, instantly penetrating into the dog's brain.

- **The click empowers the person clicking.** There are no age limitations, and it doesn't matter who clicks. With most training methods, a child can rarely control a dog. With marker training, anyone can click. An adult can click for a child, and when the child is the source of the reward, guess who the dog looks to.

- **Achieving results with a clicker is faster than not using a clicker.** With such clarity, you can quickly train complex behaviors that are difficult or impossible without using a clicker.

- **As if this isn't enough, clicker training is fun!**

If I use a clicker, will I have to carry it with me for the rest of my dog's life? No, absolutely not. A clicker (or anything you choose to mark your dog's behavior) is a teaching tool. Once your dog is trained and he performs the behaviors on cue, you don't need the tool except to teach something new or brush up a behavior.

When we are someplace like a clicker class, won't my dog be confused hearing other clicks? No. A dog trained with a clicker will alert to the sound of a click, but the dog quickly realizes that other people's clicking has no relevance to him. When *you* click he gets a reward—that's significant to him.

In a class or seminar situation, with clicking going on all around, your dog quickly learns that other clicks have no significance. A dog pays attention to the person who is marking his behavior and rewarding him.

I clicked, and my dog didn't come. What am I doing wrong? A click is not a command. It doesn't mean "come." It is simply a sound that marks a behavior that earned a reward. You don't call your dog with a click, but you can certainly click when he comes to you. Clicking his arrival lets him know that this behavior (coming) is treat-worthy.

I compete with my dog. You can't use a clicker in the ring, so why train with one? Competitive events demonstrate what you and your dog have accomplished, not how you got there. No "tool" that is used in training (clicker, lure, leash correction, ball, food, or other reward) is allowed in the ring. A clicker is the same as any teaching tool—if you still need to use it regularly, your team isn't ready for competition.

If my dog does something particularly well, should I click several times? No. Multiple clicks blur the behavior that earned a click. One click (the in-out sound) marks the behavior you want to reinforce. See Jackpots (page 143) for information about extra rewards for excellence.

What if I click and I shouldn't have, or I didn't mean to. Do I still give my dog a treat? Yes. Even if you goofed, pair a reward with your click. Especially early in your clicker training when you're teaching your crossover dog what the click means, it is important to give a reward every time you click. If you don't have a treat, you can always praise your dog as a reward following a click. On the other hand, as you advance through this training (and through the book), you will find some *rare instances* when you might not give a reward after a click. (See the Random Reinforcement Game in Chapter 8 and sidebar "Double Click" in Troubleshooting the Down in Chapter 12.) But in the beginning, if you click, reward your dog.

"I *won't* use a clicker!"

From the moment I began transitioning my training classes, I've met both cross-over and new trainers whose reactions range from curiosity and mild skepticism to a declarative, "Clicker training is bunk. If that's all you do, I'm training elsewhere!"

Talking to a friend about trying to overcome misconceptions about clicker training, she asked why I even use the name. "After all," she said, "you didn't call your previous method anything. You just trained dogs well and kindly."

I call myself a clicker trainer for a reason—clicker training is the best thing to happen to dogs since the dawn of dog training, and I am proud to be at the forefront of the "clicker revolution." That said, the philosophy, principles, concepts, and specific methodology are often lost in confusion and misconceptions about what "real" clicker training is. Now that you understand what the clicker *is*, it's important to understand and clarify what clicking and clicker training are *not*.

Gadget, gimmick, or gizmo: It's a clicker!

There are many possible reasons for confusion about and seeming resistance to clicker training, especially with potential crossover trainers who have some alternative training experience. At the top of the list, clicker training has an identifiable name with a recognizable feature—the clicker.

- **Preconceptions and misunderstandings surround this little tool, including the very role of the clicker itself.** These include:

  - **A click is a command.** It is not. It's a behavior or event marker.

  - **A clicker must be used forever or the dog won't listen.** No—its use is reduced over time, and is unnecessary once a dog has learned a behavior.

  - **A clicker is not manly.** Honest! A school in my area says this to potential students. I can't fathom how this makes sense.

  - Other significance is attached to the sound such as the click indicates:

    - 🐾 "Good dog"

    - 🐾 "Keep going"

    - 🐾 And even, as one school in our area uses it, "No!"

    None of these represents "true" clicker training. Clicker training uses the sound of the click for just one thing: information that says, "For that precise action, you win a prize." It marks a moment of behavior, period.

- **A frequent objection is that clicker training requires coordinating too many things for just two hands. Holding a leash, a dog, food...that's enough.** This is a valid point, but there are simple strategies to compensate for our physical limitations. More importantly, the advantages far outweigh the difficulties (see "Create a third hand" on page 58).

- **"The clicker is a gimmick, a gizmo, a gadget, and it's not necessary."** A clicker is a tool, not a gimmick. Necessary? It's not essential. Helpful? Absolutely!

- **Then there's the erroneous belief (often perpetuated by trainers with their own method to protect) that clicker training is a flash in the pan.** As I pointed out in the history in Chapter 1, it's been around a long time, and it's not going away.

The power of the click

The next likely factor that has impacted wide acceptance of clicker training among crossover trainers is the fact that when used with other training methods, the clicker can radically speed learning. Such improved success actually strengthens the trainer's attachment to their current method and provides little impetus to learn "pure" clicker training.

Further, the improvement lends credence to many trainers' belief that they are clicker training when they are lure-reward-with-a-clicker training. Adding a clicker to lure-reward training makes it faster, but not as fast, effective, easy, or as much fun for the dog and the trainer as clicker training.

My Crossover Journal

A seminar participant who lure trained with a click said that her husband and children had named her Shepherd/Rottie mix "Stupid" because he was so slow and disengaged in training. As she shaped him (no luring) to touch a target, it became apparent that far from being slow, he caught on extremely quickly. She first shaped him to nose touch a small traffic cone on the floor, then a ball on a stick with a weighted base. When I asked her to demonstrate something for the group, she brought him to the front of the room along with her container of uncut, full-sized sausages.

We waited as she broke the sausages into smaller pieces. At first, her dog watched patiently, but losing patience, he noticed me holding the ball on a stick. He turned to me and emphatically bumped the base. Getting no response (other than a murmur of recognition from the audience), he went directly to the traffic cone on the floor by her chair, nose-targeted it and looked back at his owner. Again, getting no response, he grabbed the cone and brought it to her.

Far from "stupid," this dog was simply bored by lure training. His owner had not engaged his brain, and he was just disinterested. Once challenged and turned on—once he started thinking—he earned not only her respect, but also the name "Brilliant."

As the example in the My Crossover Journal entry above demonstrates, if you're already using a clicker in your training, you're part-way there. But don't stop now. You've started the journey to crossover, keep going. It's worth it!

Marker training

It would be wonderful if people would stop using the term "clicker" unless they are truly clicker training. This one change would reduce confusion about and resistance to "clicker training." Faced with ambiguity about the name "clicker," we also call what we do **"marker"** training. A marker **"marks"** the behavior, communicating information to the dog: Thumbs up! That's the behavior!

Shifting Focus

As I wrote in the Introduction, crossover trainers are familiar with exercise-based approaches that focus on a method's *mechanics* to teach the *exercises*—the specific behaviors. We know, for example, the precise motion to make in training a dog to lie down with lure-reward training, or where to place our hands and how to move them when physically placing a dog into a sit. Not only does clicker training not include such mechanics, but part of the shift of focus for the crossover trainer means moving away from the very idea of training by exercise.

It is clicker training's focus on *concepts* that is the most radical difference setting it apart from any other approach. Marker training is not about "how to," that is, the mechanics of training an exercise. There is no set formula, no recipe of instructions. Rather success—the dog's behavior—is based on the trainer's understanding and application of concepts. This will become clear as the story unfolds, so let's examine a major aspect that sets clicker training apart from all others.

Command-based training

A significant departure from all other methods of training is that clicker training does not pair the command word with the behavior from the start of training. Other methods are **command-based**. The trainer says, "Sit," as she lures, tucks, or pushes the dog into position. "Down" as the trainer lowers, pulls, or lures the dog to lie down. When the trainer uses a luring motion, with or without saying a word, the motion functions as a "command."

Command-based training attempts to form the association between the command word or signal and the action from the very start. Not with clicker training. With clicker training, *the signal or voice command is not added until after the dog is performing the behavior on his own.*

Crossover trainers may be resistant to this different approach. Pairing the word with the object from the beginning is consistent with how we humans are taught. For example, a mother teaching her child says "Mama" while pointing to herself. Most significantly for crossover trainers, it is consistent with our prior successes training dogs. *While keeping quiet may seem counterintuitive, as you'll soon see, eliminating commands and signals speeds learning.*

Just say the word and I'll do it…or will I?

One of the issues encountered by the crossover trainer is semantics—the words used in clicker training for some of the most basic things are different from other methods. Take the word "command."

With most training methods, the "command" is the word the trainer uses to direct a behavior such as "sit," "down," or "come." In clicker training, these words are termed **cues**. There are both objective and subjective reasons for using the term "cue" rather than "command." Subjectively, a "command" implies an imperative, "Do it or else," boss/underling, a dominant/subordinate relationship that is not relevant to clicker training. The concept of a "command" is incompatible with a training method that focuses on forming a partnership and collaboration with a thinking dog.

Objectively, a cue is more than just a command word. It is any **prompt** that triggers a behavior, including a spoken word, hand signal, whistle, head bob, and the like. A cue lets the dog know that he has an *opportunity to earn reinforcement* by performing the behavior. Chapters 8 and 9 cover how to teach cues and achieve a reliable response.

Command-action sequence

Putting the word "cue" aside for the moment, let's explore how other training methods embrace teaching the prompt. Referred to as the **command-action sequence**, giving the prompt followed by the behavior presumes that the word or signal prompts the dog's response. In behavioral terms, it's **Antecedent-Behavior-Consequence** or A-B-C.

> A. The antecedent comes before the action. It is the prompt that tells the dog what behavior to perform.
>
> B. The dog performs the behavior.
>
> C. The performance earns a consequence.

A-B-C in a command-based approach, consistent with virtually every dog training method other than clicker training, looks like this:

Antecedent	→	Behavior	→	Consequence
Give the prompt	→	Perform the behavior	→	Win the prize
Say "Sit" as trainer lures or places dog	→	Dog sits	→	Praise/reward

Giving the prompt prior to performance of the behavior makes sense once a behavior is learned, but is it the best way to *train a behavior from scratch?* Is it the fastest way for the dog to learn the behavior that wins the reward? The simple answer is, "No." When training new behaviors, pairing prompts with actions actually slows learning.

"Helping" isn't helpful, it impedes learning

Until a dog can voluntarily perform the behavior, anything that distracts the dog, diverting even a tiny part of his focus from performing that behavior, interferes with learning. Some distractions are obvious: kids running around, the cat hopping into your lap while you're training, a family member noisily munching chips nearby, the doorbell ringing. But distractions can be far more subtle, and include many things that trainers use, often with the mistaken belief that they help learning:

- **Sounds.** The sound of your voice is just noise to the dog—even a single word intended to act as a cue when *the dog does not yet know what you mean.*

- **Movement.** Your motion as you signal or lure.

- **Touch.** Manipulating your dog into a position, or petting him.

- **Food.** Using food as a lure or bribe.

Such distractions impede learning, directing your dog's focus away from your primary objective, which is for your dog to concentrate on performing the desired behavior—and getting you to click and reward.

Once the dog is trained, A-B-C—or put another way "give the cue–perform the behavior–win the prize": *Cue-Do-Win*—is the proper sequence of events. Once the dog is trained. Learning a behavior, however, is faster when the dog can focus simply on Do–Win without sight, sound, tactile, or food distractions. (More on this in Chapter 6.)

A huge departure from the traditional concept of dog training, with clicker training you say *nothing* as your dog tries different behaviors. Let the click speak to your dog, providing critical information.

Common questions about the cue

How will my dog know what behavior I'm training if I don't use a cue word? The bigger question is: How can your dog know what you're training when you use a word for a behavior that he doesn't yet know? The answer is, he doesn't. Hearing a word is not what teaches your dog. Your dog learns by associating his *behavior* with a *payoff*: Do–Win. Before he's learned the behavior, a word is a meaningless sound. When the dog makes that association between behavior and reward, he'll readily offer that behavior, then you can attach a name or signal to it.

If I don't use a cue word, how will my dog know when I want to switch focus to work on a different behavior? The click, not the word, tells your dog what behavior you're rewarding. Changing the behavior you're training is easy. Chapter 5 tells you how.

How do I teach the cue? When will I be able to tell my dog to do what I want? The process of "attaching the cue," teaching the word or signal that tells your dog what behavior you want him to perform, is easy. It's covered in Chapter 8.

Clicker training versus training-with-a-clicker

Even with people who think they're clicker training, misunderstanding abounds over the difference between clicker training and training-with-a-clicker training.

My Crossover Journal
Attendees at an Advanced Clicker Training Seminar all said they were experienced clicker trainers with a complete grasp of the basics. When we began working it became apparent, however, that about half those in attendance were "training-with-a-clicker," not clicker training. When she realized the difference, and used the clicker "properly," one participant exclaimed, "Ohmygosh! I thought clicker training was great, but this is so much better!"

In the following chapters you'll find references to the differences between clicker training (CT) and training-with-a-clicker training (TWAC). Chart 3-1 is a brief rundown of some of the major differences for you to test your current method versus clicker training.

Clicker Training (CT)	Training-with-a-Clicker Training (TWAC)
• Click is an event marker	• Click marks only complete behaviors such as lying down, being in heel position, etc.
• Click ends the behavior	• Dog is required to perform an additional behavior to earn the treat
• Click marks the behavior; the treat follows	• Click may mark an on-going behavior (keep going); a treat may or may not follow each click
• Click represents a high-value reward	• Click is paired with lower value reinforcers such as verbal praise
• The dog is in volitional control of his own behavior	• The trainer controls the dog's behavior with luring, placement, or even with corrections
• Treat delivery follows the click regardless of the dog's position	• Treat delivery is dependent on the dog remaining in position
• Treat delivery is used to advance training in a variety of ways	• Treat delivery is always or almost always related to the dog's position when receiving the treat
• The trainer is the observer; the dog is the performer	• The trainer actively leads (e.g., lures or guides); the dog follows the trainer's lead
• The dog is given time to "figure it out" with the overall goal of future speedy learning	• The trainer relies on prompts (luring, guiding) with a short-term goal of speedily learning a behavior
• Heavy reliance on positive reinforcement and negative punishment	• Click marks compliance following the use of positive punishment or negative reinforcement
• Training employs the full potential of the dog as a cooperative partner-in-training	• The click is a tool that speeds learning regardless of training method to achieve behaviors

Chart 3-1. If you already use a clicker to train your dog, see if what you're doing is clicker training or training-with-a-clicker training.

Chapter 4

PITFALLS AND PAYOFFS TO CROSSING OVER

My Crossover Journal
I was watching one of our trainers train a dog on the agility dog walk. A crossover from lure-reward training, when the dog hesitated on the up ramp, the trainer unconsciously pulled out a treat to lure. "What are you doing?" I asked. Oops! Even after more than ten years, from time-to-time, we still fall back into insidious habits that we either drift toward, or never quite got rid of. Old habits die hard.

It seemed like a better mousetrap: a fast, kind, effective approach to dog training that gets food out of the dog's face. And it is. Clicker training—pure, true clicker training—is an incredibly powerful approach, superior to other methods in many ways: speed of learning, clarity of communication, respect for the dog, and the exhilaration of seeing the dog think. Clicker training creates a true training partnership—once you get there. The process of crossing over, however, can be stressful.

I came from a method I had happily used for years, was totally comfortable with, and could perform automatically without conscious thought. Stepping off into the unknown was, to say the least, often confusing, unsettling, and even anxiety producing. Starting over is not easy, especially learning a method that is fundamentally different from your previous training.

My Crossover Journal
I recently met with a potential new client who had owned dogs all his life, and trained them by compulsion-praise methods. A busy executive whose unpredictable schedule involved a great deal of travel, he could not commit to group classes, and was investigating private training and trainers to entrust with his puppy's education. Committed to working with a trainer and participating as much as his schedule would allow, he was intrigued and attracted by the philosophy I presented. He expressed concern, however, that his prior training, his deeply entrenched habits, would undermine our approach, confuse his pup, and potentially damage their relationship. I could identify with his apprehension, but assured him that although he might struggle from time-to-time, dogs are resilient and most can easily move past an occasional "oops," an occasional back-track, or an occasional regression into "old" methods.

If a crossover dog can learn "new ways," certainly a crossover trainer can too, and won't ruin his dog in the process. Ultimately it is far better to take the first step, occasionally slip up, learn from errors and redouble our efforts than not to crossover at all.

Having gone through the process of crossing over to clicker training, and in teaching other crossover trainers, I have identified three major factors that contribute to the ease or difficulty with which a dog and handler will crossover. These are:

1. Your previous training methods.

2. Prior experience—the amount of training and length of time you've trained with your previous method.

3. Temperament—both yours and your dog's.

Methodology: Your previous training

Command-based training methods fall into two broad categories: lure-reward (L-R) and compulsion-praise (C-P). All command-based methods include elements of one, the other, or both. As I wrote previously, any training method works at least some of the time, meaning that there are pros and cons to every approach. To assess both where you're coming from, as well as where you want to go in your training, it is helpful to consider the strengths and weakness of any method. The following is a rundown of the two basic methods crossover trainers come from.

Lure-reward (L-R) training

How it works. Holding food, the trainer lures the dog into position and rewards with the treat. The reward is immediate to the behavior. The dog focuses on and follows the lure.

Pros:

- A food-oriented dog responds quickly to food lures. The lure quickly induces the desired response, and simply following the lure earns the reward.

- Just as significantly, the dog's response (success) is highly reinforcing for the lure-reward trainer.

- The luring motion easily becomes a hand signal cue.

- Simple behaviors are easily lured, making this training suitable for unskilled trainers starting off with an untrained dog.

- L-R training offers fast, short-term results for some behaviors.

Cons:

- In order to work, the dog must be interested in food treats.

- At the opposite end of the scale is the dog that is so overly-focused on food, that it's impossible to train with food in sight.

- The dog's response is dependent on the handler luring with food. Food is an *enticement* rather than a reward: no lure; no response.

- L-R is ill-suited for training complex behaviors.

- Because this training is so reinforcing for the trainer (a pro), most L-R trainers have difficulty fading the lure (a con). Further, when faced with non-compliance, many L-R trainers quickly fall back to luring with a treat, which reinforces the dog's non-responsiveness.

- The lure motion must be **faded**: gradually reduced, then eliminated; a step that can be time-consuming, prolonging learning.

- The dog's focus is on the lure, not the behavior. The dog is learning to follow the lure rather than to perform the behavior on his own. Gaining understanding of a specific behavior is slower than when the dog is able to focus on his behavior. Here's an analogy provided by a participant at a seminar: You ask for directions to a restaurant. A friend says she's going right by it, so just follow her car. Keeping her red Toyota in sight, you twist and turn through town, passing intersections and lights until she waves goodbye at the restaurant. Do you know how you got there? Could you get there on your own in the future? What if she had given you directions, telling you where to turn and what landmarks to look for? Could you find your way again? Having found your own way to the restaurant, future success is more likely, even if you make a few wrong turns along the way.

Luring is following the red Toyota. You're mindlessly unaware of what you did to get to your destination. When you find the way yourself, you experience the satisfaction—even the joy—of accomplishment and discovery. So it is for your thinking dog.

Issues crossing over from L-R

Dog issues. Once food is out of sight so that the dog can focus on his behavior rather than on food, L-R trained dogs generally transition easily to clicker training. After some initial confusion and hesitation (waiting for a lure), L-R crossover dogs quickly catch on and begin to use their initiative, to think. Chapter 6 has recommendations that will help your dog with this.

Trainer issues. Crossover trainers from a L-R background often have a harder time than their dogs do. L-R trainers must concentrate on breaking old habits. First, focus on not holding food. Next, concentrate on holding still, eliminating body language, and finally, working on proper delivery of the treat, as covered in Chapter 6. It is helpful to the L-R trainer to *get the food out of the hand and off the body*. L-R trainers who are accustomed to achieving results quickly with a lure must be patient with their dogs and themselves while crossing over.

The biggest pitfall: the lure of the lure. L-R trainers need to fight the inclination, the magnetic attraction of luring. When you think your dog seems confused, do not "help" by pulling out a treat and luring. Doing so *reinforces waiting and looking confused*. Once you've reinforced waiting, you'll have a harder row to hoe the next time. Further, avoid staring at, leaning toward, or using your body movement to achieve the performance of a behavior. You may think of these as "helpful hints," but they're crutches both you and your dog have relied on in the past, and need to eliminate.

Compulsion-praise (C-P) methods

How it works. C-P training uses physical placement with verbal praise and/or a food reward. For non-compliance or incorrect behavior, C-P relies on a collar "correction" (a pop or check) followed by verbal praise with or without a treat. For example, if the dog fails to sit, breaks a stay, or moves out of heel position, he is "corrected," then praised for being in position. C-P training relies on creating a dichotomy between behaviors that earn a correction and those that earn praise. Avoid the former; offer the latter.

Pros:

- With dogs of a specific temperament, in the hands of a skilled trainer, C-P training successfully follows the principles of how dogs learn (see Chapter 2).

- C-P training quickly suppresses undesirable behavior, at least on leash and/or in the presence of the skilled trainer, so the results are reinforcing to the trainer.

Cons:

- C-P training punishes behavior the dog may not know how to avoid, making it unfair and potentially depressing, especially for dogs with softer, more compliant temperaments.

- Mistakes with C-P training can have a detrimental effect on the dog and the handler-dog relationship. Unless used with skill, dogs may associate the trainer with the corrections, so the unskilled owner is at a disadvantage.

- C-P training requires a high degree of expertise in reading the dog. Applying a "proper correction" is a physical skill that requires coordination and timing often beyond the abilities of the average dog owner.

- C-P training does not transfer well from the skilled to the unskilled handler.

- C-P training does not transfer easily from on-leash to off-leash.

- C-P training does not result in the dog learning self-control. Rather, control is dependent on the presence of the trainer.

Compulsion is bad...Isn't it?

"Compulsion" is not synonymous with brute force and pain. In dog training, it simply means physical guidance, manipulation, or placement. Gently tucking a dog into a sit compels him to sit, but it doesn't hurt. Training the dog to walk on a loose leash with a head halter or front-connection harness compels him to walk with you. It's not a dirty word; compulsion simply means the dog has no choice.

Issues crossing over from compulsion-praise:

Dog issues. Crossover dogs trained with C-P have learned to wait for commands, to wait to be told what to do, so it may take longer for this dog to offer behaviors spontaneously. They've learned that experimentation earns a collar pop: moving on "stay," hesitating on a recall, sitting farther away, and the like all earned "corrections." Spontaneity and creativity were corrected. The C-P trained dog often takes time to learn to try new things—to trust that he won't be corrected for offering a behavior without a command. It may take weeks, or as with my crossover dog Mayday, even months for a well-trained dog to begin to use his initiative—to think.

Trainer issues. Perhaps surprisingly, C-P trainers have an easier time making the transition to clicker training than lure-reward trainers do. C-P trainers are not in the habit of holding or luring with food—the biggest pitfall for the L-R trainer. However, since the C-P trainer's dog may be more cautious, C-P trainers may need more patience. As with L-R, the crossover trainer from a C-P background is accustomed to compelling results quickly, so your patience may be challenged. Be prepared to meet the challenge.

The biggest pitfall, feeling loss of control. C-P trainers may feel as if they have relinquished control of the dog's training. Since C-P training is generally dominance-oriented, giving the dog permission to initiate behaviors takes getting used to. C-P trainers must watch themselves, avoiding a sigh, tongue cluck, or verbal reprimand when the dog makes a mistake. As the C-P crossover dog begins to experiment, especially in the beginning, any negative feedback can dampen or even destroy his initiative. A C-P trainer may feel as if they are tolerating unruly behavior, but honestly, they're not. Ultimately, the trainer is in control. As you learn more, this will become clear.

Prior experience: How much, how long, how effective?

The extent of both the trainer's and the crossover dog's prior experience influence how quickly and easily each will transition to clicker training. Here's the rundown of each:

The crossover dog's level of compliance

The more training your dog has had prior to crossing over, the more he has learned to wait for a command or a lure. In non-clicker methods, when a dog performs a behavior unrelated to what the trainer wants, it will be handled in one of two ways. For example, with lure training, the trainer will ignore the "error" and lure the desired behavior. With compulsion-praise training, the trainer will either physically maneuver the dog into performing the desired behavior, or may discourage (punish) non-compliance with a correction. In either case, the dog is not using his mind to actively participate in learning the behavior.

As the dog becomes better trained, he becomes more reliant on the trainer to lure him (with or without food), or to give a command, telling him what to do, what behavior will be reinforced. The result is that crossover dogs with considerable prior training are reluctant to experiment, generally taking longer to begin offering behaviors than dogs with little or no training.

It isn't that a dog with extensive training can't crossover—he can. It just may take a bit longer before the dog starts to use his brain, which can be frustrating for the trainer. Believe me, I know. But stick with it; fight the urge to switch back and forth. Once your well-trained, crossover dog catches on, the fun begins…for both of you.

The trainer's experience

If you have been using a method for a long time, and/or have trained several dogs, you've developed habits and skills that you perform without conscious thought. In any endeavor, when you switch from prior learning to a new skill, you have to consciously break old habits. This means not only focusing on your dog, but also paying attention to your own actions. Here are a couple of real-life analogies most of us have experienced:

> You drive to work following the same route every day, getting off the highway at Exit 10. You get a new job located off Exit 12. When you drive to your new job, at first you have to concentrate or your auto-pilot will take you off at Exit 10. Daydream and you'll find yourself pulling into the parking lot at your former job.

And a forehead-slapping experience I live nearly every day:

> Several years ago, I rearranged my kitchen cabinets, switching the mugs and glasses to a different location. Even years later, nearly every morning, I open the wrong cabinet to get a mug for my coffee. I'd like to blame it on early-morning fog, but I also do it when I'm fully awake, unconsciously going to the wrong cabinet to retrieve a glass.

You will go through periods of discomfort as you cross over. Where you used to train routinely, naturally, and without conscious thought, you will need to purposefully focus both on your actions and on your dog's. As in "My Crossover Journal" entries with the trainer I observed in agility and the new client I reassured, you will occasionally fall back into old habits. Over time this will change as you recognize them, adjust, and develop new habits. Best of all, once you get into clicker training you'll find that your new skills become automatic, too.

Temperament

The final factor affecting the ease or difficulty in crossing over is temperament—yours and your dog's.

Your dog's temperament

Marker training works beautifully with dogs of any temperament; however, the individual crossover dog's temperament may affect how quickly he takes to it. An active, bold, out-going dog is more willing to try new things than is a quiet, timid, or mentally sensitive dog. Further, a mentally sensitive dog will be affected by the trainer's attitude, especially sensing the trainer's frustration. It is imperative for the trainer to remain calm and patient. Avoid reacting to your dog's behavior or lack of behavior with physical or emotional responses such as tongue clucks, heavy sighs, or even rolling your eyes heavenward. Take a deep breath and relax.

Crossing over to clicker training may seem stressful to your dog, especially to the mentally sensitive dog, but crossing over is *far less stressful* than the effects of traditional training. Once your dog catches on, the rewards, including your dog's excitement at being an active participant in his training, are well worth the effort. The thinking dog clearly enjoys figuring out what behavior will get the trainer to mark and reward his behavior. Any stress from the change is quickly overcome by success.

One temperament characteristic that can affect clicker training is **sound sensitivity.** A small number of dogs are extremely noise-sensitive and are frightened by sharp sounds, including a clicker. You'll find strategies for both preventing sound sensitivity to the clicker and working with sound sensitive dogs in Chapter 6.

The trainer's temperament

Dog trainers want immediate results. When you are used to instant results through luring or manipulating a dog into position, it is hard to consider waiting days or even weeks to see results. And you don't have to.

Tactics in some clicker training books include several days devoted to "charging the clicker" (clicking and treating a number of times in quick succession) to form the association between the click and treat. Some books give little guidance on getting behavior other than "watch and wait," even recommending reading a magazine while waiting for your dog to offer a behavior. Such recommendations give the impression that clicker training is interminably slow, and is only for those with relaxed, even lethargic temperaments. I don't know many trainers that thrive on such lack of immediacy and delayed gratification. Lord knows, I'm not one. Fortunately, this impression is not correct.

Most difficult for me when I crossed over was dealing with my frustration when Mayday didn't immediately "play the game." If you have such a dog, you won't have the instant gratification most of us seek. Fight your frustration, and focus on being patient. It is just for a little while. Working through this behavioral barrier pays untold dividends in just a few short weeks. Once your dog starts offering behaviors, when you see evidence of your dog starting to think, new learning will quickly erase any frustration in getting there.

Different people find transitioning to a new method—any new method—frustrating, confusing, and unsettling. Some people are better able to handle the unfamiliar, new and different. As you transition from the familiar and comfortable to the unfamiliar and unknown, focus on your skills (and your breathing), and be patient with yourself and with your dog. If you feel frustrated or impatient with your dog's progress, talk to a clicker trainer who can coach you to help get your dog over the hump.

Moving back-and-forth: Using two methods

You're making the switch—you're crossing over—but you still want to rely on your familiar (comfortable) previous methods for some training. Perhaps you use clicker training for obedience and your previous method for agility. Or maybe you introduce new behaviors with a clicker, but "polish" for competition with corrections. Or do basic training your old way, and work on other "fun" behaviors with a clicker. Here's my best advice about switching back and forth—don't. It's not fair to your dog. Settle on one approach and stick to it. Whether you're a lure-reward trainer, a compulsion-praise trainer, or a combination, there are pitfalls to switching back and forth. Here are some:

Clicker with lure-reward

If you give yourself permission to use luring, that is, more than just to jump-start a new behavior (covered in Chapter 8), you may want to use it to help your dog out of a confusing situation. Here's a typical scenario: Jane was working with her lure-reward trained crossover dog. He didn't respond quickly and perform the behavior Jane wanted, and he looked confused. Jane felt bad—he looked so helpless. It wouldn't hurt to help him just this once. So she lured the behavior, then clicked and treated. Then she tried again, waiting for her dog to offer the behavior she had just lured.

Again, he sat there looking confused. Jane waited, thinking, "Surely he'll get it if I just wait a bit longer." But it went on for minutes—what felt like hours—and nothing happened. His look of confusion turned to disconnection. Once again Jane pulled out a treat and lured him. After that, Jane's dog stopped offering behaviors altogether.

Despite what she thought, Jane wasn't "helping" her dog. Rather, she was reinforcing his helplessness. Think about the behavior the dog was offering and the resulting consequence. The behavior: "Look confused and wait…and wait…and wait…" The result: Jane pulled out a lure and "helped." The treat rewarded "Wait; help is on the way."

What if you are really clear with your dog, using shaping and marker training in one endeavor, say agility, and lure-reward training in another, such as obedience behaviors? Won't the dog get the difference? He may, but what's the point? If you believe that clicker training is better, faster, clearer, and fairer to the dog, why not use it for everything? Or if you believe your previous method is perfectly acceptable, what are you missing that led you to this book? If you're looking for a better way to train, give it a try—an honest, whole-hearted try. That's the ultimate in fairness to your dog…and to you.

Clicker with compulsion-praise

Switching back and forth between clicker training, where the dog is free to make choices, and compulsion-praise training is really confusing to your dog. Which trainer are you today: the one who wants him to think, or the one that doesn't? Are you Dr. Jeckyl, enjoying creativity, or Mr. Hyde, punishing it with a correction? Just as importantly, in twelve years of clicker training, I have never found a reason to need another approach. Being a clicker trainer does not mean that you can't "correct" (i.e., fix) undesirable behavior. It just means that you fix it within the framework of clicker training without collar "corrections." Honest, it works for everything you want to do with your dog, including service dog training. After all, if marker training works for dolphins swimming free performing tasks in the ocean—no collar, no leash—shouldn't we be able to get a dog to perform a competitive ring routine or service task without resorting to collar pops or ear pinches?

The bottom line: It is less confusing and more fair to your dog to stick with your traditional training than to switch back and forth between two antithetical approaches.

More common questions: What about a dog that already knows "stuff?"

The following answers will help clarify some questions and concerns you may still have about crossing over with a dog that has already had some training. Here are the most common questions I've been asked by crossover trainers with crossover dogs:

Do I have to start all over? Absolutely not! You can build on your dog's training, and rapidly add new behaviors to his repertoire. Your crossover dog doesn't unlearn what he's previously been taught, but you can improve on what he already knows…in minutes, rather than months.

When I first tried clicker training, I met resistance from several of my instructors who had already been through a radical change in their training while being coached by a top competition trainer. They had had to start from scratch to re-train several core behaviors, and having gone through this frustrating exercise once, they were unwilling to do it again.

My Crossover Journal
Ann was training her yellow Lab, Connie, in Open obedience. Connie was doing well on all the exercises except Drop-on-Recall. Her recall was fine, but she was slow to drop. Ann had been clicker training just a short while, and was still skeptical. Further she refused to even consider start-ing from scratch with something Connie already knew. Despite her skepticism, Ann agreed to let me see what I could do. In less than five minutes of shaping, Connie was throwing herself down, dropping like a stone. I hadn't used any cue, so then it was simply a matter of "naming" the new behavior (the fast drop) calling it something other than "down." Using the old cue would elicit the old behavior—the slow response.

Once she learned "lie down fast" as a "new" behavior, Connie could not have dropped more quickly.

What about using commands my dog already knows? Evaluate your dog's responses to the commands you've trained. If you're happy with your dog's performance, great! On the other hand, if you'd like a faster drop, a quicker recall, firmer stay or the like, once you understand the principles of clicker training and your crossover dog under-stands the process, you can "spiffy up" previously learned commands. You'll see how in Chapter 8.

If I'm not happy with the behavior, should I stop using the commands he knows? Use your dog's training. Regardless what method you've been using, you've spent time and effort, and achieved results. Utilize the fruits of your labors. If you need to call your dog, even if his response is slow and needs improvement, call your dog. If you want your dog to "go lie down," so what if he needs to be told twice. Use what he knows. When you're working on improving a behavior as with Connie's drop, you can train it as a new behavior. Once learned, the "new" improved behavior will have a different cue word. (You'll find information on changing cues in Chapter 8.)

I'm used to talking to my dog. Can I? Some crossover trainers have trouble getting used to not giving commands and verbal encouragement, but that doesn't mean you can't talk. You can. If you want to praise your dog, go ahead—*after* you click. On the other hand, don't chatter or carry on a conversation with your dog while he's working through a behavior. Remember, sound is a distraction at best, and at worst, you're teaching your dog to tune you out.

What if I give a cue and my dog doesn't respond. What should I do? There are reasons dogs fail to respond to a cue—just as dogs will occasionally fail to respond to "commands" learned by other methods. Regardless of the reasons, virtually none are the dog's fault. Help your dog be successful, even if it means repeating the cue. Don't "correct" your dog for failure to respond. This is covered in detail in Chapters 8 and 10.

What about the stuff I already know? It's hard to ignore! Learning clicker training means abandoning preconceptions and comfortable habits. New learning may not be easy, but it will be rewarding! You'll see.

How do I get my dog to offer behaviors? The crossover dog's prior training has taught him to wait patiently to be told what to do, so he has to learn that offering behaviors is good. Paradoxically, the "better behaved" a traditionally trained dog is, the longer it takes for him to offer a behavior. *But it will happen!* The exercises in Chapter 6 will get things rolling.

This is all new to me, and it's a little daunting. I'm not sure I can do it without messing up my dog. If I really mess up, what will happen? Here's the thing: Clicker training can't mess up your dog or your relationship. Late, early, or imprecise clicking may result in a behavior that you hadn't meant to train. Learn from it! Your dog's behavior will tell you if your timing was off. Stop clicking that behavior, and improve your timing so you are marking the behavior you want.

My Crossover Journal
At a seminar for advanced clicker trainers, one of the participants presented a problem with her dog dropping the dumbbell just before she reached to take it from him. He'd retrieve it just fine, but he released it a split-second too soon. Observing her timing, I noted that she was clicking as her dog was beginning to open his mouth, not while he was firmly holding the dumbbell. That small change in timing improved the dog's behavior in just three or four clicks.

I'm skeptical. Every time someone comes up with a "new" method, it's touted as the best thing since sliced bread, but it's usually just some slight variation of what I've been doing. How do I know you're not just selling snake oil? The best answer to this is to observe a clicker trained dog in action.

My Crossover Journal
The first night of our Manners Class is a workshop without dogs.
We ask only one or two students to bring their untrained dogs so
we can demonstrate clicker training, and show them what to practice. A few
days before a new class session, one of the students who was enrolled in the class
brought her 13 week old Rottweiler puppy to our Doggie Daycare, and asked for
three training sessions so her pup would have a head start on the training. Just
wanting Rozzie to learn to learn, her owner didn't care what we taught her, so
I decided to shape Rozzie to skateboard. Using her for the workshop demonstra-
tion, I was candid with the students, explaining that Rozzie had already had
some training—three sessions, each lasting little more than 5 minutes, and that
I had trained her to ride a skateboard. When they saw the tiny, three-month-old
Rottie, their skepticism was almost palpable. I removed Rozzie's leash, put the
skateboard down a few feet away, and was thrilled to hear the gasps of astonish-
ment when, with a look of pure glee, Rozzie leapt onto the skateboard and took
a ride.

"Just do it!"

The best way, really the *only* way to learn clicker training, is to *do it*. Crossing over may not be easy for either you or your dog. As someone who's "been there, done that," you have my understanding, empathy, and encouragement. Hang in there and fear not. You won't harm your dog or your relationship by marking behaviors to reward. As your training builds, so will your understanding. So relax and enjoy "the game" with your dog.

You're embarking on an adventure that isn't easy—learning a whole new paradigm of dog training. This adventure may make you feel uncomfortable, uncertain, even impatient, and anxious. Putting up with short-term discomfort will be well-rewarded by the joy of training your thinking dog. It is so well worth it!

II

PART II: Crossing Over...Just Do It!

"If you ever get a second chance in life for something,
you've got to go all the way."

—*Lance Armstrong*

Overview

This section includes everything you need to know to get started, from practicing your timing skills before you work with your dog, to connecting with your dog. You'll learn how to get behaviors, starting with a mere hint of a subtle movement, taking them all the way through to the cue, getting the dog to understand and to perform the behavior anywhere and everywhere, building your dog's repertoire of trained behaviors. This is the meat of clicker training. C'mon in...the water's fine!

Chapter 5

BUILD YOUR CLICKER SKILLS

My Crossover Journal
Almost invariably the first time someone plays the "Training
Game," they mention a new awareness of and profound respect
for three things: the importance and helpfulness of the "trainer" having good
clicker timing, the frustration and confusion of poorly timed clicks, and that
despite our failings, how exceptionally brilliant dogs are in being able to figure
us (humans) out.

This chapter contains information on what you need before you start training including equipment, training regimens, goal-setting and planning your sessions, connecting with and reading your dog, key concepts, and suggestions for exercises and games that will build your clicker skills. If your crossover dog has not been introduced to a clicker, don't start clicking yet. Occasionally a dog may be initially put off by the click, and how you introduce it can make a difference. Until you start working with your dog (in the next chapter), practice your clicker skills out of your dog's hearing.

Training tools

As a crossover trainer, chances are you have a good idea of what equipment you need for dog training, and you may already have many of the following items for clicker training.

Clickers

Starting with the basic behavior marker, you have choices. You'll find some sites listed in the Resources section where you can get specialty clickers: digital, foot-operated, wrist clickers, and clickers for people with big fingers. Some trainers make a clicking noise with their tongue on the roof of their mouth, a mouth click. You can certainly do that, although it is likely slower than using a mechanical clicker. Or save it for when you don't have your clicker, if you prefer it to "yes."

How loud is your clicker?

Some box clickers make a sharp, loud click that may be painful to some dogs' ears. When you purchase a clicker, test several to see if one has a duller, softer click than others. If you already have a loud clicker, you can dull the sound by putting a piece of masking tape on the metal tongue. Or consider a clicker with adjustable sounds (see Sources and Resources).

Treats

Prepare plenty of treats, more than you think you'll need—then make even more! To motivate your dog, treats should be enticing, small, and easy-to-swallow. Avoid less appealing, hard, or crunchy treats which create crumbs that can be distracting or may reinforce your dog at the wrong time. In addition crunchy treats take time to chew, which slows training. Treats do not have to be large to reinforce behavior. In fact, smaller, faster-to-swallow treats are better.

If your dog is overweight, cut the amount of his regular meals and use low fat treats. If your dog is on a special diet, consult your veterinarian for permissible treats, keeping in mind that they must be appealing to your dog to be a valuable reward.

Preparing treats

There are lots of soft treats you can use such as cheese or treats sold at specialty pet shops or online. Hot dogs are easy to prepare and appealing to most dogs. I prefer low fat turkey hot dogs or better still, health food hot dogs without chemicals. For large dogs, cut the hot dog in half lengthwise; for medium to small dogs, cut it into quarters. Then slice it into pieces a little thicker than a nickel. A small treat is just as rewarding as a more sizeable one, as long as it's something your dog likes. Spread the pieces onto several thicknesses of paper towel and microwave it to reduce moisture and fat, about 5-7 minutes for three hot dogs. Refrigerate leftovers.

Hot dogs cut up and microwaved make them easier to handle.

Bait bags and containers

Have your treats readily available in a bait bag or container that you can access easily. "Readily available" means you can deliver a treat in under two seconds, so don't keep them in a zipper plastic bag, or zipped in a fanny pack. Your container or bait bag should be large enough to easily reach in with your hand to get a treat. More on treat delivery in Chapter 6.

Leashes and collars

I recommend a flat buckle collar and a plain six-foot leash with a simple bolt snap of the right weight for your size dog. Since clicker training can often be done off-leash, the leash and collar are for walking your dog, or whenever you need your dog on leash. If your dog pulls out of a buckle collar, use a Martingale limited choke collar.

Create a "third hand"

A common complaint about clicker training is that we have only two hands. One hand holds the clicker, the other is needed for delivering treats. That leaves a leash with no available hand. Here are some suggestions to get around this:

- If you're training in a safe place, don't use a leash. If your treats aren't enough to motivate your dog to stay with you and train, find better treats!

- Drop the leash and step on it.

- Thread your belt through the loop end of the leash.

- Wear the leash in "umbilical cord" position: Pass the leash around your body, thread the snap through the loop end, pull it tight, and attach the snap to your dog's collar.

- There are "walking" leashes that go around your waist and so free up your hands that are available from sources on the Internet and specialty stores.

What not to do: Do not put your dog's leash loop under a movable piece of furniture and walk away. We've had students' dogs try to follow them, dragging a flopping chair, terrifying themselves and the other dogs.

Head halters and harnesses

The instructions for loose leash walking in Chapter 12 are designed to train your dog to walk without pulling regardless of equipment. In the meantime, before your dog is trained to walk politely, you need a strategy to stop him practicing the behavior that you want to eliminate. A front-connection harness or a head halter may help. Keep in mind that these are tools—a means to an end, not the end itself. If your goal is a dog that walks on a simple, flat collar without pulling, you can easily achieve it.

Targets

Virtually anything can be used as a target from target sticks to sticky notes, placemats, carpet remnants, and furniture. You can purchase items specifically made for clicker training, or use things such as retractable pointers, pencils with erasers, or nearly limitless possibilities you'll find in your home. Consider your dog's perspective when using visual versus tactile targets. For example, if you're teaching your dog to back up onto a carpet remnant (tactile), it's easier to use if you're not placing it over carpet.

What not to use

Retractable leads

Although they appear to offer the advantages of a long line without getting tangled, unless the dog is well-trained, retractable leads are unsafe and even dangerous. Here are just a few of the disadvantages of a retractable lead with an untrained dog:

- You cannot pull your dog away from danger. Your dog may run into the road, or be as far as 26 feet away from you, and you have no way to control your dog without grabbing the cord, a sure-fire way to cut your hands or get a rope burn.

- The cord-type retractables are garrotes; they can sever a finger or lacerate a leg. Serious injuries can occur from having the cord slash a person or dog.

- You cannot judge when the dog will hit the end of the lead, causing whiplash or worse. One of our staff was taking a dog from the lobby down the hall to daycare on a retractable lead she thought was locked. When the dog suddenly bolted down the hall, she was literally pulled off her feet, falling on her face and breaking her nose. We have since banned retractables altogether.

- A retractable lead (and on the same subject, a bungee lead) only works if your dog pulls…which rewards pulling. This should be a "Duh!" for anyone who wants a dog to walk without pulling.

Choke collars

The purpose of choke collars is to give collar checks. Since clicker training does not use collar corrections, there would be no reason to use a slip, choke type collar.

Training sessions

If your dog is awake, your dog has an opportunity to learn—whether or not you are training. Learning takes place in:

- Planned, prepared training sessions

- Informal opportunities to teach something to your dog

- Unplanned "oopsies"—lessons you wish your dog never learned, but he did. Now you have a problem, so deal with it (see Chapter 10).

There are no hard and fast rules about training sessions, but the following guidelines will help acclimate your crossover dog to clicker training, keep your dog in a "teachable" frame of mind, and allow you to get the most out of both planned sessions and informal opportunities.

Training session goals

Whether your ultimate goal is a fun companion and playmate, enjoying a competitive dog sport, having a helpful service dog, or all the above, articulating your goal helps you to visualize and plan the behaviors to reach them. Write down your goals: short term for a specific training session or a specific behavior; and your long-term, ultimate goals.

The first short-term goals for the crossover trainer are to learn the techniques and skills you need to master and to teach "the game" to your dog. Your initial sessions will teach your dog what the clicker is all about. Once that's accomplished, have fun with it—train new behaviors, or spiffy-up previously-learned ones.

It is helpful to prepare a training plan before you start a lesson, including what you hope to accomplish in the session and how you think you'll get there, listing the likely steps you plan for each behavior. When you first start clicker training, it is helpful to break each behavior into small components, and then break each of those into even smaller ones. You likely re-think and adjust as you train, but it's important to visualize a plan before you start.

Many trainers think of training in terms of "don'ts." "Don't pull on the leash," "don't jump on visitors," or "don't take cookies from the baby." To train positive behaviors, it's important to visualize what you want and phrase your goals as "do's." "Walk by my side on a loose leash," "sit calmly when company arrives," or "lie quietly when the baby is eating." The behavior you *want*, your training goal, is a "do." Thinking of behavior as a "*don't*" focuses you on what's wrong, not on what's right. (More on this in Chapter 10.)

Remember that any opportunity for your dog to learn (for good or ill) is not about this moment. It's about the effect of learning on your dog's behavior in the future. So every opportunity for your dog to learn represents an opportunity for you to move closer to or achieve your ultimate goal.

Starting a "formal" training session

Before you start training, gather all your equipment and supplies: clicker, treats, collar, leash, bait bag, and anything else needed for the session. Once you're ready, let your dog know that you're going to be working together starting…now! How do you tell your dog? It's simple. Smile, look at your dog, and softly tell her you're going to train. You can even give her a tasty treat—a freebie. Your pleasant affect (smile) and calm demeanor (soft voice) combined with the treat get your session started off right for both of you! What a nice way to start learning.

Be ready the moment your session starts, including making sure your clicker is held properly for the click so you don't miss important, helpful opportunities to communicate with your dog.

My Crossover Journal
For her homework assignment, one of the students in our Professional Trainers Academy sent in a video of her training a Labrador retriever to "settle" (go to the blanket and lie down). Before starting the session, she turned on the camera, put the blanket on the floor, and went to get treats.

While she was out of the room the dog went to the blanket, walked off it, sniffed it, touched it, and turned away several times. When the trainer returned, she engaged the dog's attention, and waited for him to offer a behavior with the blanket. He didn't. He was done. Having gotten no reinforcement for his efforts, there was no reason to continue that behavior.

Dax pounces on the mat the moment Shari puts it down. A well-timed click at this point will focus Dax on the mat. (Note Shari's enjoyment. This is clicker training!)

Crossover Cornerstone #1

"If the task is available, the trainer must be awake."
I love the way Norwegian dog trainer Anne Lill Kvam expresses this concept. Stay focused and keep your eye on your dog from the moment you let your dog know you're "in training."

How many repetitions?

Clicker training gets the dog thinking. While this is one of the most exciting aspects of training, it is mentally taxing, especially for a crossover dog just starting out with a clicker. Work in short time frames, taking frequent breaks for your dog to clear his mind and refresh. A short break can keep your dog sharp and able to learn.

An easy way to enforce breaks is to count out the number of treats for how many repetitions you want to do before a break. A good rule of thumb is five to ten repetitions of a behavior, then take a break. Some crossover dogs, especially older dogs or those who don't really enjoy training, may need a breather after just one or two repetitions. Judge the quality of the behavior more than the number of responses. For example, if the third repetition is a good one, take a break. Or you may even take a break after one good rep, assessing your dog's demeanor, and focusing on success.

It is human nature to go for "just one more," but that's often one too many. End with a good rep, take a break, and train more after the break. You want to stop training before you see signs of stress (below).

65

What constitutes a break?

A break is as short as a few-second, brain-clearing floor sniff or a trip to the bathroom (for either of you). It's going to the kitchen for more treats, or ending for the day. A break can be as simple as moving to a different place in the room. While many people think of playing with the dog as taking a break, play is a reinforcer, not a mind-clearing breather. The best break is to just let your dog veg-out for a bit, after which you can return to the same behavior or start training a new one.

How to break

After you click a behavior and deliver the treat, smile, praise your dog and give her a cue that signifies you're taking a break, such as "all done." Communicate this as a good thing so she won't construe the removal of your attention as "punishment."

For a short break, just let her relax a moment, sniff the floor, take a drink, etc. To refocus her, show her a treat (see "Jumpstarting behaviors" on page 130) to send the message, "We're back on. This is for you when you get me to click."

Interruptions

Gratuitous interruptions, the removal of your attention and focus, constitute punishment. Don't do it. Answering the phone, suddenly thinking of something you need to do and doing it—these are not emergencies. A non-emergency should not take your focus away from your training.

OK, that's not always realistic. Things happen, and chances are you will be interrupted at some point. Recognize, however, that clicker training is cooperative. Your dog is cooperating if he is working, thinking, and trying to figure out what behavior you are looking for. Out of respect for your training partner and the effort he's making, communicate when you need to stop training. If, for example you need to answer the phone, give your dog a cue that tells him he's off the clock—that you're "all done."

> ## Crossover Cornerstone #2
>
> **Your dog is your partner—tell him when he's "off the clock."**
> Whether it's an interruption, taking a break, or ending your training session, make it clear to your dog. Don't just stop and walk away. Give him a cue that says he's on his own. After that, your dog may continue to perform the behavior you were training on his own. For example, if he wants to lie down, that's fine—but your "all done" cue says you will no longer click and reward it at this time.

How long should a training session be?

Some dogs are so into the game that they can continue playing virtually as long as you like. Go by your dog's attitude and attention rather than by the clock. When you first start to crossover, five to ten minutes will likely be long enough. At times you'll do more, and other times you may be done after a minute or two. You can accomplish a great deal in a just a few minutes of clicker training.

My Crossover Journal

Shortly after I began experimenting with clicker training, I decided to start shaping Mayday to do a High Five. I trained for just a minute or two, watching for any foot movement of his right forepaw, and clicking it. As sometimes happens, after this session it was several weeks before I had the opportunity to train him again. When I picked up the clicker again, I vaguely recalled having worked on a new behavior before the break, and paused as I tried to think what it was. Mayday had no such memory problem. Raising his right foot, he whacked me on the leg—the behavior we had briefly worked on over a month before—an astonishing demonstration of the power and memorability of clicker trained behaviors after just two minutes of training.

Remembering the High Five with barely two minutes of training, Mayday whacked me on the leg.

Ending the training session

End with success. Smile and say "all done." Don't rev your dog up with strenuous play. Let him rest quietly to chew a bone, relax, or do whatever he'd like. He's earned it.

If you miss the opportunity to end with success, and your dog is no longer offering the behaviors you want, smile nonetheless and give your "all done" cue. It's not your dog's fault that you trained too long. Consider what body signals you missed that your dog was sending to indicate he was finished, and try to end on a better note the next time.

Informal training

Opportunistic training is taking advantage of any opportunity to practice and reinforce your dog's behavior. Consider Crossover Cornerstone #1 ("If the task is available, the trainer must be awake.") from a slightly different perspective: "If the dog is awake, a task is available." Every waking moment of your dog's life is an opportunity for learning. When you see such an opportunity, use your verbal marker ("yes") to mark it, and use either a reward (see Premack Principle) or verbal praise to strengthen your dog's behavior.

It is important for your crossover dog to learn that you may mark and reinforce behaviors at any time, whether or not you're in a training session, and whether or not you're holding a clicker. Dogs easily learn that the sight of the clicker and availability of treats means "in training"—helpful when it comes to encouraging your dog to offer new behaviors. But the potential downside of this association is that your dog won't respond if he doesn't see the clicker or if you're not carrying treats. Being spontaneous and unpredictable can prevent this—mark a behavior with a verbal marker, use life reinforcements, and give your dog treat rewards at unexpected times.

Kathy Sdao, an outstanding clicker trainer, "salts" her outings with her dog. Before taking her dog out, she walks the trail and puts a hamburger in the branch of a tree. As she approaches the place where the hamburger is stashed, she asks for a behavior, and surprise! The message to her dog is, "You never know when you might get a hamburger. After all, I know where they grow on trees!"

You never know when you may come across a Hamburger tree!

*5→10 reps. Break
Whole session max 10 min*

Recognize, respect, and respond to the signs of stress

Learning involves some stress, but you can minimize it. Watch for the subtle signs that indicate your dog is reaching his limit of training. Especially in the beginning with your crossover dog, when you see signs of stress, take a break or end your training session. Your dog is your friend. Consider his mental well-being.

Here are just a few of the things you'll see that mean your dog could use a break:

- Turning or looking away
- Sniffing the floor or ground
- Lip licking
- Panting, especially with corners of the mouth pulled back

yawning? she did not a... of this

Clicking versus connecting

In the "Training Game," described at the end of this chapter, there are two rules: no touching and no talking. This ensures that the crossover trainer focuses on practicing the simple mechanics of using a clicker for shaping behavior. With a marker, good timing, positive reinforcement, and an understanding of a species' subtle "intention" movements, a trainer can shape behavior in virtually any live creature without physical or verbal guidance—from fish to fowl to fox to friend, and, of course, dogs. Learning happens faster without touching or talking, but it takes more than mechanics to make a connection with your dog.

The wonderful bond we share with dogs is what makes them special above all other species. Connecting is not about science, techniques, timing, or procedure. It's about the magical: the imprecise, inexact, non-scientific connection between dogs and people. It is our role and responsibility as human beings to elevate and improve this partnership—to value and cherish the dog, striving for the deepest relationships imaginable.

Talking and touching are two important aspects of creating this bond, but because during clicker training we avoid both touching and talking in the early stages of learning a new behavior, some trainers mistakenly take this to mean hands off and shut up…*always*. Both species miss out on a huge part of our unique partnership if trainers fall victim to this misconception, discounting the importance of verbal and tactile communication in our relationship with dogs. So let's address these two aspects of the bond, not required for clicker training, but necessary to make the human/canine connection the best it can be.

Talking to your dog

I talk to my dogs all the time, just not so much during training. I often praise after marking a behavior, but I don't talk while the dog is working, while he's figuring out what behavior will make me click. Remember that sounds, including the sound of your voice, are a distraction. But at other times, when your dog isn't concentrating on his own behavior, there's no reason not to talk. Talking to your dog can enhance your relationship. You don't need to be silent just because you're clicker training.

Touching your dog

Physical touch is good on so many levels. It can calm an over-excited puppy and lower your blood pressure. Your touch is one way to communicate with your dog, and get her attention. But probably the best part of touching is that it feels good—to both of us. Stroking, scratching, and massaging feel great to your dog, and to you.

Since clicker training doesn't involve touch, it's important to make touching your dog in a training context a part of your practice.

My Crossover Journal
Shortly after we crossed over, Jean, our Agility Training Director, came to me with a problem. To introduce some obstacles in her beginner agility classes, the instructor or assistant holds the dog—the owner goes to the other side of the obstacle and calls. As the dog comes through the tunnel for instance, the owner clicks, treats, and takes hold of the six inch tab on the dog's collar. Jean reported that some of the dogs were shying away when their owners reach for the tab. Every dog that did this was a graduate of our clicker Manners class. While their dogs were responsive, and quickly caught on to the agility training, their prior training had not included any physical handling.

To acclimate dogs to being handled, we introduced an exercise in our beginner program for students to "examine" their dogs: pick up a foot, touch a leg, look in the dog's ears, rub their shoulders, all the while marking the dog's willing compliance with "yes" (not a click) and giving treats. Further, we introduce students to the connection that comes from massaging their dogs.

Massage to calm and connect

How wonderful to make a calm connection that is rewarding, healthful, and pleasurable to both you and your dog. Massage can do this. A simple massage or any stroking is good for both of you. It not only calms your dog, but you, too.

During your dog's massage, breathe deeply, and talk softly and calmly. Start by stroking in long, gentle movements from your dog's head, down the muscles along the spine to the base of your dog's tail. Repeat this three or four times, then continue along your dog's tail, gently squeezing along the length of the tail from base to tip another two or three times. With your fingertips, rub gently behind your dog's ears, then stroke along the muscles that extend down his neck to his shoulders. With your dog's ear held between your thumb and forefinger, gently massage his ears from base to tip. With small circular movements, massage his skull and cheeks. Lightly massage his eyes, then stroke up his muzzle from his nose up over the stop, the space between his eyes. Stroke along the length of his forelegs, squeezing lightly from armpit down to his paws, and gently hold each paw for a few seconds. Move to your dog's rear legs, massaging along the thigh muscles, then squeeze along the lower leg to his rear paws, holding them gently as you did with the forepaws.

Journey and MaryBeth share the connection, a calming massage, enjoyable and bonding for both of them.

Reading your dog

Learning to read your dog, to understand, recognize, and respond to the physical signals that tell us what the dog is thinking and feeling, is a huge part of connecting with your dog. Making this connection is more than talking, touching, and recognizing body language. It is tuning into your dog. Once you've experienced the connection, you want it again and again. As powerful as an addictive drug, the ability to connect, to create a true cooperative partnership, is what sets clicker training apart. Clicker training is not just about what we train our dogs to do, but is about how we act toward them; how we are with them. It's not just about what we *do*—the mechanics of training; it's about who we *are*.

Connectedness springs from our ability to communicate with our dogs, and to recognize, understand, respect, and respond to our dogs' communication—to understand what the dog is "saying." As Norwegian dog trainer Turid Rugaas says, "Dogs want to be visible," which means that we respond to what they communicate, from joy expressed by a huge grin and ecstatically wagging body, to the subtle signals that say, "I'm feeling anxious. Please rescue me."

In her beautiful book *Bones Would Rain from the Sky*, Suzanne Clothier refers to it as "dances with dogs."

> The dance is not a result of specific techniques. It springs from a life lived according to the philosophy crafted by your heart, a philosophy that informs all you do. This cannot be achieved by bringing your awareness and effort only to those moments you call "training." The dog is a dog, twenty-four hours a day. His world is shaped by what you say and do, not just in training

sessions but in every waking moment he is with you. Incapable of dishonesty in his own communications, a master of observation, the dog not only notices what you do, but he believes what you do to be an accurate reflection of the relationship between you. The relationship—the pivotal point on which all else turns—is built (or undermined) in every interaction…[F]or those who have the desire, those who would dance with a dog as their partner, this reality is a welcome opportunity to use every moment with awareness and purpose.

This dance, this connection is something I believe crossover trainers desire, by the mere fact that they (you) seek information about a "new" way. By focusing on and responding to our dogs' subtleties with positive training and proactive advocacy, clicker training supports and enhances our bond as no other method.

"Calming Signals"

A key to reading your dog is learning about what behaviorist Turid Rugaas terms "calming signals," which include everything from subtle deference and appeasement gestures to overt signs of fear, avoidance, and stress. Taken as a whole, they are the dog's communication system: a visual language that enables us to "listen" to our dogs. Turid calls it the "language of peace."

Here's a list of many signals dogs use. Some are offered *only* when the dog is feeling anxious; others as a stress-reliever for self-calming. Still others are used in several contexts. For instance, sniffing the ground can be investigatory or a sign of anxiety. Panting can be heat- or stress-related…or both. When you see a signal, assess the situation to decide if you need to intercede to help your dog. The asterisk (*) indicates those we can use as calming signals to communicate with our dogs. Dogs' signals can be subtle. When you use them, be subtle too.

Eyes and head

Look away*	Turn head*	Dip/lift head*
Lick lips*	Lick at face	Panting
Blinking*	Lowering eyelids*	Smile*
Ears down/back		

Body

Turn away*	Turn side*	Turn your back*
Avoidance	Lower/reduce posture*	

Movement

Move slowly*	Curving approach*	Walk away*
Move stiffly	Slow; stop*	Freeze*
Crawl	Lie down (heaviest!)	

Behavior/Activity

Sniff ground	Yawn*	Splitting up*
Redirected behavior	Sneeze	Submissive urination
Pawing at	Stretch (play bow)	Scratching (as an itch)
Dig ground (pawing)	Tail wag	Sit*
Shake off (as water)		

My Crossover Journal
A student in an advanced class complained when her Bernese
Mountain Dog kept stopping to scratch whenever it was their turn
for a run-through in class. She thought he must be allergic to something. He
wasn't. He was just a bit anxious. By relaxing her expectations she helped him
acclimate. He stopped scratching after just two classes.

Key clicker concepts

Before moving on to specific skills, let's review three key concepts that all crossover trainers must master:

1. Behavior markers

2. Timing

3. New training "rules"

All about behavior markers: But you don't have to click

A behavior marker can be virtually any sound or sign—a whistle, kiss, tongue cluck, thumbs up sign, hands clap, word, even a smile. You may use as many different markers as you like. Once your dog understands the game, you can easily change or introduce additional markers. Simply pair the marker with your dog's behavior, then present the reward: behavior/mark…reward.

In addition to the clicker, you can use a verbal marker such as "Yes" or "Yup." A marker is just a marker; it is unemotional. Don't confuse a marker with praise. Rather than a yippee-do, enthusiastic "YEEESSSS!!" to mark a behavior, use a crisp, truncated utterance—a combination of yes and yup: "Yesp."

No marker gets the point across as definitively and clearly as a clicker; however, this very power is a detriment to someone whose timing is off. No trainer has perfect timing 100% of the time. Occasional badly-timed clicks (early or late) are no big deal, but repeatedly ill-timed clicks lead to unintentional behavior, confusion or even a shut down (see Crossover Cornerstone #3 on page 75).

As with any skill, clicker timing may improve with practice, but even with practice, some people simply will not develop good timing. Lack of good clicker timing does not mean a dog owner can't be a clicker (or a marker) trainer, however. Think of it as any talent such as natural rhythm, artistic ability, or being able to carry a tune. You don't have to be an artist to enjoy art, have good rhythm to love to dance, and even the tone deaf enjoy belting out a song in the shower. So, too, can a crossover trainer with less-than-perfect clicker timing successfully use the principles and instructions in this book—and have fun training!

Assess your timing

As you go through the following exercises to build your clicker skills, work with a training partner, if possible, or video yourself and try to objectively assess your timing. Even if you don't have a helper or video, ultimately your dog will let you know if your timing is off. If your dog continually offers "wrong" behaviors, chances are it's your timing: You're marking that wrong behavior.

My Crossover Journal

Wanting to train her dog to stand still rather than jump on people, a student in class timed her click, she thought, just before her dog's feet left the floor. I was giving instructions to the whole class when I became peripherally aware of a dog bumping my leg with her nose. Hearing the click, the dog returned to the handler for a treat, then came back to touch my thigh. Finished with my instructions, I turned to the student to ask what she was shaping. "To stand before she jumps up," she replied. "Not exactly," I explained, pointing to the wet spot on my leg. "You're clicking her for targeting my thigh."

To change the behavior, the student simply timed the click just before her dog made contact. The first time the dog heard the "early" click, before she touched my leg, I saw a momentary look of puzzlement, followed by an expression that could only be interpreted as, "Gee...she must not have seen that I didn't touch... but Heck! I'm gettin' a treat anyway!" It took just two more well-timed clicks before the dog stopped short of thigh contact on her own.

Confused on hearing a click before he touched my thigh, the wet spot showed what the owner had been clicking: nose-targeting my thigh rather than stand on the floor without jumping up.

Another sign of poor timing is confusion. Your dog is trying different behaviors, but just doesn't seem to get the behavior you're looking for. Or your dog may lose focus and interest, shut down, or walk away.

Some crossover trainers (especially the skeptical) are quick to blame the method or even the dog when all they get is a confusion of behaviors. It's easy to say "clicker training doesn't work" or "clicker training isn't for my dog." Don't give up on clicker training. The problem most likely is your timing.

> ## Crossover Cornerstone #3
> **If you missed the moment to mark the behavior, don't click late.**
> Having missed an opportunity to click, many trainers will click anyway, several seconds after the dog has performed the behavior hoping the dog will realize it was for what he did three seconds ago. He won't. Since what the dog is doing at that moment is not the "clickable" behavior, the late click is counterproductive, marking that unrelated behavior. If you miss the moment, don't try to make up for it by clicking late. Occasional missed opportunities are no big deal. Learn from them, watch your dog, and improve your timing the next time.

If your clicker timing doesn't improve with practice, switch to a verbal marker. For the trainer whose clicker timing is off, the less precise timing of the verbal marker can be a help. So if you find you can't click well, don't beat yourself up over it, and don't think you can't be a clicker trainer. You can be. If you're not sure about your timing, seek out a knowledgeable clicker trainer for an assessment and some help.

New "rules" for training (and for life)
Clicker training is fun, and should be for both you and your dog. These are some general guidelines and recommendations for your practice both with and without your dog:

- **Smile.** Relax your face. Avoid frowning and/or staring eye contact with your dog. Are we having fun yet? Yes!

- **Display patience**. Previous training taught your crossover dog *you'll tell him what to do*. It may take a while before he realizes that not only *can* he offer behaviors, but it's up to him to do so. In the meantime, don't be impatient. Relax.

- **Be generous with clicks.** Called a **high rate of reinforcement (ROR)**, this keeps your dog both interested, and motivated. Stingy clicking, a low ROR, will cause your dog to disengage. Stingy clicking gives your dog no reason to play the game. Especially when you first start working with your crossover dog, a low ROR leads to disinterest in participating. The antidote is loads of clicks and treats. If your dog does lose interest, take a break and try again later. When you start again, train briefly, with lots of rewards, at a high ROR.

My Crossover Journal
Understanding just what a rapid rate of reinforcement means
in concrete terms can be helpful for new clicker trainers, as new
and crossover students have difficulty grasping precisely what a high rate of
reinforcement is. I find it has an impact when I describe an event that happened
shortly after we began crossing over. I was watching Shari train a Westie pup
that was attending our daycare. I timed and counted the number of clicks and
treats as she shaped the dog to go to the blanket. In sixty seconds, she clicked and
rewarded twenty seven times.

- **Give a treat each time you click.** Your dog will quickly learn that the click is for his having done something. Important for all dogs, but especially with crossover dogs, your dog needs to trust that you'll reward his efforts. As you progress through your training, there might be a time to click without a treat (see Chapter 9), but in the beginning, it's important to pair each click with a reward.

- **Don't treat without a click first.** An occasional "freebie" won't hurt, but regularly getting something for nothing delays your crossover dog getting the message that it's his behavior you're rewarding. He must learn that he can get you to be a treat dispenser by doing something.

- **Avoid something-for-nothing.** Having to earn a reward is a good policy whenever you want to give your dog a treat, even when you're not training or using your clicker. It doesn't have to be a huge or complex task, any behavior will do. Giving loads of freebies can create disinterest in training. After all, why work for something if you get it for nothing?

- **Fight the temptation to help!** It is difficult to fight your natural inclination to lure, guide, or even mold a behavior "just once." For your crossover dog to figure out that *he can offer a behavior on his own* he has to do it himself…on his own, without help.

- **Don't cheat.** Beyond the temptation to help, cheating includes subtle movements like leaning in the direction you want your dog to move, gesturing, head movements, or staring at the target to aid your dog. This can be especially difficult for lure-reward trainers, but such subtle movements are not helpful in the long run, and create dependency. You want your dog to offer behaviors on his own, not because your body language is leading him toward your goal.

- **Be flexible.** Most dog training methods move sequentially from point A to B to C and so on until you reach the goal behavior. With clicker training, progress often advances in leaps and bounds: point A to B to M to Z. Be prepared to embrace major advancements. You don't need to force your dog to go through each step of a behavior.

Also, be flexible when your dog offers a different behavior from the one you are focusing on. It may be a behavior you really like or have wanted to train, but haven't been able to. When you see that behavior, consider clicking it. For example, I've always wanted to train a sneeze, so no matter what behavior I might be working on, if my dog sneezes, I mark it. Once you've done this a few times, your dog may continue offering that behavior for you to mark and reward. So when you're working on one behavior and your dog offers a different "clickable" behavior, go ahead and click it. Think of each clickable moment as a deposit in your bank account of behaviors (more on this in Chapter 7).

- **Watch your dog.** When you're in training mode, keep your focus 100% on what your dog is doing or you may miss an important opportunity to click.

- **Think small.** In fact, think *tiny*. Shaping means reinforcing incremental behaviors (even infinitesimal movement) toward the desired goal. Crossover trainers tend to visualize and focus on the end behavior, paying less attention to the steps it takes to get there, but shaping involves marking progress. On the other hand, this doesn't always mean baby steps, taking an interminable time to achieve any goals. Once you get started, you'll get results quickly—as you'll see in the next chapter.

- **Have fun!** Clicker training opens a whole new world to you and your dog, creating a true training partnership. Relax, enjoy the process, have fun watching your dog think, and even more importantly, enjoy learning.

Building skills through games and exercises

I know you're eager to begin training with your dog, but practicing your skills first will greatly benefit you both. Crossover dogs can be confused by simply having the opportunity to offer behaviors on their own. Ill-timed, infrequent, or missed clicks will cause further confusion, and may cause your dog to disconnect, prolonging your crossover journey. Practicing without your dog first can save weeks or even months of confusion and frustration.

There are a number of activities and games you can play with friends or family, critiquing each others' timing, and giving important feedback that will enhance your skills and understanding before you start training with your dog. Additionally, Appendix B has a number of websites that can be helpful for developing clicker coordination.

The following are some activities you can do either alone or with a helper. When you're practicing with a friend, take turns so you each have a chance. Your training partners will help you determine if your timing is early, late, or just right. Make sure each person is successful with each exercise before moving on.

Tennis ball bounce
1. Stand with the clicker in your dominant hand and a tennis ball in your other hand, chest height.
2. Let go of the ball, and click as it hits the floor. Your timing is right if you click the moment the ball hits the floor. Practice until the click and the precise instant the ball bounces are simultaneous.
3. Next try it with the clicker in your non-dominant hand.

Tennis ball toss
1. Stand with the clicker in your dominant hand and a tennis ball in the other.
2. Toss the ball straight up, and click the highest point of the toss. You'll likely find this a bit more of a challenge, since the apex of the toss is not a fixed point, as is the floor.

3. Practice different height tosses.

4. Switch hands.

Tennis ball toss and bounce
1. Combine the first two exercises: Click the high point of your toss, and again when the ball hits the floor.

2. You can also practice bouncing the ball against a wall. Click when it hits the wall, and again when it hits the floor.

The "Training Game"—Hot and Cold

Karen Pryor has popularized this take-off on the children's game "Hot and Cold": "You're getting warmer…warmer…colder…freezing…" The games are similar, but where Hot and Cold is about a place or object, the Training Game is about shaping actions or behaviors. For example, Hot and Cold could lead you to a chair, where with the Training Game the trainer could shape you to hop to the chair, climb up onto it, or pick it up and move it. You will learn a lot about clicker training by playing this game with friends.

It is best played with more than two people—one as the trainer, one as the trainee, and the others observing and helping the trainer develop and build observational and timing skills. Everyone except the trainee should know the goal behavior. Send the trainee out of earshot and agree on what behavior to shape with the following guidelines:

- Select a human behavior, not a dog behavior. It shouldn't be something like sitting on the floor and scratching an ear with a foot.

- Choose a behavior that does not involve touching another person.

- Select a behavior you would perform in public when sober; nothing humiliating or embarrassing.

When playing the game:
- No talking: Pretend you have no common language with your trainee.

- Follow the "New Rules for training" on page 75 especially frequent clicks (ROR) and watching for and marking small movement toward the goal.

- After each click, present a treat. You can just pretend to give something, but get into the habit of providing a treat for each click. Treat delivery is an important and useful training skill—don't ignore it.

Practice treat delivery. You'll read more about treat delivery with your dog in the next chapter. In playing the Training Game, experiment with treat delivery to develop a feel for some of the different strategies you might use. Here are a few to consider:

- Either have the trainee come to you to get the treat, or you go to the trainee and reward. This is a helpful option to consider during the game since *where you reward* can help advance your training. Not just true with your human trainees, this is critically important for your dog, too.

- If your trainee seems to have grown roots, and seems unwilling to move, hold the treat far enough from her so she has to move to you for the treat.

- Position yourself in the direction you want your trainee to move so after you click, as she approaches to get the reward, you can click again. Yes, I know, that is two clicks for one treat…but this goes under the heading of "be flexible." Don't continue acting as the lure, however, or the behavior will become dependent on your position.

- Use proximity to you, if it's helpful. For example, to get the trainee to back up, it can be helpful to bring her into your "personal space" by holding the treat close to your body. It's a natural inclination to take a step backward to back out of this uncomfortable proximity, providing you with an opportunity to click.

- And sometimes it is helpful to deliver the treat to the trainee so she doesn't move away from a location.

Suggested behaviors. Start your first game session with something simple such as go to a chair and sit in it. Then try something more complex such as to pick something up and carry it to the trainer. Want still more? How about pour soda in a glass, pick it up, and give it to the trainer. Remember, the trainee's job is to get the trainer to click, and each click means you're on the right track. Don't forget to follow each click with a treat.

Postmortems. After each behavior, talk about it. Even if you were unsuccessful shaping a behavior and decide to stop, talk about steps you might have clicked, and review those you did click that perhaps you shouldn't have. Consider if there was another element of the behavior you hadn't considered. For example, in a class demonstration, the task selected was to shape my class assistant to pick up my clipboard. She touched every item on the table but my clipboard. Clearly, in her mind, there was a stricture against touching "my stuff." This postmortem can be the most helpful part of the game, giving everyone a chance to critique timing, missed opportunities, and to make suggestions for alternative ideas for getting the behavior.

The Training Game is more than fun. It is helpful for teaching timing and the process of shaping to everyone in the game.

Crossover Cornerstone #4

Click progress toward the goal behavior.

Avoid clicking the same step more than two or three times in a row. Multiple *consecutive* clicks solidify the behavior. To make this point to our new students in our first class workshop, we ask the class to shape the instructor to walk toward the white board. As I step forward on my right foot, the students click. I shift back onto my left foot at the starting point, and step forward with my right foot again, click. Then back onto my left foot and again step forward on my right, click! And then a fourth time. Since each click was for precisely the same behavior—taking one step with my right foot with no movement beyond this one step—I continue to rock back and forth from my right to my left and back again, demonstrating the behavior the class trained: rock in place.

Keep in mind this is more than two or three *consecutive times*. As you'll see in Chapter 7, when you're shaping a behavior, there will be times you'll need to click an earlier progression.

Now that you're prepared and you've practiced without your dog, you're ready to put it together with your dog.

Chapter 6
GETTING BEHAVIORS

My Crossover Journal
Crossover trainers at a seminar were working in groups, four trainers with one dog, learning to shape a behavior from a starting point. After a few minutes, a trainer from one of the groups came to tell me that their dog wasn't offering any behaviors. Fearing the dog had lapsed into a coma, I rushed over to find that they were observing an active, year-old Bearded Collie. In the perpetual motion typical of the breed, she bounced around, jumped up, and alerted to every movement around her. What she didn't do was sit, lie down, or stand still. The dog offered infinite starting points, but they were waiting for a "complete behavior." After being reminded that "a behavior" is a jumping off point—a movement no matter how small—they were on their way. They marked a slight head turn, then another and another. Soon the Beardie was offering lots of head turns.

Crossover trainers are used to achieving behaviors by luring or by placing a dog in a sit or a down, each easy to recognize as a "behavior." Come when called, retrieve a dumbbell, or jump a hurdle are each clear behaviors. Less clear are subtle behaviors like a glance, head movement, or a slight lowering of the body, yet these, too, are "clickable" behaviors.

What is a behavior?

In judging what constitutes a behavior, clicker training adheres to the Dead Man's Rule: *If a dead man can do it, it ain't a behavior.* Everything else is. So a behavior may be as small as a glance (the mere intention of movement) or as big as running over an A-frame or retrieving a duck from the water. A sample breakdown of behaviors that when put together constitute "settle" (go to your bed, lie down, and stay there until released) is shown on the next page.

Some behaviors such as a sit or hand targeting are easily achieved with just one step. Others are incremental behaviors shaped in steps, and then there are **behavior chains**—a series of linked behaviors performed one after the other.

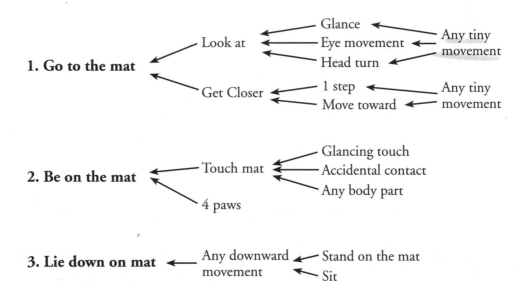

Some of the elements of the behavior chain resulting in "settle." The subtle movements and actions on the right side are potential starting points to shape toward the goals on the left. Each of the three elements of the goal behavior is shaped separately.

Whether the behavior is simple, incremental, or part of a behavior chain, getting a behavior started happens in one of two ways:

1. The behavior is achieved, start to finish, with just one action.
2. You shape the behavior in progressive, incremental steps.

Simple, one-action behaviors

Virtually every dog owner has experienced one-action behaviors. You can easily lure a puppy to come to you by crouching down, smiling, and calling "Pup-pup-pup-pup" in a happy, high voice. Your inviting body posture, facial expression, and happy tone of voice can elicit a recall in one step.

Sit, too, is easy to achieve. Hold a treat over a puppy's head, chances are the puppy will look up and sit, another one-action behavior. Getting your dog to "hug" (jump up on you) is a one-action behavior—so is "stay."

Cannon easily learned to "hug'" when invited up.

By simply getting her to look up, Marybeth induces Stella to sit, a one-action behavior.

Incremental behaviors

Arriving at the goal behavior in incremental steps is what shaping is all about. Visualize the process much like frames in a movie—each frame is one segment of the whole picture. The first frame leads to the second; frames one and two lead to the third; one, two and three lead to the fourth frame; and so on. Performed all together in sequence from beginning to end, the frames create a movie: a complete behavior.

The ability to shape a finished behavior starting from a subtle, initial movement is one of the profound advantages of clicker training. Some crossover trainers may feel discouraged with the idea of watching for subtle movements rather than *making it happen*, but shaping can progress in huge leaps with exciting, mind-boggling break-throughs. You'll see. (More in Chapter 7.)

Behavior chains

A behavior chain is the linking of several discrete behaviors. The first behavior triggers the second, which triggers the third, and so forth. The cue starts the chain, and the reward comes at the end. "Settle" is an example of a behavior chain—the dog goes to his blanket, then lies down, then rolls over onto one hip, puts his head down, and remains there until released. The obedience Retrieve over the High Jump is another example. On the "fetch" cue, the dog clears the jump, goes to the dumbbell, picks it up, carries it back over the jump, sits in front of the handler, and holds the dumbbell until cued to release it.

Chains may be trained going forward from the first behavior, adding each additional task, or backward from the last behavior working toward the first. Each behavior in the chain is shaped separately, and then linked with the others.

Shaping, whether for one behavior or part of a chain, relies on observational skills and timing. You practiced timing in the last chapter; now let's work on your powers of observation.

Seeing a behavior

British dog trainer Elizabeth Kershaw developed an exercise for her classes to sharpen their observational skills, focusing them on tiny changes and subtle movements. Chart 6-2 is an Observation Checklist to help you notice subtleties you might otherwise disregard, helpful in shaping behaviors from scratch.

In addition to helping you start shaping behaviors, when you put being able to "see" your dog together with the Calming Signal information in the previous chapter, this exercise will help you learn to recognize when your dog is in a "teachable" frame of mind, and when he is anxious, stressed, or distracted. By recognizing and responding to your dog's body language, you will maximize both your training sessions and your dog's overall comfort.

Chart 6-2 Observation Checklist

Head Movements	Body & Legs	Vocalizations
• Up	• Lean Forward	• Whisper
• Down	• Lean back	• Squeak
• Right	• Stretch rear legs	• Bark
• Left	• Bow in front	• Growl
• Tilt Right	• Turn left	• Squeal
• Tilt Left	• Turn right	• Sing
• Nod	• Crouch	• Talk
• Shake	• Scratch	• Grumble

Tail

- • Up
- • Out
- • Down
- • Under
- • Tip twitch
- • Circle wag
- • Full wag
- • Slight thump
- • Full body wag
- • Tip wag

Body & Legs (continued)

- • Lift front right foot
- • Lift front left foot
- • Lift rear right foot
- • Lift rear left foot

Vocalizations (continued)

- • Howl
- • Groan

Nose & Mouth

- • Lip lick
- • Nose lick
- • Tongue flick
- • Sneeze
- • Snort
- • Sniff
- • Smile
- • Snarl
- • Pant
- • Click teeth
- • Yawn
- • Sigh

Eye Movements

- • Alternate eyebrows
- • Eyebrows up
- • Eye contact
- • Glance left
- • Glance right
- • Look up
- • Look down
- • Wink
- • Blink

Ears

- • Up
- • Forward
- • Back
- • Right ear flick
- • Left ear flick
- • Alternate ears

Other

- • _____
- • _____
- • _____
- • _____
- • _____
- • _____
- • _____
- • _____
- • _____
- • _____
- • _____

This checklist gives you an idea of some subtle and not-so-subtle behaviors you may observe. For one week, watch your dog for three minutes each day. Choose a different time of day, and check off any movements and behaviors you see. Don't stare, and don't influence your dog's behavior. Simply watch as he goes about his business normally.

Getting behaviors

The first step of any dog training method is getting the dog to do it—to perform the behavior. All training approaches use one or more of five possible ways to get behaviors to happen: capture, shape, lure, mold, and correct.

Crossover trainers from a lure-reward background are familiar with getting behaviors with a food lure enticing the dog into performing. Those who have used compulsion-praise training methods are familiar with molding (physically placing) a dog into position and some may be familiar with using corrections. Clicker training relies on luring, shaping, and capturing. The following breakdown explains how each approach works, the pros and cons of each, and how it fits with clicker training…or not.

Capture

How it works. One way to get a behavior is to catch the dog spontaneously performing it on his own, and "capture" it with a mark. Some crossover trainers erroneously believe that capturing is the primary focus in clicker training—simply waiting for the dog to do something. While capturing is certainly a valid way to get behaviors and does play a role in clicker training, it is a bit part. Captured behaviors fall into three general categories: **predictable, typical-but-unpredictable,** and **serendipitous.**

Predictable behaviors are those your dog offers regularly at predictable times. As you'll learn in Chapter 8, when you are confident that the dog is about to perform the behavior, give the cue. Mayday would stretch (bow) every time I let him out of his crate. With such a predictable behavior, every time I opened his crate I said "bow." It didn't take long before the behavior was on cue and I could give the cue in other locations, too.

Capturing a predictable behavior such as a stretch (bow) makes it easy to put it on cue.

Typical but unpredictable behaviors are those your dog offers in the normal course of events on a regular basis, but whose occurrence you cannot predict, such as lying down. Even though you know that sooner or later during the course of the day your dog will lie down, trying to capture unpredictable behaviors for training purposes can be frustrating. Certainly you can mark the behavior when it occurs spontaneously, whether or not you have a clicker, but capturing typical but unpredictable, behaviors requires great patience, and can be time-consuming.

Once your dog understands the process of marker training, when he knows you're looking for him to do something, he'll likely offer a variety of typical behaviors on his own. At that point, watching for a new behavior becomes part of the game—lots of fun and very rewarding. On the other hand, for most typical behaviors, there are easier ways to get them than waiting to capture them.

Capturing serendipitous behaviors (those that "just happen") includes such things as sneezing, yawning, scratching, and shaking off. As with typical but unpredictable, you cannot cue the behavior until your dog offers it predictably.

Advantages. Capturing works well for spontaneous behaviors which are predictable that your dog readily offers such as stretch, bow, yawn, and the like. Further, capturing is practically essential for behaviors that are virtually impossible to lure, elicit, or shape.

Pitfalls. Waiting for a behavior can seem interminable to some trainers, so most clicker trainers save capturing for predictable behaviors and those that cannot be shaped or lured.

How to incorporate with clicker training. Simply mark the behavior when your dog offers it spontaneously. Even if you're not in a training session, or you are actively training another behavior, it doesn't hurt to mark any spontaneous offering of a behavior you want to capture. Each time you do, it becomes more likely that your dog will begin purposely offering the behavior, allowing you to mark it, and then put it on cue.

Kochi frequently engaged in a scratching behavior. It took very few clicks to "train" Kochi to put this behavior on cue.

Shape

How it works. Shaping is selecting and marking incremental movements leading toward the goal behavior.

Advantages. Shaping incremental movements toward the finished product yields fast results, enabling the trainer to quickly train behaviors as complex as finding and bringing you your keys, or teaching your dog to go to his bed and lie down. Complicated behaviors, useful or fun behaviors, tricks, specialized tasks—anything you want—can be achieved in minutes. Shaping works better with clicker training than with any other method, bar none. It is possible to shape behavior without a clicker, but doing so is less precise and takes far longer.

Pitfalls. Timing is critical—the behavior you click is the behavior you get. Mistimed clicks can result in a "mis" behavior learned just as quickly as the one you're trying to achieve. The good news is that you can correct the error just as fast.

My Crossover Journal
A student in my Rally-O class needed to work on downs. Her Springer Spaniel would begin to drop, go about half-way, and then bounce up expectantly. The problem was early clicks, before her dog's elbows and chest touched the floor. By delaying the click until the dog was all the way down, she was able to shape a new "down" in a matter of a minute or two.

How to incorporate with clicker training. Shaping is what sets clicker training apart from any other approach. More on this in the next chapter.

Lure

How it works. Like a magnet eliciting a behavior, lures fall into three categories: **Hand-held lures** that the dog follows, **target lures** that the dog goes to, and **directing lures** the handler uses to guide the dog.

Hand-held lures to follow. Holding food or a toy, the trainer lures the dog into the desired position, for example, luring up over the dog's head to elicit a sit or motioning down toward the floor to prompt a down. Virtually any object that attracts a dog can be a lure, such as a ball, toy, or your hand with or without food. It's important when using any hand-held lure—especially food—to eliminate it early on, before it becomes part of the cue, unless using the motion is your goal.

Targets as lures. Targeting is especially helpful to focus the dog. Using a target elicits behavior without requiring food or trainer proximity. A target can be a destination, such as the dog's bed or the arrival point for a Go-out. Or it can be something the dog touches such as the contact zone on an agility obstacle. Targets can be as big as a piece of furniture or a person, or as small as a spot on the floor, a Post-it® note or a butterfly clip. Targets are helpful for training a wide variety of behaviors from heeling, to agility directions or contacts, to ringing a bell to go outside, and more. You'll find recommendations of specific uses for targets in Chapter 12.

Some of the things you can use as lures are a telescoping pointer or target stick, free-standing rod or dowel, a target stick, carpet remnants, plastic lids, Post-it notes, or a bell.

Handler's location as a lure or target. Your position can act as a lure to help get a behavior started. For example, stand on one side of the mat and toss the treat to the opposite side. Your dog will likely turn and move toward you after he eats, enabling you to click him for approaching the mat. For behaviors such as sit-in-front, the handler-as-target is an integral part of the task.

Directing lures. These include lures that lead your dog in an action, such as using a finger motion or a target stick to direct your dog to spin or twirl. You can also use a directing lure to transfer your dog's focus, such as from a target stick onto an object or location.

Advantages. Hand-held lures get a fast response to get a behavior started, effective in the short-term. Targeting and directing lures are helpful in eliciting behavior without focusing the dog on food.

Pitfalls. Reliance on hand-held lures, especially with food, interferes with the dog's focus on his behavior. In the short-term luring can be helpful, but the dog is mindlessly performing while the trainer does all the work. As long as the trainer recognizes the addictive qualities of luring (Chapter 2), the necessity to quickly eliminate lures, and the body language that accompanies them, there are few other pitfalls.

How to incorporate with clicker training. All three areas of luring, hand-held lures, targeting, and directing are consistent with clicker training. You'll find specific recommendations in Chapter 12.

"Rules" for Using Food Lures

When using a food lure short-term to jump-start a behavior, follow these "rules" to get the dog to perform a specific action:

- Lure up to three times with food in your hand, but no more than three times.
- Then lure up to three times without food held in your hand. Again, no more than three repetitions.

- Each of these six times, the moment the dog assumes the desired position, click and treat.

- After these six repetitions, discontinue luring and shape the behavior. If the dog loses focus, use a nose tease to motivate the dog (see "Jumpstarting behaviors" on page 130). Do not confuse a nose tease with luring. It is a reminder that a reward is available if the dog performs.

- If your dog stops working, do not return to luring in that training session. Doing so teaches your dog "helplessness," that is, to wait for food to lure him into performing the behavior.

Mold/Compel behavior

How it works. Molding is physically manipulating the dog into position. For example, tuck or push the dog into a sit, pull forward on the collar to lift into a stand, or physically guide the dog to your side for heel position.

Advantages. Molding can be used to achieve simple physical positions. However, from a learning perspective, there are few advantages to using physical compulsion—even gentle manipulation.

Pitfalls. Physical touch masks learning and prolongs the process, making molding an inefficient approach for teaching behavior. Methods that employ molding generally require dozens of repetitions for the dog to recognize the behavior being trained. Further, any role the trainer plays in physically achieving a behavior will have to be faded—a process of gradually and progressively weaning the dog off the help.

How to incorporate with clicker training. From a learning perspective, even gentle physical handling of your dog is unhelpful. Since there's no advantage to physical manipulation for training behaviors, I can't think of a reason to use it.

Note: Using equipment such as a head halter or harness to restrict the dog's movement technically falls into the category of mold/compel. Although many clicker trainers use these training aids to prevent pulling, relying on them means the trainer will either need to continue using them or will need to fade their use.

Collar corrections

How it works. Collar "corrections" (also called "checks," "pops," and "jerks"), are used to coerce the dog into performing a behavior or to avoid making an error. For example, if the dog strays from heel position, he gets a collar check for being out of position and is praised when he arrives in the proper position. Or if he breaks a stay, the check punishes the error.

How to incorporate with clicker training. Because it "punishes" creativity, spontaneity, and thinking, trying to introduce behaviors with correction-oriented training is antithetical to clicker training. The answer to "how to use it with clicker training" is…don't.

Using treat delivery to further behavior

In addition to the benefits derived from physically separating the marked behavior from the treat, the clicker trainer gains additional advantages through controlling and manipulating treat delivery. With training that does not utilize a behavior marker, the dog associates the treat with whatever he is doing at the moment he receives it. Of course this association can happen even when using a behavior marker, so clicker trainers must be aware of not repeatedly reinforcing undesirable behavior. Such associations are easily avoided by having a treat delivery plan that includes where and how to reward your dog.

Before establishing a plan, we must first address the question, "Does the dog need to remain in position to get the treat?"

Click ends the behavior…or does it?

There are two viewpoints on whether or not the click sound means the end of the behavior. The "click-ends-the-behavior" side says that anything happening after the marker is immaterial to the behavior that earned the mark. If the dog moves out of position after the click and before he gets the reward, he still gets his treat.

The "click-does-not-end-the-behavior" camp holds that the dog must remain in place until released by the trainer. If the dog does move after the click, but before being released, he does not get a treat, and may be replaced in position. Here is the rationale for each.

Click ends the behavior (CEB). The click marks *the behavior* that is worthy of reinforcement. It provides *information* about the successful behavior, that is, whatever the dog was doing at the moment he heard the click. Since you cannot mark a behavior that has not yet occurred, anything that follows the click is, by definition, a *new* behavior. Therefore, the click marks the completion (the end) of "the behavior" that earned a click. How and where the trainer presents the reinforcer (*motivation*) cannot change the information provided by the click, *information* about the behavior that ended with the marker.

Click does not end the behavior (CDNEB). This viewpoint may derive from a training adage among some trainers who use a clicker for training, "Click for action; feed for position." While the adage is "feed *for* position," not "feed *in* position," it has morphed into the latter. Feed *for* position means using treat delivery to advance your training, as you'll read below in "Treat delivery options." Feed *in* position implies that the dog must not move after the click until he's gotten the treat, adding an implied "stay" to any behavior the dog offers.

Another likely reason trainers adopt this approach is that some clicker trained dogs tend to bounce from behavior to behavior, barely completing one before they offer another. Such rapid-fire conduct can make training feel chaotic and out-of-control, even making it difficult to find a behavior to mark. The solution offered by CDNEB trainers is to require the dog to wait for the treat. But here's the rub…

Requiring the dog to remain in position is a *different* behavior from the one that was marked by the click. Such insistence changes the meaning of a click from simply providing information about the behavior just performed. Used in this way, the click is both a behavior marker and a *cue* for a behavior chain. The chain of behaviors is: perform the behavior; remain in position while you wait for your treat; get and eat your treat while continuing to hold your position; and finally, wait for a release or if you aren't released, repeat the behavior. That's a lot of meaning for one small sound, and changes the click to a cue, rather than its most powerful use: *information* about the precise event that earned the reward.

Confirmed CDNEB trainers argue, even convincingly, that training is speedier when the dog stays in position, saving time between repetitions. However, even when click ends the behavior, there is no reason the dog cannot remain in position after the click. As you'll see below, there are many behaviors when treat delivery will, in and of itself, encourage the dog to remain in position, often until released. *Requiring* the dog to hold a position after the click means that the reward is withheld if the dog moves, resulting in "punishment" for moving after the click—punishment that is antithetical to clicker training.

Finally, requiring a dog to remain in position after the click limits rewards to those that can be delivered *in situ* (food and praise) making unavailable all other forms of reinforcement. For example, how can a dog remain in position and be rewarded by chasing a ball, going outside, or being free to play with other dogs? Such rewards would come only after the dog is released. Rather than being related to the behavior that was marked, the reward is a consequence of being released—an outcome that is rewarding in and of itself.

Certainly a trainer can choose CDNEB, but it is training-with-a-clicker, not clicker training (see Chapter 3). Further, as you'll see, requiring the dog to wait for a treat eliminates treat delivery options that can be advantageous to training.

Treat delivery options

Here's a rundown of some different ways to use treat delivery that can greatly facilitate and speed training (you'll find recommendations on treat delivery for specific behaviors in Chapter 12):

- **To re-set the behavior.** A helpful use of treat delivery is to get the dog into "start-over" position, ready to repeat the behavior right after eating the treat. For example, when working on "down," the trainer clicks and holds the treat so the dog must stand up, or tosses it a short distance so he gets up to get it. After eating the treat, he is in position to repeat the behavior. If you reward in place, you will need an additional step to move the dog so you can repeat the behavior. In lure-reward training, this is often done through luring between two positions, such as luring up then luring down again. **Note**: If the dog bounces from behavior to behavior too quickly, rather than insist the dog remain in position after the click, a better solution consistent with clicker training is to simply delay the click so that the behavior is assume-the-position-and-wait-for-the-click (be patient).

To reset the behavior, Marybeth places the treat a short distance away after clicking Dharma's sit.

- **Reward in place**. The trainer may choose to reward the dog in place, eliminating the need to re-position the dog to start over. For example, when working on building duration for "stay," click marks the end of the time frame. Rewarding in place can also be helpful when working on a positional behavior such as "heel" or "finish," but it is not required. If the dog moves from position after the click, he still gets his reward, since click ends the behavior.

- **To affect demeanor**. How you deliver the treat can help increase animation or calm a high-energy dog. For example, rewarding in place or with little movement of the dog may help settle an overly excited dog, resulting in a calmer response. On the other hand, skipping the treat across the floor for the dog to chase can create enthusiasm in a lethargic dog.

To affect Kaylee's demeanor, Carolyn tosses the treat along the floor to build her enthusiasm.

- **To increase distance**. Since the trainer doesn't need to be close to the dog at the moment of success to deliver the treat, the clicker trainer can quickly build distance from the dog. For example, with lure training when teaching a dog to go to a target or when working on cues at a distance from the trainer, the treat must be either strategically placed at the target (a complicated maneuver to set up properly), or distance must be built slowly, in small increments. On the other hand, with clicker training, click marks the behavior no matter how far the dog is from the trainer.

- **To bridge a time lapse**. An event marker buys some time after the behavior until the presentation of the reinforcer. By using a marker, the trainer can choose virtually any activity as reinforcement, rewards that are unavailable with other approaches. For example, to use a reward such as going outside to play, there may be a time lag between the behavior earning the reward and getting to the door, opening it, and letting the dog out. Ideally you want the reinforcer to be presented within two seconds or less of the click. This may mean a game of "let's run to the door" or "run to the kitchen" (to get a treat) starts right after you click—a game that is reinforcing, too!

Separate the click and treat

Allow a separation between the click and the delivery of the treat—a brief, fraction-of-a-second pause after the click before moving to deliver the treat. When your treat delivery is too closely connected, even intertwined with the click (click-treat), the dog's brain doesn't register the association between the behavior and the marker. Perfect timing is click…then…move to deliver treat. After you click, think of a two syllable word, such as your dog's name, and pause for the time it takes to think the name, *then* reach for the treat.

Delay…but not too long

While the marker buys time between the mark and the presentation of the reinforcer, it is not unlimited time. Picture yourself in conversation with a friend, and each time you say something your friend waits five seconds before reacting or responding; consider how interminable and puzzling such a pause would seem. So it is to your dog.

A delay of more than a second or two after the mark leads to a variety of possible results, the three "F's": frustration, futility, and fitful behaviors.

- **Frustration.** "What the heck are you waiting for?!" How does a dog display frustration? The most common outlet is barking. A reward presented after frustration barking would…you guessed it—reinforce barking.

- **Futility.** Why stick around? "Nothing's happening. I'm outa here!" (mentally or physically). After your dog has shut-down a few times, you'll likely have trouble motivating him to train. After all, you're not giving him any reason to participate.

- **Fitful behaviors.** Many dogs start offering a variety of erratic, arbitrary behaviors during the delay. As with frustration barking, there's a danger that you'll unintentionally reinforce whatever behavior the dog is engaging in when you deliver the treat. With several repetitions of such reinforcement, the dog will repeatedly offer the erratic behavior as a learned behavior.

A common treat delivery delay occurs when the trainer keeps treats in a difficult-to-access zipped plastic bag in a pocket or bait bag. Worse still, some trainers use a zipped fanny pack, with a zipped baggie inside it. Yikes! The poor dog has to wait seemingly interminably as the trainer fusses and fidgets getting food out of the bag. The simple solution is to have your food treats easily available. Don't delay.

Reward associations

There's good news and bad news. The good news—dogs quickly learn behaviors that result in valuable rewards. The bad news—what they're learning may not be what you have in mind. To avoid your dog learning unintentional behaviors, it's important for the trainer to be aware of associations that may affect learning. The two most common associations are with the *availability* of treats, and with the behavior the dog is performing when he *receives* the treat.

Availability associations

Clicker trainers (in fact, all trainers) want a responsive dog in the absence of food rewards. I've worked with clients to rehabilitate dogs who will only perform if the client is holding food treats, the dogs having learned that when there's no food readily available, there's nothing in it for them to comply—no reward is forthcoming. This leads some potential crossover trainers to suggest using a punishing consequence such as a collar check for non-compliance in the absence of food. While I understand the crossover trainer's "past-life inclination" to resort to a correction in this instance, it is both counterproductive and unnecessary. There are far easier ways to both fix this association, and to avoid the dog forming it in the first place.

The easiest way to achieve this is to prevent your dog from learning the treat-related associations: Food = behavior, No food = no behavior. Here are some strategies to prevent this:

- **Food in your hand**. You can pre-load your hand with a few treats for rapid repetitions, but train without food in your hand, as well. Pre-loading is helpful for speedy training, but when you pre-load, remember the sequence is still click, pause, treat. Allow that brief, second or less pause between the mark and the delivery of the treat, and during the pause, remain still.

  When holding food in your hand, place it behind your back, or away from your dog so the food doesn't act as a lure or otherwise interfere with your dog's performance. You want your dog to focus on his behavior, not on the food in your hand.

Shari holds her treat hand (and clicker) behind her back so the treats don't distract Siku as she shapes him to lie down.

- **Bait bag.** Using a bait bag forms an association that treats are available. This means that when you aren't wearing a bait bag, your dog may not be as responsive. To avoid your dog forming this association, move the bait bag so it is on your left, your right, in front or behind you. Sometimes place it on a table or on chair across the room. Train wearing an empty bait bag, and retrieve treats from a bowl on the table, and train without the bait bag anywhere in the picture.

  In addition to preventing an association with a bait bag, your dog may form an association with your hand position if you keep your hand in or near the bag, or reach for it simultaneously as you click. To prevent this, hold your hand in a neutral position when you click, and wait until after the "do-nothing-pause" before reaching to retrieve a treat.

- **Pocket.** As with a bait bag, if your dog can sniff your pocket, he'll know when you do and don't have treats. Use different pockets, as well as training without having any food on you.

- **Bowl of treats.** Using a container other than a bait bag or pocket is a good strategy for getting food off your body, but an association with the bowl will still form, so train away from it and without it, as well. And remember, keep your hand out of the bowl until after you click.

My Crossover Journal

My trainers and I worked with prison inmates teaching them to train dogs as Service Dogs. During a training visit, one of the men complained that his dog, a bright Golden Retriever, wouldn't do anything unless he had a container of treats nearby. To demonstrate, he moved away from the bowl and sure enough, Morgan was unfocused and distracted, failing to respond to even the easiest cues. I had him click once for nothing. Hearing the click, she immediately alerted. He rushed over to the bowl and gave her a treat. That's all it took for this smart dog to get it: "It doesn't matter where the bowl is—a reward is available if I click you."

- **Chipmunk cheeks.** OK, I admit to a pet peeve—spitting food at a dog. I shudder when I hear the "thwoop" sound of food being extruded from the trainer's mouth for the dog to catch. The theory behind food-spitting is, I guess, to encourage the dog to focus on the handler's face. It's far easier to train this as a rewarded behavior by clicking attention, and rewarding with a treat, eliminating food thwooping. Just as importantly, as with the visual stimulus of the bait bag, your dog learns when your cheeks are pre-loaded, forming an association that you'll need to eliminate.

  If my opinion about this isn't enough (and honestly, why should it be?) the Discovery Channel program *Mythbusters* tested the germs in the human mouth versus a dog's mouth to see if it's unhealthy for us to let our dogs kiss us. The end result: It is not healthy...for the dog! Your mouth has far more bacteria than your dog's mouth.

- **Anything else that the dog learns to link with the availability of food.** You may discover other associations you've inadvertently taught your dog. You'll know you've done it when your dog doesn't respond without it. Examine your behavior and the environment to figure out what the association is. Once you recognize it, it is easy to eliminate.

Some associations can be helpful. As Jean Donaldson says, they signal "The bar is open," so the dog is encouraged to offer behaviors. Use a conditioned association when it will advance your goals, but also set up training situations without food, so your dog doesn't become dependent on the availability of food treats. Use other high-value rewards, or have food hidden to surprise your dog. (See Chapter 12 for specific suggestions.)

Delivery associations

In addition to associations made with the *availability* of treats, undesirable associations can be formed with the *delivery* of the reinforcement. Repeatedly rewarding the dog when he's performing a behavior unrelated to the behavior that was clicked, such as jumping up on you after the click, can result in the dog learning that behavior.

You can easily avoid such learned behavior by varying your treat delivery. Sometimes give the treat to the dog in place and sometimes give the treat to the dog right after he moves. Or try having the dog come to you, throwing the treat to the dog, or tossing it on the floor, and the like. And always remember the timing: click…then…treat.

Superstitious behavior

Finally, sometimes an extraneous behavior becomes paired with the trained behavior, forming a "superstitious" connection between the two behaviors. Maggie the Pug featured in Chapter 1 was well on her way to learning to bark as she lay down. Had noisy downs been continually reinforced, barking would have been a superstitious behavior she performed with lying down.

Watch for any unnecessary behavior that is offered in conjunction with the one you're clicking. When such an unrelated behavior is offered more than once or twice, focus on getting and clicking the core behavior without the superstitious one.

My Crossover Journal
A crossover trainer at a seminar was shaping her dog to touch a ball on the end of a target stick. Her dog repeatedly nosed the middle of the stick then slid her nose towards the ball. Wanting her to touch the ball without touching the stick, the handler asked what she should do. I suggested withholding the click and see what happens. (Experiment!) When she didn't get a click, the dog tried different behaviors—including touching the ball, not the stick.

Just give me something to click

With an understanding of how treat delivery can affect your dog's behavior, it's time to put what you've learned to work. The first step in clicker training the crossover dog is teaching "the game." That is, play along and do something—*anything*—to get me to click you. This important first step in getting your to dog start using his initiative—to start to think—is for your dog to grasp that *his* behavior makes you click. The *dog* controls your treat-dispensing. This is a new and different concept for the crossover dog, many of which have been conditioned to wait to be told or shown what to do. Some dogs catch on quickly and you'll see their mental wheels start to turn right away. Others take longer.

Teach "click" to your dog

To start your dog's training, keep in mind the four things your crossover dog needs to grasp about the marker sound:

1. Click means a payoff is coming.
2. Click marks the *dog's* behavior.
3. The dog is in control of getting you to click.
4. Click ends the behavior.

Clicker don'ts and do's

Don't:

- Point the clicker as if it's a remote control.
- Thrust the clicker toward your dog as you click. Doing so can lead to fear of the clicker, or your movement can become a secondary (associated) signal.
- Click near your dog's ear. Doing so is painful to some dogs, leading to dislike or fear of the clicker.
- Click multiple times for one repetition of a behavior.

Avoid moving the clicker toward your dog when you click. Note the look of concern on Mazzie's face (and the Calming Signal, see page 72), when Shari thrusts the clicker at her like a remote control.

Do:

- Hold your clicker in a relaxed fashion.
- Hold the clicker still as you click.
- Click just once for each behavior.
- Follow each click with a treat.

Fear of the clicker

If you've already tried to use a clicker with your crossover dog, and she exhibited discomfort or fear of the sound, here are some strategies that can help:

1. Muffle the sound of the click by putting it in a pocket or a sock, put a piece of tape on the metal tongue, or get a quieter clicker (see Resources).

2. With your dog out of hearing range, test the sound to make sure it is dull and not as loud as what you have been using.

3. Get some good treats—really good ones! Sit in a chair or on the floor and toss a bunch of treats around, broadcasting them across the area. With the sound muffled, click as your dog eats a treat. Repeat a few times, then time the click after your dog eats a treat and is moving toward another one.

4. Repeat this three or four times in different rooms, timing the click so it is associated with "find a treat." Your dog should exhibit calm behavior with no signs of stress or distress as she's eating the treat.

5. You should now be able to follow the "normal" introduction to the clicker.

If even hearing a click in another room is too much for your dog, and your dog is not otherwise sound sensitive (afraid of loud noises like a dropped dish or pan), try desensitizing your dog to the sound. When she is eating her meal, go into another room and click once or twice, pausing between clicks. If your dog continues eating without pause, over the next several days continue desensitizing her by clicking a few times while she's eating, gradually moving closer. Your goal is to click and then put down her meal. When you are able to do that without your dog exhibiting apprehension, you are ready to begin training with the clicker.

To charge, or not to charge: That is the question

The significance of the click is based on the dog forming the association between the marker and the payoff: that click means "a reward is available." Some trainers "charge up" the clicker—click and treat repeatedly, sometimes over several sessions, until the dog demonstrates a positive association, alerting to the click.

When I first crossed over, my trainers and I charged the clicker with each dog. Seeing apprehension and even fear of the click in some dogs, we thought it might be that the "strange sound" had no frame of reference, so we tried a different approach. Connecting the click with performing a behavior, we introduced it using a simple behavior such as a hand touch or a sit, both easy to capture. With this frame of reference, few dogs reacted negatively to the sound, so we discontinued "charging" the clicker without connecting it to a behavior.

Getting started: Touching a "target"

The first two aspects to get your dog's clicker training started are getting a behavior, and getting your dog to offer it repeatedly. Select a behavior that you have not trained previously. While some crossover dogs may have learned to go to a specific spot, which is an aspect of target training (covered in detail in the next chapter), few non-clicker-trained dogs have been trained to touch a specific object with their nose or a paw. That makes the "hand touch" a good place to start, using your hand as the "target." Here's how:

Step 1. Teach your dog Click = Payoff. This first step teaches your dog the association between the click sound and the consequent reward. Hold a treat in your non-clicker hand, make a fist and hold your hand directly in front of your dog at his nose level, palm up, just a few inches from your dog. When your dog sniffs or touches your fist, click and immediately open your hand to let your dog have the treat. Repeat 3-5 times. If your dog does not actually touch your hand, click any movement toward it.

Concentrate on holding your hand still so your dog touches *you*, rather than moving your hand toward your dog to bump against your dog's nose.

Step 1. Vision touches her nose to Kris' fist holding a food treat.

Step 2. Next association—click is for behavior. Get the dog to focus on his behavior, not on the treat. To accomplish this, briefly delay delivery of the treat, separating it from the behavior.

As you did in Step 1, make a fist, but without food in your hand. Have your treats in a dish nearby, in a pocket or bait bag. Hold your fist in front of your dog, and click as you did in Step 1. After the click, reach for and give a treat to your dog. To avoid your hand movement or hand placement becoming an associated signal, hold your hand still and do not move it toward the food container until *after* you click. Repeat three times.

Continue working on this step moving your target hand slightly, just a few inches to a different spot with each repetition. Incrementally move it so that your dog turns his head to touch your hand. Then hold your hand far enough away so your dog has to reach towards, and then get up and move to touch your hand. Be patient. With many crossover dogs, this step may take more than one training session. Once your dog is doing well on this, move on to the next step.

Step 3. Your dog controls getting you to click. Switch to a different object to use as a target, such as a plastic yogurt lid. Hold the target in your hand and click any interaction—a glance, head turn, or movement toward the target. If your dog shows no interest, rub the target lightly with food, or hold a treat under it for up to three repetitions—but not more than three! Be sure to wait until *after the click* before moving to deliver a treat. Click progress, moving closer, touching more firmly, and the like. Once your dog is touching the target in your hand:

- In incremental steps, gradually move it to the floor.
- Once the target is on the floor, gradually move your hand away from it.
- When your dog is readily touching the target on the floor, move it around to different locations, and farther away from you.
- Re-set the behavior by tossing the treat away or having your dog return to you to get the treat.

Chapters 7 and 12 have more information on the specifics of Target Training.

 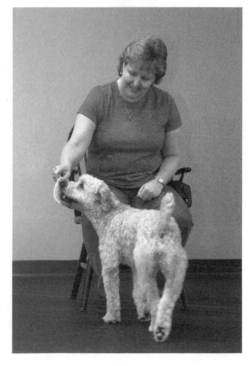

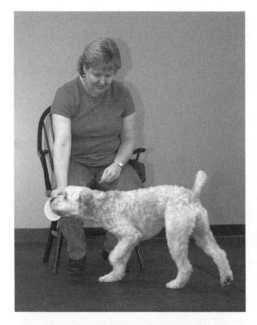

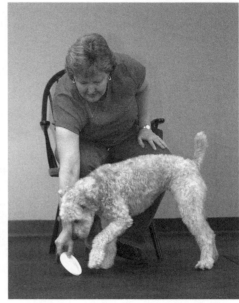

Carolyn shows Kaylee the target in her hand, clicking (and rewarding) a glance, then a touch, then lowering incrementally until it is on the floor.

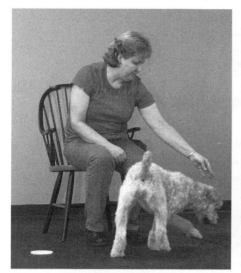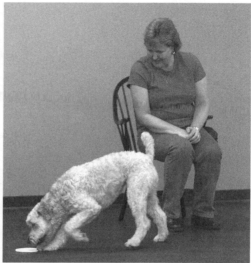

Moving the target further away from her, note how Carolyn rewards Kaylee away from the target to re-set the behavior after she clicks.

Step 4. Click ends the behavior. As you work through different behaviors, experiment with different treat delivery options to both enhance and advance your training. Regardless how you deliver the treat (toss it, hand feed, drop it, etc.), click means "the behavior *you just did* is the one that has earned the treat."

Take your time with these four steps. The knowledge you are providing your dog forms the foundation for his clicker training now and into the future.

Click-a-lot

Click and treat at a high rate of reinforcement. Since the click provides information, the more information you provide, the faster your dog will get it, the faster training progresses. Each click bolsters your dog's efforts, encouraging him to keep training, to participate, to "play the game."

At first, many crossover trainers are "stingy clickers," perhaps hoping that the next response will be just a bit better, or waiting for the complete behavior. The result is not only a missed opportunity to click, but no reward for your dog's efforts. Without the motivation provided by the rewards, the dog disengages and stops offering behaviors. So provide information; the more the better. Click a lot, click often!

It's not working?

It's possible that your crossover dog, much like mine when we first started, doesn't offer any behavior, waiting for you to lure or to give a command. Of course your dog does lots of things, but not (yet) in a "training" context. The remedy is to let your dog know that you not only want him to offer behaviors, but you'll even reward him for it! Here are some ways to start.

101 things to do with a box

Popularized by Karen Pryor, this creative exercise can be helpful with crossover dogs that have been trained to wait for you to lure, or whose spontaneity has been suppressed by corrections. You can follow the progressions below using a box, or use another prop—a paper bag, plastic milk jug, or virtually anything. The idea is to use a prop to get the point across to your dog that *his behavior* gets you to click and toss him a treat. Once your dog figures this out, you're on your way to having a thinking dog!

To do this training exercise, use a cardboard box that your dog can step into. Take your clicker, a big bowl of small treats (good ones!), put the box on the floor, relax, and get ready to click.

Step 1. The association—do something with the box. Treats are coming! The moment you set it down, click your dog for *anything* to do with the box: A glance, a step toward it, sniffing it, *anything*! If he walks by the box on his way to get a treat, click.

Without talking to your dog—no coaxing, tongue clucking, box rattling or any "help" at all—try different ways to click something with the box. If your dog doesn't move, try standing or sitting on the far side of the box. Watch for even a slight foot movement toward the box, click! After the click, toss a treat into or near the box on the far side of it. When your dog steps toward the box either to get the treat, to investigate, or to move toward you, click again, and toss another treat.

Alternate having your dog come to you for a treat, tossing the treat into the box, and tossing it on the far side away from you. If your dog is reluctant to get the treat in the box, it doesn't matter. Treats accumulate, so when he *does* get them, it's a jackpot. If you end the session before that, pick up the treats in the box and put them away. *Do not treat without clicking first, and always click for a reason—an action on the dog's part.*

End the first session with a click and a jackpot by either dumping a bunch of treats all at once, or offering your dog the bowl for a "help yourself" mouthful. Then put everything away including the box. Consider the impact that ending this way has on your dog when you bring out the box the next time.

Some dogs may be suspicious that the box is a trap such as a distraction or an attempt to catch him doing something wrong. If so, repeat this first step until your dog recognizes that the box means that you make that funny noise and toss treats!

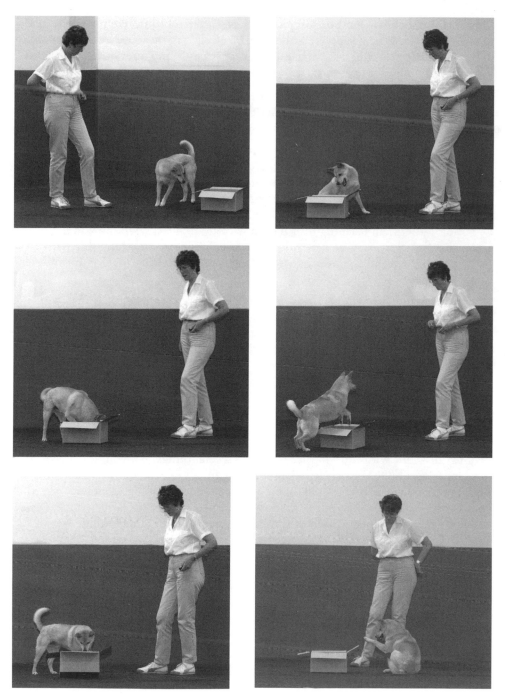

Kochi got clicked for any interaction with the box including a glance, turning toward the box, stepping into it, jumping over it, pawing it and sitting and waving at it.

Step 2. **Interact with the box—try stuff. Get Creative!** Once your dog recognizes that you're clicking "something related to the box," click more active interaction—step in it, paw at it, bite, push, lick, sniff, mouth, drag, carry, jump on it—*anything* the dog does with the box. Some reminders:

- **Click *during* the behavior, not after.** For example, click *as your dog paws* the box. Yes, the click will end the behavior, but once the dog has eaten the treat (tossed or handed to him), he'll go right back to it.

- **Clicking the same behavior repeatedly trains that behavior.** (See Crossover Cornerstone #4 on page 80.) If, after you click, your dog repeats that same behavior and you click again, you are training a single behavior. For example, your dog paws the box with his right paw, you click. He paws it again with his right paw, click. Once more, right paw, click. You are creating a single behavior, rather than teaching him the game of try *different stuff!* How to get out of this fix? Next time he paws, don't click it. Wait for something different, even pawing with his *left*. Click anything different, then keep looking for different behaviors.

- **Too many behaviors?** Great! If your dog starts doing *lots* of things with the box, terrific! If he really catches on and offers a flurry of box behavior that is too much to keep up with, jackpot and end the session. You are now ready for Step 3. Give some thought to what you might want to do in the next session to start shaping one behavior.

Step 3. **Shape a behavior.** Start shaping small increments leading to a particular behavior. For example, get in the box and lie down. Pick up the box and carry it. Carry a toy over and put it in the box. Tip the box over and hide under it. What else can you think of? Shape small movements toward your final destination.

Playing this game with your dog accomplishes several things. For you, it is a good way to practice and hone your clicker skills without any ill-effects. Early or late clicks are unimportant, since they're related to something your dog is doing, even if it's not what you intended to click. For your dog, it's a simple way for her to learn "the great game of clicker training," the first step of turning on your thinking dog's mind.

Chapter 7
THE JOY OF SHAPING

My Crossover Journal
Shortly after we crossed over to clicker training, I did an experiment in one of my first beginner training classes. Working individually one at a time, I had each student take her dog off leash and walk briskly in a circle around the class. I clicked, and the handler gave a treat as we shaped "walk at the handler's left side." The experiment exceeded my wildest imagination. In a very few minutes, each and every dog in this beginners class was heeling off lead—a behavior that normally would have taken months or even years to accomplish. Of course they weren't fully trained, but what a motivating start for all of us!

The feature that sets clicker training apart from other dog training approaches is shaping—a joy of discovery for both the dog and the trainer. Shaping creates a connection that, more than any other aspect of dog training, gives you a thinking dog. An incredibly powerful tool for training complex behaviors, shaping is helpful even with simple behaviors that are easily achieved.

My Crossover Journal
Pepper, an adolescent Great Dane, is 80 pounds of gangly uncoordination. Not quick to respond to luring, Pepper enjoys clicker training. To shape Pepper to lie down, we clicked when she moved her front feet. She soon started waving her forelegs. From that point we easily shaped her to put her feet down further from her body, until she simply lay down. Once she figured out that "down" was the behavior being clicked, this clumsy teenager began dropping as quickly as her ungainly body would allow.

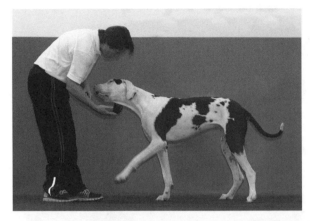

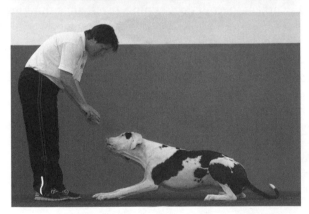

Beth demonstrates shaping Cami to lie down, starting with just a slight paw lift, then a wave, and ultimately lying down.

My Crossover Journal
Here's another example of shaping a more complex behavior in
small bits. Charlie, a Chesapeake Bay Retriever, was learning to go
to his bed and lie down. We began shaping Charlie to target the blanket, clicking
as he moved closer, and then got all four feet on it. As a separate behavior, we
shaped Charlie to lie down on the bed, then put the two together—go to your bed
and lie down.

Do the behaviors described above in the "My Crossover Journal" segment sound like a long process? The truth is, Pepper was lying down *on her own* after just a minute or two of training, and Charlie was going to his bed and lying down in just two short class training sessions with a few minutes of practice in between. More importantly, both dogs were off leash in a class situation with lots of dogs and people around, trained by novice clicker trainers to boot! After having used virtually every training approach, I have not achieved, nor can I conceive of achieving these results in such a short time with any other method.

Starting the shaping process

Building on the analogy that shaping is like frames in a movie (see page 83, Incremental behaviors), think of each discrete frame as an interim goal, a segment of the finished product. Starting with the first frame, the trainer shapes the behavior through that scene, then shapes through the first two scenes and adds a third until the movie is complete—the finished behavior.

Figure 7-1 shows the first few frames of Scene One, "Settle." The first frame starts with any behavior or hint of a behavior—a glance, a lean, a move, a head turn. The trainer marks any observable action in the direction of the mat, from the subtle to the obvious, even if it has nothing to do with the mat itself.

The second frame moves the dog closer to the mat. In the third frame, Charlie comes in contact with the mat, even if accidentally. And in the last frame, scene one ends with all four feet on the mat. The first glance, movement toward the mat, any accidental touch, all the way to having four feet on the mat—each discrete scene contains clickable behaviors.

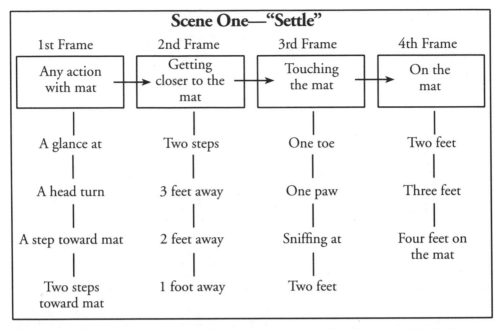

Figure 7-1 Frames in Scene One of the shaping "movie"—Charlie Learns "Settle."

Free-shaping versus targeting

Starting the shaping process, that is, getting the behavior started, can be achieved in a number of ways. The two primary approaches to shaping are with and without a prompt. Shaping without a prompt is sometimes referred to as **free shaping**. Shaping using an object or target as you did with the "hand touch" in the previous chapter, is target training. Shaping Pepper, the Great Dane, to lie down was "free shaping." Charlie's bed, on the other hand, is an example of using a physical object as a target. For clarity, I use "shaping" to refer to free-shaping, and "targeting" to refer to shaping with a target.

Targeting

In addition to being helpful for introducing the crossover dog to clicker training, targeting is useful in training a wide variety of behaviors and tasks. Tremendously helpful for crossover dogs, targeting can be used both for improving behaviors your dog already knows and for introducing new behaviors. With nearly limitless possibilities, targeting greatly speeds learning, giving the dog a focus that helps narrow the parameters of a behavior. You'll find specific recommendations for training with targets in Chapter 12.

Activities for targeting

Here are just a few areas and activities made easier with target training, helping the dog focus on specific actions, body movements, positions, locations and the like:

- **Obedience and Rally.** Heeling, finish, attention, automatic sit, recall, sit-in-front, go-out, drop on recall, jumping.

- **Agility.** Weave poles, obstacles, contacts, directions, box, jumps.

- **Conformation.** Gaiting, leading out, free-stacking.

- **Service dog.** Turn on the light, close the door, "take to," "bring to," and countless other tasks.

- **Other sports.** Flyball, Free-style, spin, bow, back-up, and on and on.

- **And, of course, basic manners and polite behavior.** Come when called, get in the crate, go to a bed, plus fun behaviors and tricks galore (see Appendix C).

The possibilities are virtually endless.

Free-shaping voluntary behaviors

Consider the observation checklist in the previous chapter and all the subtle movements your dog engages in. Shaping is as simple as selecting any one of these spontaneous, voluntary actions, and then clicking it. Doing so enables you to obtain behaviors that you either cannot achieve or would have more difficulty training using luring or physical manipulation. When you focus on a specific movement, click and reward it repeatedly, you're shaping your dog to volunteer that head turn, ear flick, tail wag, and the like.

My Crossover Journal
Using a quiet "yes" as her marker, Wendy trained her dog Cruiser to wag her tail, and put it on cue while listening to a lecture at a seminar. Before the one-hour lecture concluded, Cruiser wagged her tail when Wendy stuck out her tongue.

Starting by clicking a spontaneous action, you can shape a slight head movement into a down or a spin, a foot movement into a four-square stand, a down, or a High Five—you can even shape moving forward into hopping on a skateboard for a ride. Starting with any impromptu, random, or serendipitous action, you can shape behaviors ranging from useful to fun to manners or tricks.

My Crossover Journal
The students at our Instructor Training School (crossover trainers all) were practicing shaping. The task was to train Darby, a Border Terrier, to lie down under a chair. In less than four minutes, they went from a slight head turn toward the chair, to his touching the front chair legs with his feet, to touching the seat with his nose, to slightly lowering his head, to getting all the way under and lying down.

Darby tries different interaction with the chair: Touching it with his nose, his paw, lying near it, going under, and finally, the goal—lying down under the chair. Note how he checks in with the trainer. Do you like this? How about this?

20 rules of the shaping "art"

Whether targeting or shaping, whether starting with a subtle intention of a movement or focusing your dog on a large object such as a piece of furniture, an agility obstacle, or a blanket, I have identified 20 basic principles that make the shaping process easier for your dog…and for you.

While I refer to these fundamentals as "rules," they're really "recommendations," since very little about shaping is etched in stone.

1. Just start…Get your dog involved.

You control shaping your dog's actions from any starting point toward your ultimate goal behavior. While it's important to know your end goal, your starting point doesn't have to be at all related to it.

Let's revisit the Bearded Collie in the introduction to Chapter 6, whose trainers didn't think the dog was offering behaviors, and examine some potential starting points. Virtually any click gets the process going, even with the most subtle intention movement toward a behavior. Chart 7-2 is a sampling of some behaviors that might have been shaped with this Beardie, and where the trainers might have started clicking and rewarding.

What the Beardie did	To start shaping, click	Some potential behaviors
Eye movement	A glance	Go to an object or person, attention, come when called
Look around	Any tiny head movement	The above, plus tricks such as spin, head shake, others
Sniff the ground	Any downward movement, slight head or shoulder dip downward	Down, bow, nod head up and down, nose target touch
Walk around	Any visible paw movement	Back up, "High Five," dancing moves, turn, spin, foot target touch, "Go to," conformation training
Stand still	All four feet still, even for a brief moment	"4-on-the-floor" (polite greeting), stand for grooming, stack for conformation

Chart 7-2. An example of some possible behaviors that could be shaped from virtually any starting point.

2. Click and reward *every response* related to the shaping sequence you're focused on.

Called **continuous reinforcement**, take advantage of every opportunity to let your dog know he's on the right track. Doing so provides information to your dog and keeps him actively involved. This relates to "Click-a-lot," in the previous chapter. As you progress through the behavior, you'll change to a variable schedule of reinforcement. (More on this in rule #4 below, and in Chapter 8.)

3. Behaviors that aren't reinforced tend to extinguish.

When a previously reinforced behavior is no longer rewarded, especially one that has been rewarded every time, the dog will stop offering it and the behavior will **extinguish**. If this doesn't happen, examine what might be rewarding the behavior. You may find that you are doing something that unintentionally reinforces it. (More on this in rule #4, and Chapters 8 and 10.)

4. You control shaping your dog's actions toward your ultimate goal behavior.

This may seem too simple to mention, but by choosing what to click, you control moving the behavior along. The process of progressing toward a goal behavior by reinforcing a new aspect and discontinuing to reinforce the previous level, is called **differential reinforcement**.

Differential reinforcement is a schedule that involves rewarding behaviors moving closer to your goal and ignoring, and thereby extinguishing earlier sequences of the behavior. Figure 7-3, the brainchild of Corally Burmaster, is a graphic representation of this concept. Each circled "shaping cluster" is a group of like behaviors. Cluster 1 represents clicking the dog for any and all intentions or subtle actions toward the mat, a glance, a lean, a movement—anything that brings the dog closer.

Cluster 2 is any behavior involving touching the mat, even a glancing touch. The process of differential reinforcement means you no longer click a glance or lean, as you did with Cluster 1. Without reinforcement, the dog stops offering Cluster 1 behaviors. Once the dog is regularly touching the mat, the trainer ups the ante, requiring the dog to have more paws on the mat—two paws, then all four paws—no longer clicking just a toenail or one paw.

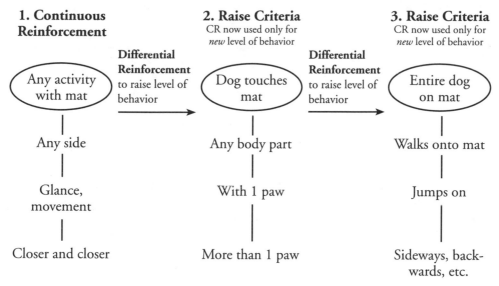

1. Continuous Reinforcement

Any activity with mat

Any side

Glance, movement

Closer and closer

Differential Reinforcement to raise level of behavior

2. Raise Criteria
CR now used only for *new* level of behavior

Dog touches mat

Any body part

With 1 paw

More than 1 paw

Differential Reinforcement to raise level of behavior

3. Raise Criteria
CR now used only for *new* level of behavior

Entire dog on mat

Walks onto mat

Jumps on

Sideways, backwards, etc.

Figure 7-3. **Differential Reinforcement**. *Each of these three sequences represents a step toward the goal behavior "settle," using continuous reinforcement within each shaping cluster, a group of like behaviors. Differential reinforcement is continuously reinforcing a new level of behavior, represented by the new cluster, and discontinuing reinforcement of the previous level.*

It would be great if dogs read this book, but they can't—so differential reinforcement is not as clear-cut as illustrated in Figure 7-3. The overlapping circles of the Venn Diagram in Figure 7-4 more closely represent how shaping progresses. The left circle represents Cluster 1—the beginning of the behavior. The right circle represents the next clear step. The overlap area, where the dog moves back-and-forth between Clusters 1 and 2, and 2 and 1, is a decision-making area for the trainer—to click or not to click.

For example, the dog's front paws are on the mat, click. The dog moves off the mat to get the treat re-setting the behavior, then takes a few steps away from the mat. Moving away from the mat is clearly not click-worthy—but then the dog turns and moves toward the mat. The trainer has decision to make—delay the click until the dog is on the mat again or, to re-focus the dog on the goal, click for moving closer to it. Since waiting too long for the previous successful behavior (front paws on the mat) risks the dog losing interest or changing direction, the trainer may click to remind the dog that the behavior has something to do with the mat—a click in the "overlap" area. (If you hesitate too long and lose the behavior, don't despair. It's just a brief setback. Keep clicking and you'll get it back. See rule #15.)

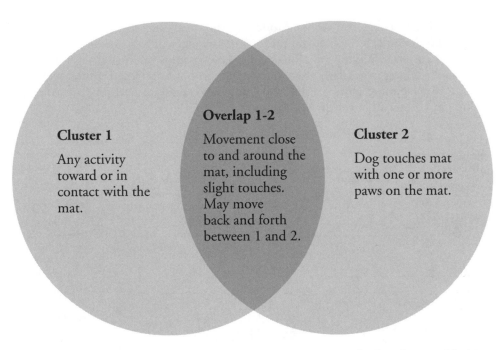

Cluster 1

Any activity toward or in contact with the mat.

Overlap 1-2

Movement close to and around the mat, including slight touches. May move back and forth between 1 and 2.

Cluster 2

Dog touches mat with one or more paws on the mat.

Figure 7-4. The overlapping section of the two circles represents the "gray" area of decision-making, where the behavior may move back and forth between Clusters 1 and 2.

With practice, you'll develop a feel for when it might be more advantageous to wait, or when to click more frequently. As you shape behaviors, play with this aspect, noting your dog's responses and speed of learning. In the beginning of any new behavior, especially for your crossover dog as she is learning the game, click more often.

5. Accidents count.

An "accident" is the serendipitous performance of the behavior, such as the dog walking over the mat as he heads to the window to check out something he heard. Accidents are your friend—be grateful and welcome them. Many trainers avoid clicking an accident, thinking that the dog didn't "know" that the accidental behavior is related to the goal. The truth is that with any new behavior, the dog doesn't "know" what you're shaping. He has no idea of the goal behavior, so treasure accidents as opportunities. At the very least, they keep the dog actively involved and working.

6. Shape one thing at a time. Don't try to shape two behaviors simultaneously, or try to shape two aspects of the same behavior.

One of the questions crossover trainers ask is whether you have to limit a training session to just one behavior. Certainly you can work on more than one behavior in a training session, but shape just one element at a time of any behavior you're working on. For example, in teaching "settle," different elements of the behavior include "go to the blanket," "move onto the blanket," "lie down on the blanket," and "remain down until released." Each aspect will likely need to be shaped separately.

Even a simple one-step behavior has different aspects such as the speed of performance, the duration or distance of the behavior, its location or proximity to an object or person, and the like. Work on one characteristic at a time. For example, working on stays, build duration with close proximity, then build distance for short durations, then combine those two elements. In shaping weave polls, the separate elements to work on include correct entry, number of poles, speed, and the like, each shaped separately, not simultaneously.

7. Move forward in small enough steps so the dog continues to be successful and is reinforced frequently.

Shaping isn't a question of what the dog is capable of, but rather what you are communicating. For example, we knew Pepper the Great Dane was capable of lying down, but clicks communicated to her that moving her feet, lowering her head, then her shoulders were behaviors that would be rewarded.

Rewarding small steps with a high rate of reinforcement keeps the dog actively involved and progressing. Crossover trainers feel frustration when a dog shuts down, often as a result of missed opportunities to mark and reinforce small steps. You'll keep your dog involved through informational clicks, with a high rate of reinforcement. Ideally, make the goal within each shaping cluster easily achievable so the dog is successful (gets a click and treat) for 80% to 90% of her efforts.

8. Be prepared for quantum leaps.

Don't limit your shaping to miniscule steps if the dog takes a giant leap. Shaping doesn't need to progress sequentially: A to B to C. Sometimes a behavior will leap from A to the end of the alphabet in a short move. It may be that performing the goal behavior is simply easier for the dog than moving in increments. Or it may be that your dog suddenly "gets it"—the "Aha! moment." When a behavior takes a quantum leap, don't hold your dog back by withholding a click. Go with it! This is what a thinking dog is all about—that moment when it "clicks" for your dog, when he clearly communicates to you that he's got it, he's figured it out.

My Crossover Journal
During a seminar in which I was a participant, I was quietly shaping my puppy Cannon to put his head down on the mat. I marked head lowering several times. It took just a few quiet "yes" marks before it was just more comfortable for him to put his chin on the mat. Voilá—that was what I was looking for. It could have progressed in inch-by-inch increments, but most often it doesn't.

Just as importantly, don't hold your dog back by insisting on free-shaping when another approach will get the job done far more elegantly and easily. I once read instructions on shaping the agility tunnel recommended on an Internet clicker list. The writer described shaping step-by-step getting closer and closer to the tunnel, then putting one paw near it, then one paw in it, then two feet, etc. Advice included ignoring the dog if it jumped ahead and went through the tunnel! While you certainly could shape a dog to go through the tunnel in this fashion, it's just silly to ignore the successful goal behavior. Consider how much easier it might be to have a helper hold the dog, go to the other end of the tunnel and call the dog through. Click as the dog enters and throw a toy or provide a treat as he exits the tunnel.

9. Be flexible; don't be afraid to "bank" behaviors for future use.

You'll often find that while shaping one behavior, your dog may offer a serendipitous, unanticipated one. Don't be afraid to capture such unexpected opportunities with a click; putting them in the bank, so to speak. They may pay dividends later. This is especially useful with behaviors that are difficult to obtain or shape and are best captured, such as a sneeze or yawn.

Ultimately you're in control of what you click, so you can choose to change tracks and go with a new behavior if the opportunity arises. If you click a new behavior, and the dog continues to offer it, that's fine. If he doesn't, you can return to the original behavior you were working on. On the other hand, be careful that such behaviors don't become superstitious.

Since clicker training does not follow a step-by-step recipe, experimentation and flexibility are part of what make it fascinating and exciting. While many crossover trainers embrace this with enthusiasm, some may find it off-putting, or even anxiety-producing. Your dog's training won't necessarily suffer if you lack flexibility, but rigidly adhering to achieving a single behavior means you may miss opportunities to capture interesting, exciting, and even breakthrough behaviors.

My Crossover Journal
A student in our Trainers' Academy was shaping Kochi, a bright Shiba Inu mix, to lie down. He happened to scratch, a calming signal, at the moment he got clicked. When it happened a second time and then a third consecutive time, the student had a decision to make: go with it and train scratching, or watch for and click "down" behavior without the scratching.

Kochi, the dog who had been repeatedly clicked for scratching, started out offering "trial" scratches when we were working with him to settle on the mat. When he didn't get clicked for scratching, he quickly tried other behaviors, enabling us to shape lying down.

10. "Fix" the behavior as you shape it.

Traditional training involves getting the behavior, then "fixing" elements of it. For instance, you train your dog to sit on command, then correct it to make it faster, straighter at heel position, balanced on both hips rather than a sloppy "puppy sit," and the like. With clicker training, you shape the sit, shape a fast sit, shape a straight sit at heel, shape a sit up from a down, etc.

Sometimes the crossover trainer is tempted to use the criterion "well at least he did it." Using "at least he did it" as a benchmark usually means marking a distant cousin of the desired behavior, or perhaps marking other, superstitious behaviors he "did" at the same time.

Crossover trainers may be tempted to return to their former method to fix a behavior they've shaped. Remember, combining methods is not advantageous to your dog or to your dog's training. More importantly, you don't need to—the "fix" exists, and can be found with clicker training.

> *My Crossover Journal*
> *Mary was training her dog Shannon to stay. Extremely excited, Shannon vocalized quietly, with an eager whine. Working on increasing duration, when Shannon reached the time goal, Mary clicked her for the stay at precisely the same moment Shannon uttered a louder whine. The same thing happened when she repeated the exercise. Mary continued working on the behavior thinking "at least she's staying!" If Mary didn't focus on clicking only when Shannon was quiet, Shannon's learned behavior would be "whine-and-stay."*

11. The behavior you see is the behavior you clicked. That is, "You clicked it; you trained it!"

Crossover trainers sometimes get frustrated when the dog is offering something other than what the trainer is trying to shape. Here's the truth, sad though it may be: your dog demonstrates the results of your clicker timing and proficiency. When you get the behavior you thought you were clicking, you're doing fine! If you get a different behavior, don't blame your dog.

When you see a behavior you didn't intentionally train, examine how it happened. Often a simple adjustment of your clicker timing is the "fix."

> *My Crossover Journal*
> *A student complained that she couldn't use food in training, because all her dog did was stare at the treat bowl—she couldn't get her to do anything else. On questioning, I learned she had "warmed up" the clicker, repeatedly clicking and giving her dog a treat. She didn't notice that her dog was looking at the treat bowl every time she clicked. In just four or five repetitions, she trained her dog to stare at the bowl.*
>
> *Here's another example: One of our agility instructors attended a training clinic where obstacles were introduced by tossing food onto the low A-frame, dog-walk plank, or into a tunnel, then clicking as the dog approached the treat. She decided to try this with her Beginner agility class. Repeated with each obstacle, by the time these dogs started Intermediate agility, they were well-trained...to search for food. The Intermediate class instructor noticed the problem immediately: While dogs from other Beginner classes had learned the obstacles, the dogs from this class had been clicked for finding food, learning "search for food"—they had learned the lesson well.*

12. Don't get stuck. Avoid clicking a sequential level of a behavior more than two or three *consecutive* times before raising your standards.

This is Crossover Cornerstone #2, but it bears repeating. Even with something as simple as a sit, if you repeatedly click the precise moment the dog's rear end hits the floor, you are shaping "sit briefly" and will have a harder time teaching "sit and hold position." When shaping down, if you click your dog for lowering her head several times in a row without any other related movement, you'll get beautiful head-bobbing. Not that you cannot advance to another level of the behavior, but doing so is much easier when you simply raise your standard after just a couple of clicks.

This rule refers to *multiple consecutive* clicks. On the other hand, if a behavior regresses, and you need to get it back, you can return to an earlier sequence and click it. Clicking in this case falls into the overlapping area 1-2 in Figure 7-4. From time to time you will need to click earlier sequences of a behavior.

13. When you change an aspect of the behavior, be prepared for regression. Temporarily relax your expectations and standards for the behavior.

In the learning stage, behaviors regress when you change something, even something as seemingly insignificant as how close you are to your dog, or your body posture. When shaping a new aspect of a behavior, or changing the context such as location or distractions, be prepared for deterioration in the dog's performance. You may have to back up a bit in the shaping process to an earlier step. After just a very few "reminder" clicks of that earlier progression, the dog will once again offer the behavior without hesitation, and you're good to go. (More on this in Chapter 8.)

14. Be prepared for the dog to test the premise—to test the parameters of the behavior.

Every behavior has countless possibilities for different associations. Your dog will have to work through some or many of these to get to the explicit, core behavior. The setting in which the behavior occurs, the environment, location, and context all offer possible associations the dog needs to work through, eliminating those that are irrelevant. In the same respect, the dog must discover relevant correlates with the behavior.

My Crossover Journal
Denise had unintentionally shaped Duke to lie down in front of her. When she started Rally-Obedience, she discovered this association and had to change the premise so Duke would lie down at her side. At first Duke would curve himself around to be in front of Denise. When he didn't get a click to tell him that this was the correct behavior, he tried something different so Denise could shape the goal behavior: "lie down wherever you are, regardless of my position."

With a different chair in a new location (see page 114-115), Darby tested the premise, trying different things with this chair before trying to go under it and lie down.

15. Don't be concerned about "losing" a behavior. It's not "lost," it's just temporarily missing, and is easy to regain.

Shaping is a joy of discovery. To experience the joy, you need also to be open to the possibilities. Experiment, try different things, and don't worry about losing behavior. Any behavior your dog stops offering can be regained, easily and quickly. It's simply a matter of clicking and shaping the behavior that you want; the one you thought was "lost."

There's another, positive side to this. In the process of "losing" one behavior, you may discover an even better one. Be open to the possibilities!

My Crossover Journal

When I attended class with my young Beardie, Cannon, our instructor, Marybeth had the class shape "crawl" with a foot target by clicking movement toward the target in the down position. After a few training sessions, Cannon no longer stayed in place when cued to lie down. It took just three or four repetitions of cueing "down," click and treat, and withholding the click if he moved, before Cannon recognized that "down" meant "lie down and remain in place."

16. If a learned behavior deteriorates, review your shaping procedures.

Just as with a "lost" behavior, if the dog seems to have "forgotten" one, review a few earlier steps of the shaping process to recover the behavior. This review moves quickly, usually taking just a few clicks. Deterioration of a behavior occurs for a variety of reasons. Dogs, like people, occasionally forget things. Lack of practice, insufficient reinforcement, and a variety of other causes can lead to regression in a learned behavior. When in doubt, back up a few steps, and the dog should progress quickly.

A caveat: If this happens repeatedly, especially with a crossover dog, it may be that the dog is "playing dumb." Consider the possibility that your dog has learned that you make it easier for him when he acts as if he doesn't understand. When your dog seems not to understand on a regular basis, review your actions. Are you unintentionally reinforcing "forgetfulness?"

17. Explore variability, don't fear frustration.

Varying reinforcement schedules—how often you give a treat—and varying the reinforcements themselves will trigger variations in your dog's behavior.

- **Vary the reinforcement schedule.** Behaviors can be dramatically changed and improved by introducing a variable reinforcement schedule that encourages variability in behavior. You'll learn more about using reinforcement schedules in Chapter 8.

My Crossover Journal
Susan was training Hein to retrieve. He was doing everything short of actually putting his mouth on the dumbbell. He'd touch it with his nose, rest his chin on it, paw at it, but not open his mouth. Susan tried varying the reinforcement schedule and, in a burst of frustration, Hein bit the dumbbell—click!

- **Vary the reinforcement.** Try giving your dog a **jackpot**, an extra-large treat, and see what happens. Especially in the beginning of shaping a behavior, jackpots most often lead to a different behavior from the one you jackpotted. You'll read more about jackpots in the next chapter on page 147.

When you play with variability, you'll likely see frustration, a powerful spark for behavior. Don't be afraid of it. Some trainers feel it's important to do everything possible to avoid frustration, concerned that it stresses the dog. All learning involves some stress, and frustration can actually be helpful. Trying to avoid frustration is like trying to prevent a child from ever experiencing disappointment or opposition—it's not real life.

It is the same for dogs. Once your dog figures "it" out, he's truly got it!

My Crossover Journal
I am not a techie. My ten-year-old niece knows far more about technology than I do. When I got my new iPod I was tempted to call her for help, but I resisted. It was frustrating as I learned to upload music and use it, but ultimately well worth the effort! Despite, or perhaps because of the frustration, having been successful, I'm better prepared for other new advances.

18. There is no "one right way." If one approach doesn't work, try another.

When you run into a problem, be creative in thinking of new ways to get the behavior. Shaping and targeting provide countless approaches. Add to that the changes you get using variability, and you have virtually infinite ways to get behavior. If your dog is physically capable of performing a behavior, you can train it with shaping.

The more you get into shaping with your crossover dog, the more helpful your dog will become. Clicker-trained dogs often seem to relish their role in finding a starting point for you to click—your thinking dog working with you. What fun!

Here are a few different ways our students have shaped behaviors when the first approach didn't work.

- A student couldn't get her Rhodesian Ridgeback to move from a bow into a down. Shaping her to go under the coffee table, it took just a few clicks before the dog was lying down willingly.

- Another student couldn't lure her Greyhound into a sit from a stand, so she shaped the sit rising up from lying down.

- A student's Golden Retriever puppy who was too keyed up to lie down, was continually jumping up. She timed her click for the moment her pup lowered her front end as she gathered herself to jump. After two or three clicks, the pup paused in that position, and shaping "down" progressed from there.

Verne, the illustrator of this book, came up with a creative way to eliminate a problem she encountered in the obedience ring. Her Portuguese Water Dog, Kayak, barked the moment Verne left the ring for the three-minute sit-stay. Uttering just one, "Hey! Don't forget about me!" bark, he stayed put, but this one vocalization had to be eliminated. To give him something to concentrate on, Verne shaped him to balance an object on his head. She gradually reduced the size and weight of the object as she increased the time he held it, combining this "trick" with her going out of sight. Ultimately Verne could simply brush her fingers against his head to have him concentrate when she left the ring.

Concentrating on holding his head still, Kayak learned to stay without uttering a peep.

19. Try to end on a high note.

At the end of the session, stop with a good response. Give your dog a jackpot to reward her for a good training session, and as motivation for future training sessions. Use a cue such as "all done" to tell her the session is over.

The last behavior your dog performs can have a lasting impact. This is true for individual behaviors within a session as well as the training session as a whole. When working on several behaviors in one session, if possible, end each with a good, reinforceable response.

Since our dog's success is incredibly reinforcing to us, the trainers, it is tempting to go for "just one more good one." Sometimes this is successful, but more often you'll mentally kick yourself for not stopping with the last good one.

Virtually every other method of training requires multiple repetitions, so crossover trainers are used to drilling behaviors many times. Some crossover trainers may have difficulty trusting that learning takes place with just one or two good repetitions. But it does. In the absence of prompts, when the dog is afforded the opportunity to figure it out for herself, it is amazing to see how significantly faster learning takes place. You'll find that a few well-timed clicks replace dozens of unmarked, prompted repetitions.

20. They're *all* tricks to your dog—have fun!

Is there a difference to a dog between the manners (obedience) behaviors "sit," "lie down," and "heel" versus the "fun" behaviors "sit up," "play dead," and "dance?" Without question, there's a difference: *We* behave differently. The difference is *our reaction* to a trick. We laugh and enjoy a dog performing tricks, but we tend to be serious about obedience commands. To the dog, however, the process of learning "lie down" is precisely the same as "bang, you're dead." Except for the change in *our attitude,* they're *all* tricks to the dog.

There's often a difference in a trainer's attitude toward training a puppy, and the change that occurs when the dog is mature. When cueing "sit" with a puppy, for instance, the cue is a light, upward sounding, two syllable word, "Si-iT." Suddenly, when the dog turns a year of age, the cue becomes a militaristic command, "SITTT!!!" Same behavior, different attitude. No fun for the dog...and not necessary!

Approach all behaviors as tricks—relax and enjoy training. After all, it's not critical—it's a *trick.* This doesn't mean you can't have reliable behaviors. Of course you can! But enjoy yourself. To help develop your clicker skills, play with different behaviors, thinking of them as "tricks." Appendix C contains over 200 useful, helpful, and most of all, fun behaviors.

Review the fundamentals
Shaping behavior is fluid, often elegant, and artful. The more you play with it, the more you'll learn about it, and the more your dog will get it, too. Review these fundamentals from time to time. As you add new behaviors to your dog's repertoire, various aspects will become relevant and instructive.

"Clicker-wise"
Usually when a trainer talks about their dog being "something-wise"—ring-wise, food-wise, correction-wise, and the like—it's a bad thing. It means the dog fails to perform in the ring, or performs only in the presence of food, or when he knows a correction is in the offing. Being clicker-wise, on the other hand, is a *good* thing.

A clicker-wise dog gets into the process of shaping, offering behaviors, and quickly narrowing the parameters of the behavior to accomplish your goals in minutes. She quickly learns the rules of the "shaping game," repeating a behavior if she is clicked, and trying a different behavior if she isn't. The more you get into shaping with a clicker, the more your crossover dog will become your partner-in-training—a thinking dog. Clicker-wise, thinking dogs are inventive, trying new behaviors or new wrinkles on old behaviors. Such inventiveness makes learning fun, spontaneous, creative, and fresh for both of you—another joyful element of your partnership.

Chapter 8

BUILDING BEHAVIOR

My Crossover Journal
Judy, one of our Instructors, laughingly claims that it took her five
years and three minutes to train her Golden Retriever, Maddie,
to do a High Five. Five years of repeatedly lifting Maddie's foot and praising/
rewarding her, then three minutes of clicking foot movement, then shaping it
higher and higher to a High Five.

Crossover trainers often come from a background of command-based training, introducing the cue or command from the very start. Consequently, it can be confusing and even a bit unsettling to contemplate getting a behavior without saying a word, and only later putting it on cue. The process is not as perplexing as it may seem. Some behaviors get there easily and quickly, while others take a bit more focus.

Four steps to a trained behavior

In general, follow a four-step sequence to take a behavior from a mere hint to being on cue:

1. Get the behavior. *no cue, no duration or distance*

2. Put the behavior in perspective to help the dog figure out the specific parameters and context.

3. Use a variety of reinforcements to perfect the behavior.

4. Name the behavior—add the cue.

Know your goals

How long you spend on each step varies from dog to dog and behavior to behavior depending on your ultimate goals. Do you want a well-mannered pet, or are you interested in dog sports such as obedience, dancing with your dog, agility, or Rally? If you participate in dog events, are you enjoying a fun activity together with your dog, or are you competitive and want to win first place?

The focus you place on details and finer points depends on what you plan for your dog. With your ultimate goal in mind, visualize the elements of your dog's behavior that will provide the results and precision you desire. Table 8-1 contains some of the differences in behaviors depending on your goals.

How it looks

Form follows function: Shape the behavior to fit your goal

Behavior	Pet manners	Obedience and Rally	Agility
Sit	No particular posture No particular position	Hips square and balanced Different positions Lined up straight at heel Square in front At a distance (Go-out) With other behaviors	Square and balanced for fast take off
Down	Sit then down	Fold-back down from stand Down in motion	Fold-back down from stand, fast down in motion to drop on the table
Stand	Informal for grooming and other husbandry	Stand up from sit Stand-stay Stand for exam	Stand for measurement
Walk on Lead	Without pulling	In heel position	Without pulling
Stay	Informal—tolerating posture/position shifts	Hold posture and position Handler across the ring Handler out of sight	Remain in position Handler leads out Wait on the table

Table 8-1. Some possible goals for each behavior, depending on the activity.

Knowing where you want to end up, let's get started. Here's a run-down of each step of the process:

Step 1. Get the behavior

Starting from scratch, this step takes the behavior from non-existent toward your goal. This is not as daunting or as lengthy a process as it may seem. For example with "sit," the process might begin with a puppy standing in front of you. As you smile down at your pup, perhaps showing him you have a treat then holding your hand against your chest, chances are outstanding that the puppy will look up at you and sit. Few behaviors are this easy to capture, but "getting the behavior" can be that fast.

To train "settle," getting the behavior involves first shaping the dog to go to the blanket, then get onto it with all four feet. In other words, Step 1 is simply accomplishing the behavior—no cue, no duration, no distance—just get the behavior.

There are many ways to get your dog to offer behaviors. Don't be afraid to experiment as I did in the beginners class described in the introduction to the last chapter. In that experiment, we used the handler's brisk walking as an attraction to get the dog to follow along and get clicked. This was just one way to start the process. You may even start by luring…*briefly*. Many crossover trainers will want to take advantage of the opportunity to lure, but remember the rule on page 89 about luring with food: *no more than three times with food, followed by up to three times without food; then shape the behavior without further luring.* This is important for all dogs, but even more so for crossover dogs from a lure-reward background who are well-trained to wait for and follow a lure. Avoid reinforcing this reliance.

Ideally, think of ways to put your dog in a position to easily perform the behavior without interference, body language, or help. For example, to shape "sit at heel," you might begin standing next to a wall or other object to help your dog be in position for success. You'll find specific recommendations in Chapter 12, but don't be limited by these ideas. Experiment and consider strategies with and from other clicker trainers. The more you experiment, the bigger your creative bag o'tricks.

Crossover Cornerstone #5

"Discovered" behaviors are learned with greater retention than lured or molded behavior.

Most crossover trainers know how to get a dog to execute a behavior instantly using a lure or physical placement, and consequently may initially feel frustrated with shaping. But training isn't about one training session, or getting one behavior quickly. It's about the dog discovering and *learning* the behavior. One of the greatest joys of clicker training is that the dog is the trainer's partner, actively participating, considering various options and zeroing in on the behavior the trainer is looking for—*thinking*. Time spent on this step is time very well spent. Much as Maddie learned the "High Five" in an earlier example, dogs *learn faster, remember, and retain* behaviors far better having figured them out for themselves.

Jumpstarting behaviors

Dogs that are new to clicker training, especially crossover dogs, often need motivation and reminders that mean "the game is on." If your crossover dog is not offering behaviors, try stimulating him to action with a nose-tease. Hold a treat in your fingers, and waft it *briefly* in front of his nose, then *put it out of sight* behind your back, and wait. The message the nose-tease sends is, "*This treat is available to you if you figure out how to make me click.*"

Shari shows Mazzie a treat as a nose-tease, then puts it out of sight. The nose-tease says, "This can be yours if you…" Mazzie lies down, and gets a click.

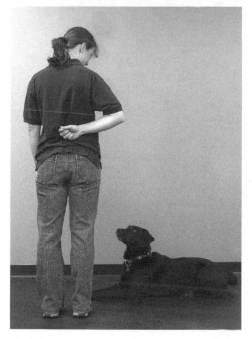

You'll need to repeat the nose-tease from time to time when your dog gets distracted, loses focus, or stops working, but don't automatically assume your dog isn't focused just because he isn't doing anything. Often a dog is actively engaged in training even when he doesn't move. He's thinking. As long as your dog doesn't disengage, move away, or focus on something else, don't distract him. Let him think.

When your dog does disengage, use the nose-tease to re-focus him to the task. If this doesn't motivate your dog, consider why. Is your treat appealing, or does your dog need a mental break?

After a nose-tease your dog will likely try something, maybe even several different behaviors. That's fine! You have the opportunity to choose a behavior to click, ignoring elements that don't relate to your immediate goal.

Distracted...or needs a break?

Appearing to be distracted often means your dog needs to take a break. When your dog suddenly starts sniffing the floor, looks off into the distance at nothing in particular, or scratches an itch, she's likely telling you that she needs to take a moment. Remember, clicker training is a mental process for your dog, and can be tiring, especially when the crossover dog is first learning it.

Some training methods advocate correcting the dog for disengaging. Doing so is unfair at best. Dogs, like people, are better able to perform when they have an opportunity to clear their heads for a moment, and can then re-focus to give full attention to the task at hand.

In the middle of a training session when this picture was taken, there was no distraction in the yard. Could Mazzie's message have been any clearer? She saying, "I need a break!" Note Shari's delight in their shared communication. (After Mazzie went to the bathroom, she was back on track.)

A break can be as simple as taking a head-clearing moment to sniff the ground as Duke and Vision are doing.

When you and your crossover dog first start clicker training, you may need to nose-tease frequently, even several times in a row to let your dog know she's on the right track…keep trying. Getting your dog to offer behaviors on her own may take awhile, but your patience will be rewarded as long as you resist the temptation to help, to lure, or physically place her. You'll soon see your dog get the behavior you are clicking when she consciously, thoughtfully offers that behavior.

This is such an exciting moment. Treasure it! It not only demonstrates that your dog is getting it, but it rewards your faith in the process. We crossover trainers need this reinforcement, just as our dogs need the click and the treat.

Energizing your crossover dog

Sometimes a crossover dog's behavior is so restrained that it is difficult to get him to volunteer behaviors. Since clicker training requires *active* participation, here are some strategies to energize the lethargic or non-participating dog:

- After you click, skip a treat along the floor for your dog to chase, as if you are skipping a stone on the surface of a pond.

- Instead of a food treat, briefly play an active game such as retrieve or chase.

- Prior to training, confine your dog in isolation.

- Confine your dog and train another dog in front of him. When you bring him out, he'll be highly motivated to work with you.

- Consider an activity that gets your dog's blood pumping, and incorporate a few seconds of training with it and build from there.

No hesitation

The time will come when your dog no longer needs a nose-tease—he will offer the behavior without hesitation between repetitions. Here's what you're looking for:

1. Dog does the behavior
2. Click
3. Give the dog a treat
4. Dog eats the treat
5. Dog does the behavior again

When there is little or no hesitation between #4 and #5, your dog is clearly offering the behavior you're clicking. When he does this several times in succession, you're ready for the next step in the process.

Step 2. Putting the behavior in perspective

As a crossover trainer, you've likely felt (or heard) the most common lament of the dog training student in class: "...but he does it at home!" Of course he does; that's where the majority of the dog's training takes place. Dogs are not quick to **generalize** trained behaviors, that is, perform the behavior in different contexts—here, there, and everywhere.

The process of getting your dog to understand what is and is not relevant begins with putting the behavior in perspective. In this step of training, you specify the framework of the behavior so your dog learns both the specific behavior, and the context in which it is performed. For example, in the first week of our beginner class, students introduce and reinforce "sit," a readily offered behavior that is learned quickly. After several repetitions, we have them trade places with the student directly opposite them in class. Even with such a small change from one side of the class to the other, the dogs no longer perform as readily. After two or three repetitions in the new location, however, the dogs once again sit without hesitation.

This exercise demonstrates three things to the trainers:

1. **Dogs don't automatically generalize to "here, there, and everywhere."** If there's a difference in the dog's performance when you simply move several feet away to a new spot in the room, there will likely be a bigger difference between home and class, home and the park, and even your kitchen versus the back yard. Just because you train "come when called" at home, does not automatically transfer that learning to the park. Expecting the same response without more training is unrealistic.

2. **Backing up just a few steps in the shaping process helps the dog figure out what is and is not relevant.** Doing so helps the dog focus in on the specific behavior, learning that the behavior you clicked in the living room is the same one you're clicking in the bedroom.

3. **The dog's response quickly returns to the previous level of proficiency.** Training in different locations not only helps the dog learn to generalize, it doesn't take long! And that can be very motivating for trainers.

Confirm the criteria

Your dog needs to figure out precisely what factors are and are not relevant to the behavior. By process of elimination, you help your dog hone in on the precise behavior you're training. Until you've done so, he may associate virtually any external element or criterion with the behavior.

My Crossover Journal

At a seminar in England, I was shaping a Miniature Schnauzer to lie down on the mat. After several successful repetitions, I moved the mat to a new spot, telling the audience just what would happen next—that the dog would go to the previous location, and when he didn't get a click, would glance at or step toward the mat in the new spot. I told them that I would click that glance or movement to help him narrow his focus and understand that the criterion is the mat.

Apparently the Schnauzer wasn't listening to my prediction. He did go to the previous spot and lie down as expected, but then rather than looking around or moving toward the mat, he got up, purposefully moved away from the mat and lay down. I was flummoxed. What was going on? Then I saw what he was focused on. The first location of the mat had been by a man in the front row. And the dog was now lying down…in front of…a man. This clever fellow had formed an association with the gender of the person in front of whom he was lying down, and was testing the parameters of the behavior: If you're not clicking me for lying down in front of this man…will you click me for lying near this one? Proving you can shape virtually anything: even to find the only two men in a seminar of 70 women.

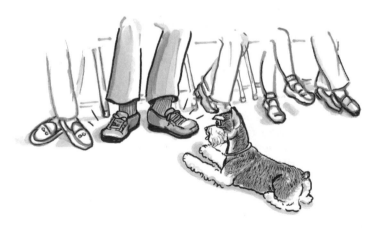

The Schnauzer found the one other man in an audience that was 90% women.

To eliminate potential associations and help your dog generalize a behavior, change just one criterion at a time. Each change gives the dog the opportunity to learn what the behavior *is not* related to—it isn't the location, it isn't the trainer's posture, and it isn't men in the front row.

When you change an element, be prepared for the dog to regress briefly while he tests the new context. Reduce your expectations and backtrack slightly in the shaping process. The more you help your dog work through each change, the faster your dog will regain proficiency, the sooner he'll generalize, the better trained he'll be.

Better still, the more behaviors your dog understands, the faster he will generalize each new behavior and context, quickly adding them to his repertoire. Over time generalization becomes a learned response, and you will not have to expend the same effort. In other words, the more your dog knows the easier training gets.

To help your dog learn to generalize, the following represent different contexts to work through.

Your posture and expression. This includes postures while sitting, standing, crouching, kneeling, lying down, your facial expression, the direction your head is turned, where you're looking, eye contact, or no eye contact. Each change in your posture or expression may alter the dog's impression, making it a *different* exercise. Be ready to backtrack a bit when you make an adjustment and make just one adjustment at a time.

Dogs, like poker players, quickly learn your "tells," subtle cues, even as unconscious as pupil dilation. If your dog's behavior regresses when you wear sun glasses, for instance, it means that your eye movement or expression has likely become associated with the behavior.

My Crossover Journal

It was late the second day of a two-day seminar. I was answering questions, sitting in a chair at the front of the room with Mayday lying quietly by my side. When he stood up, to prevent his going visiting, I quietly said, "sit." Imagine my chagrin when my well-trained demonstration dog lay down. I signaled him to sit up, which he willingly did. "stand," I said, and then repeated "sit." Once again, he lay down.

What was going on? Mayday knew what sit meant. At least I had thought he did. I stood up and tried it again. This time when I said "sit," he sat. I sat down again, and "sit" cued lying down. I stood, and "sit" triggered a sit. I puzzled over this for a few seconds and then…Aha! The answer: At home, relaxing on the couch, when Mayday asks for attention, I'd cue a sit. Both of us being "off the clock," I might vaguely notice if he lay down rather than sat, but I'd pet him anyway. On the other hand, when I stood with him the start line for an agility run, or did obedience heelwork, "sit" meant sit. My relaxed posture was a cue for Mayday's differing behaviors—a clear demonstration of the power of associations (as well as the supremacy of visual over auditory cues).

Body posture includes your hand position, which is why you should hold your hand in a neutral position rather than in your pocket or bait bag.

Julie works on sit, changing her posture and orientation. Note in each position how she re-sets Ryder's behavior with her treat delivery.

When she moved, changing position and posture to sit in a chair, Julie used a nose-tease to jumpstart Ryder's behavior. He sits and gets a click.

Your orientation. Orientation refers to how you face your dog in relation to an object or target. If you've been facing your dog or turned toward an object such as a blanket or agility obstacle, change your orientation and turn sideways, practicing on both sides. Changing your orientation helps your dog learn, for instance, that his behavior has nothing to do with being in front of you; that is, of course, unless it does.

My Crossover Journal

A student in our Instructor Training School was shaping a puppy to go to the blanket and lie down. After several successful repetitions, we suggested she turn sideways to the blanket to see what would happen. Sure enough, after eating his treat, the pup immediately moved in front of the trainer and lay down off the blanket. He needed to learn that her orientation was irrelevant—helping him figure out that the behavior was related to the blanket.

Dog's orientation/location. This aspect refers to the location of the behavior, or where your dog is in relation to you or to an object. Unless related to the behavior, this is another aspect to work through. Your dog's orientation to you or his location are inherent in behaviors such as sit at heel or lie down on the agility box, however, the dog still needs to learn to perform the behavior in new places.

My Crossover Journal

I moved Cannon's crate from one side of the room to the other. For the first few days, "Kennel up" cued the old location where he stood waiting for his meal. It took several days of repetition before he got that the cue was related to his kennel, not the location in the room. Once learned, Cannon kennels on cue in any open crate in any location.

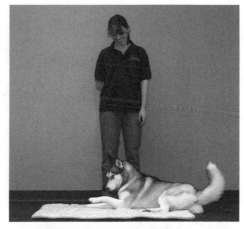

Shari changes her orientation, moving around the mat. She stands both facing and sideways to the mat so Dax learns that Shari's location or orientation doesn't matter and is not integral to this behavior.

Proximity. This includes both how close you are to your dog, and your dog's proximity to an object or other relevant factors. In the early steps of training a behavior, being close to your dog enables you to see the dog's subtle behaviors more easily. When building distance is a factor in the behavior, do it gradually (described in Step 3).

Being close to an object that is the focus of a task (a target, for example) makes it easier for the dog. When first training a behavior, space and distance hamper the dog's ability to perform the task. Greater distance means you can't click as often—and remember, a high rate of reinforcement provides information to your dog.

LynnMarie introduces "stay" standing close to Becke, and then with increased distance. With each increase, she lowers her expectations as to length of time or distractions. Once distance is achieved, she will then focus on time and distractions (see stay instructions in Chapter 12).

My Crossover Journal
Reporting to the class about her homework assignment, one of our Instructor Training School students expressed her frustration with trying to shape her crossover dog to nose-touch a target. She described how she started, putting a yogurt lid on the floor about two feet in front of her. Her dog first touched it with his foot, which she clicked once or twice, then waited for a nose touch. Not getting any clicks, her dog flipped the lid on its side, picked it up and brought it to her. Discussing it with the class the next morning, the students rightly suggested that she might have started holding the lid in her hand near her dog's face where she could more easily see and shape head movement, then a nose touch, then move it away, lower it to the floor directly in front of her, and only then build distance.

Proximity also plays a role in building your dog's tolerance for distractions. In most cases the closer the distraction, the greater its influence. As you work through things that distract your dog, start far enough away so your dog is able to focus on her behavior, then gradually work closer to the distraction. (Note: This is not always the case. For some dogs, middle-distance distractions or those farther away are more powerful. Adjust your training accordingly.)

With her reduced, inviting body posture, Shari creates a distraction for Rosie, but remains far enough away so Rosie will be successful. Her success (the mark and reward) builds Rosie's understanding that "stay" means remain in place no matter what is going on.

Wendy ups the ante, moving closer and closer using her enticing body posture and facial expression to increase the difficulty for Rosie. Notice how Carolyn, the trainer, decreases her distance to work on just one element—the increased distraction.

Environment. Indoors and out, on a hardwood floor, on carpet, grass, stone, tile, etc., this factor includes weather changes and environmental distractions such as birds, leaves blowing, and the like. Environmental elements can be used to advance your training as well. For example, consider shaping your dog to back up onto a different tactile surface such as onto a carpet remnant.

Location. Change the location where the behavior is performed, moving around in the same room, moving to different rooms, then different places, both inside and outside. Begin with small changes as simple as moving to new spots in the room.

Attractions or distractions. These include anything that takes the dog's attention off the behavior that you're clicking. A systematic approach to increasing your dog's resistance to distractions is covered in the next chapter, with specific instructions in Chapter 12.

Intangibles. An intangible is anything with which your dog forms an association, often something you're not even aware of. This may include such things as unconsciously bobbing your head every time you give a cue, or the association the Schnauzer in England formed with men. You may discover an intangible when your dog's response deteriorates and you explore possible reasons.

Combinations. As you work through these factors, combine changes in context such as postural and orientation changes in new locations and environments. The more you help your dog work through and rule out irrelevant criteria, the faster your dog will learn to generalize the behavior.

When to introduce changes

The time to start making changes is after three or four successful repetitions. This is far sooner than most trainers are inclined to change something. Most crossover trainers come from methods that recommend drilling a behavior many, even dozens of times before changing any aspect. Multiple repetitions in the same context are unhelpful and counterproductive in clicker training. The more you practice a behavior without changing criteria, the more the behavior will be learned within a narrow context and the more difficult it will be for your dog to adjust to changes. Altering the framework early and often radically speeds training, making it easier for both you and your dog.

This is an important aspect of clicker training. Unlike methods that rely on drilling, when training becomes repetitious, the inventive, thinking dog will introduce variations on her own. The sooner you introduce changes, the more engaged your dog will be, and the faster she will learn.

Step 3. Variety adds spice to reinforcement

Most people, crossover trainers among them, are eager, even impatient to start teaching cues. Coming from command-based methods that introduce the cue from the very beginning, we're always anxious to teach it—however, adding the cue too early is a common reason for poor responses or non-compliance.

At this step of your dog's training, when he is readily offering the behavior, you likely want to start using the cue. Don't do it yet. You will gain both knowledge and expertise spending time working further on the behavior before you add the cue, and your dog's behavior will be much more proficient and polished as a result. You'll get to the cue in Step 4, and your patience will be rewarded by better, more reliable behaviors.

Step 3 begins the process of weaning your dog off treats, but there are other advantages and exciting opportunities presented here. Before we explore these, it's important to know a little about reinforcement schedules.

Reinforcement schedules

How regularly you reinforce a behavior is called a **schedule of reinforcement**. Two basic schedules are helpful in clicker training: continuous and intermittent. A **continuous schedule** means marking and rewarding every "clickable" action every time it occurs. An **intermittent schedule** is variable, involving the withholding of reinforcement some of the time.

The best variable schedule has no discernable pattern—a **random schedule** that both strengthens behavior, and makes it resistant to **extinction** and to distractions. A common analogy is the difference between a vending machine and a slot machine. A vending machine delivers candy every time you put money in (continuous reinforcement). A slot machine, on the other hand, provides a payoff at some unspecified point (random reinforcement).

One of the best analogies I've ever come across explaining the difference between continuous and random reinforcement schedules is in Karen Pryor's book, *Don't Shoot the Dog!* in which she compares starting a new car versus starting a clunker. Here's a description of the two:

Continuous schedule of reinforcement: Your new car starts every time you turn the ignition switch, so when you turn the key and hear a dull click, you'll try to start it once or twice more, but quickly abandon the effort and call for assistance. Since key-turning behavior has been rewarded every time (continuous reinforcement), in the absence of reinforcement you're not motivated to keep trying, so you quickly stop offering the behavior (the behavior extinguishes).

Random schedule of reinforcement: What if your old clunker has a history of erratic starts? When you turn the key and nothing happens, you try again. Still nothing? Try again. Still no response? Give it another try, and another and—since you're never sure precisely which key-turn will yield results, you keep working, certain that one of these times you'll be rewarded. Unpredictable starting (random reinforcement) makes you work harder (strengthens behavior) and continue trying longer (resists extinction).

A random schedule of reinforcement is the most durable for solidifying and strengthening behavior. Students in Psych 101 learn about experiments with pigeons that peck a button to earn a kernel of corn. With continuous reinforcement, the pigeon pecks steadily, but not fast: peck (food drops)…eat…peck…eat…peck…eat. As with the car analogy, if the peck stops resulting in food, the bird soon gives up. But when a peck doesn't always result in food, and the pigeon is reinforced on a random schedule, pecking behavior radically increases. For instance, peck (food drops). . . eat. . . peck (no food) . . . . peck (no food) . . . . peck (food drops)—eat—peck, peck, peck (food drops)—eat—peck, peck, peck, peck, peck, peck, peck, peck, peck, peck (food drops)—eat—peck, peck, peck, and so on. With no predictable pattern to the reinforcement schedule, the pigeon tries harder—faster and longer. After all, the very next peck may be the one that results in a reward.

The best schedule: Random reinforcement

In the first two steps of the training process so far (getting the behavior and narrowing the parameters) you used a continuous schedule of reinforcement or differential reinforcement (continuous reinforcement within each shaping cluster). A high rate of continuous reinforcement provides helpful information and motivates the dog to work.

As soon as your dog performs the behavior without hesitation, begin to vary the reinforcement schedule. Select only the best to click, passing over a repetition of the behavior that is sub-par. For example, your dog lies down slowly, or sniffed the floor as he dropped, or the behavior otherwise differed from your goal. Withhold the click, get your dog up again (move to a new spot, pat your leg, or clap your hands), then wait for your dog to lie down again. If you like this repetition better, click and treat. Some trainers refer to this as a "two-fer," getting "two for the price of one." Similar, but different—with a "two-fer" the trainer chooses to not click the first response, and clicks the second response no matter what, even if the second one was not as good as the first. On the other hand, when you select *the best responses* to click, you're differentially reinforcing behaviors leading to your goal, while at the same time introducing a variable schedule of reinforcement.

> ## Crossover shut-down
> Don't be discouraged if your crossover dog shuts down when you fail to click and reinforce a behavior. You can easily get him to participate again by clicking something, even if it's not the behavior you were working on. In the beginning, try withholding a click only occasionally. If your dog shuts down quickly, rather than ignoring the first behavior completely, mark it with "Yes," and reward with verbal praise. Then when he offers the behavior again, click and treat. Over time, gradually wean your dog off continuous reinforcement.

Uh oh! He's making mistakes…or are they?

Change begets change. When you begin to vary the reinforcement schedule you will often see varying behavior including deviations in your dog's performance, and even some errors. Your dog may respond more slowly, or even try a different behavior altogether. This is good! By experimenting, your dog may well hit upon improvements such as a faster execution, a more desirable performance—just what you wanted!

As long as your dog keeps trying, don't be discouraged by errors. Even if the behavior you're working on disappears completely, you can always get it back by increasing your rate of reinforcement. The positive side of errors is that they provide an opportunity to select improvement. By choosing better responses—the faster drop, the quickest recall—you improve your dog's standard behavior.

Deviations in behavior can present wonderful opportunities for you to take behaviors to unimagined places. Let's revisit the clunker car analogy:

> When your unreliable car doesn't start the first time, not only do you keep trying, but most people offer different behaviors: talk to the car, maybe use a pet name, maybe swear at it. You might stroke the dashboard gently or slap it. You may grip the steering wheel or shake it. What if, right after you stroke the dashboard, crooning "C'mon Bessie. You can do it." Your car starts? The result: the ignition rewards dashboard stroking and sweet talk. More likely than not, the next time your car won't start, the first thing you'll try is what "worked"—stroking the dashboard and saying, "C'mon Bessie."

Can you imagine doing this in a new car? Of course not. What led to unusual car-starting behavior was *random reinforcement*. It works the same with your dog. This hugely important step is like a secret weapon for clicker trainers, a well-kept secret. *When you change your rate of reinforcement and the reinforcers you offer your dog, your dog's behavior changes, too.* This is such an exciting aspect!

Consider being able to change "lie down slowly" to having your dog throw himself to the floor faster than a dropped rock. Consider having the ability to increase your dog's level of behavior from lackadaisical to enthusiastic. You've got it; and it doesn't take months or even weeks of training. It takes just a few clicks—or a few withheld clicks—to rapidly improve your dog's performance.

Just as exciting, when your dog offers you a completely new behavior altogether, you have the option to mark it. This can lead to your dog performing an entirely new and different behavior without you needing to shape it.

Yo-Yoing: The ups and downs of reinforcement schedules

The above schedules of reinforcement are useful for a distinct behavior such as assuming a sit or lying down. A different schedule of reinforcement, called **variable duration**, applies to behaviors over the course of time, such as "stay."

Starting with the dog in the desired position (sit, stand, or down) you delay the click on a variable duration schedule starting with just a second or two, and build from there. (See specific instructions in Chapter 12.)

In my previous training incarnations, I learned (and taught others) to build difficulty gradually, lengthening a stay from a second or two to five seconds, then ten, twenty, thirty, and so on. Building distance from the dog on a stay was the same, incrementally increasing distance from two feet, to three, then four, five, ten, gradually moving out-of-sight. Increasing distance on heelwork was the same, starting with just a few steps, and gradually increasing the number of steps traveled (the duration the dog stays at heel). But I never considered the impact of this ever-increasing difficulty on the dog.

From the dog's perspective, each new level of training becomes more demanding than the last, until ultimately for many dogs, the increased stress leads to a breakdown of the behavior, such as breaking the stay. But it is easy to avoid this stress and help the dog easily learn to increase duration with few errors—by **yo-yoing.**

Yo-yoing is randomly moving between short, medium, and long distances or time frames. For example, with a duration goal for stay of ten seconds, yo-yo around a ten second average by starting with five seconds, then two, four, ten, seven, twelve, three, fourteen, etc. When you randomly change the time frame, your dog doesn't know if this will be a long or short stay. By the time he realizes it's a long one, it's over, and he is reinforced for staying. Yo-yoing distance follows the same model. If your goal is five paces—take three paces, five, one, seven, four, two, and the like—moving randomly between short, shorter, medium, long, and longer distances with no discernable pattern.

As in Shaping Rule #6, shape each aspect (distance or duration) separately, setting the dog up for success with each. With stay, for example, increase time to your desired goal, then decrease the time as you build distance. (See specific instructions in Chapter 12.) Start yo-yoing before you add the cue, and continue to build duration and distance after the behavior is on cue.

> ## Watch for the scallop effect
>
> As you increase duration, for instance the number of steps you take with your dog in heel position, you may find a drop in performance immediately following a reward. Called the **scallop effect** or **post-performance pause**, your dog learns that after getting a reward, there isn't likely to be another one for at least a few steps. The result—the behavior weakens right after a reward. Consider whether you'd stick with the same slot machine right after it gave a big payout or would you assume it won't be profitable for awhile? It's the same with your dog. To prevent scalloping, every so often, mark and reward several times in rapid succession.

Jackpots: What do they *really* do?

In addition to varying your schedule of reinforcement, varying the size of the reward and the rewards themselves impact learning, too. Enter the **jackpot**.

A jackpot is a bonus—a large, unexpected reward, or a better-than-standard treat. The purpose of a jackpot is to both reward and encourage behavior. In general, we think of a jackpot as affecting the behavior that earned the bonus—rewarding a particularly good response with a windfall for that behavior. This seems logical, doesn't it? But in reality it doesn't always work this way.

Noticing that when training a new behavior, a jackpot rarely resulted in the dog repeating the jackpot-earning behavior, British dog trainer Elizabeth Kershaw set out to study the effect of jackpots on learning for her Masters thesis. Her results suggest that jackpots do not in fact promote learning. Elizabeth found that the longer it takes a dog to eat, the more the behavior is subject to memory decay. A larger reward interrupts learning simply because it takes longer to eat. The result is a disconnect between the reward and the behavior that earned it. Rather than strengthening the previous behavior, what follows the jackpot is likely to be a *different* behavior.

A short time span between the reward and the opportunity to repeat the behavior speeds learning. So when shaping or introducing a new behavior, training progresses faster with a rapid rate of reinforcement—many repetitions, each rewarded with one, quickly-swallowed treat. There *are* times, however, when a jackpot is advantageous and motivational. Some appropriate times for a jackpot include:

- **At the start of a training session.** I give a jackpot to a new dog I'm training to motivate the dog to work with me, giving the impression that I'm a high roller.

- **To end a behavior drought.** A jackpot can motivate the dog to activity when he doesn't seem interested.

- **To trigger variable behavior.** Since the behavior after the jackpot is likely to be *different from* the previous behavior, jackpots promote variability in behavior. Play with this. You'll learn a lot.

- **If you cued it and you love it.** Promoting variability with a jackpot is a characteristic of behaviors that *aren't yet fully learned*. Once a behavior is learned and is on cue, jackpots do reward excellence.

A caveat: Use jackpots sparingly. Over-use makes a standard treat non-rewarding. Consider if you got a bonus with every paycheck. Then one week, all you got was your standard pay. Not only would you be disappointed, you'd likely feel as if you must have done something wrong.

Jackpot delivery: All at once or one at a time?

There are two main ways to deliver jackpots: a large amount to be eaten all at once—"dump-a-clump" or bowl-dive—versus dole it out piece by piece. Does it matter? Certainly. Consider that the longer it takes a dog to eat, the less the dog associates the treat with the behavior. But even more than that, consider this: You've just hit the jackpot at a slot machine. Which is more exciting, if the machine doles out quarters one at a time, or getting a landslide of quarters dumped in your lap? So it is for your dog. The conclusion—either dump-a-clump or let your dog help himself from your bait bag or bowl.

For jackpots, Becke helps herself to a mouthful from the bait bag. Cannon gets to dive into the treat dish.

Be not afraid

Does the concept of playing with variability, that is, uncertainty about what behavior your dog will offer, seem scary? If you're honest, you said, "Yes." We crossover trainers are used to predictability because our prior training techniques resulted in foreseeable, predictable responses. It's hard enough to consider making profound changes in how we introduce behaviors, from luring or touching to no-lure-hands-off shaping. As if that isn't enough, the thought of stepping off into space, freely letting the dog offer random and varied behaviors—whew! It's out of control! It's enough to make a crossover trainer hyperventilate.

Borrowing a line from Nike, "Just do it!" The least that happens is nothing, and the most is that your dog acts like a maniac, trying behavior after behavior, action upon action. While this may not sound appealing, the inventive dog is truly easy and fun to work with. Ultimately, no matter what behaviors your dog starts offering, *you* are in control. You can shape your dog's behavior from seemingly out-of-control, to the most self-controlled, relaxed behavior you desire. It's all in what you choose to click and how you time your marks.

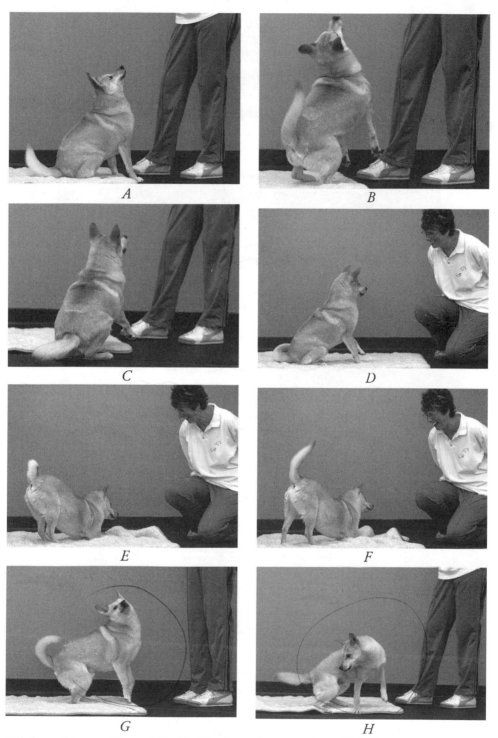

While working on "down," Kochi offered a wide range of possible behaviors to click. Here are just a few "snapshots" that could have been clicked to shape other behaviors: A-Attention; B-Hop, bounce, sit-up, pray, hug, jump up; C-Right paw lift; D-Left paw lift; E-F-Dig/ paw at or scratch the mat, back up, bow; G-H-Head turn, spin.

Save start

I love when the dog takes a moment to look you right in the eye as Kochi is, clearly asking, "What do you want?!?"

Losing the behavior?

In the worst-case scenario, when you change to an intermittent schedule of reinforcement your dog may stop offering the behavior. But this worst-case is not a disaster. You know how to get the behavior—after all, you got it to begin with. Simply regain the behavior (which will happen quickly), then click and treat it four or five times in succession with continuous reinforcement and you're back in business. When you re-introduce a variable schedule, reinforce more repetitions than non-reinforced ones, varying your reinforcement ratio more gradually.

Random Reinforcement Game

The following is a fun game to play with variability. Invented by Gary Wilkes, arguably the "father" of clicker training, it uses random rewards on a random reinforcement schedule. Play this game with a behavior-in-development—one the dog readily offers, but that is not yet on cue. In addition to being fun, this exercise can be one of the most valuable tools for improving behavior quickly and easily. Since variability affects behavior, the Random Reinforcement Game is useful for tweaking behaviors, for experimenting, and for learning...a lot! I use this in my own training, at seminars, and in classes.

The Random Reinforcement Game provides an eye-opening demonstration of what happens when you introduce unpredictability—your dog's behavior becomes unpredictable. Your dog may try new things, offering variations on the behavior you've been working on, or may even offer different behaviors altogether. Don't be frightened, this can be a good thing.

For example, your dog might sit faster, offer a stronger nose touch, or drop more emphatically. Or your dog may offer a behavior totally unrelated to what you're working on, maybe one you've wanted to train, or that would be fun to add to your dog's repertoire.

Before you play this game, plan your random schedule. While it may seem paradoxical to *plan* to be random, it actually takes deliberate effort. You might think you will reinforce randomly, but the human brain automatically establishes a pattern that will emerge over time, eliminating "randomness."

To make your plan, consider the two elements of this game—the reinforcers themselves and the reinforcement schedule. To vary the reinforcers, think of an assortment such as different food treats, verbal praise, petting, throwing a ball, playing tug, encouraging your dog to chase you, roughhousing, and the like. To create a varied schedule of reinforcement, you will click some repetitions, use a "yes" marker for others, and bypass some, using no marker and no reinforcement at all.

Putting these two elements together gives you a plan to follow that includes directives such as "click and treat," "no click, no treat," "yes and praise," "yes, praise and pet," "click and throw a ball," "click and praise," and the like. The following sample list includes 24 instructions. By making the list in columns, you can go in order down the list, go across the columns, go backwards, back and forth, do odds, then evens, changing it every time you play the game. Here's the sample:

1. Click, 10 treats	9. Verbal praise only	17. Click, throw ball
2. Click, 1 treat	10. Click, 1 treat	18. "Yes", no treat
3. No click, no treat	11. No click, no treat	19. Click, 10 treats
4. "Yes" treat	12. Click, 3 treats	20. Click, no treat*
5. Praise & pet only	13. No click, no treat	21. Praise only
6. Click, 5 treats, praise	14. Click & chase	22. Click, 3 treats
7. Click, no treat*	15. Click, 1 treat	23. Praise and pet only
8. No click, no treat	16. Click, praise & pet	24. Go back to #1

*Note: "Click, no treat" is not a misprint. Don't do it often, but try it and see what happens. You may be pleasantly surprised—even shocked by what your dog does next!

Mark a deck of cards

Here's another option. One way to make sure your reinforcement schedule is truly random is to mark an old deck of cards with Sharpie pen. Here's a sample of some options:

Aces. Click, jackpot of 10 treats, praise and pet

Face cards. Click, one treat

Tens. Click, 5 treats

Sixes. Click, no treat

Fives. Click and play

Fours. "Yes" and treat

Threes. Click and chase game or throw ball

Deuces. No click, no treat

All other Clubs. "Yes" and praise

All other Diamonds. Praise, pet, and baby talk

All other Hearts. Click, treat, pet, and praise

All other Spades. Click and pet

When you shuffle the deck before you play the game, and then turn over the cards one at a time, your instructions will be totally random.

One of our instructors, Lynn Marie, printed out a variety of instructions, laminated them as a small set of cards with a different instruction on each side, punched a hole in them, and put them on a key ring, so all she has to do is flip a card, and follow the instructions. Each card contains a suggestion for various reinforcements and can be flipped in any random order.

Instructions for playing the Random Reinforcement Game

Now that you have some ideas for creating a random schedule of varied reinforcers, here's how to play the game. Ideally, have a helper give each instruction to you. If you play it by yourself, check your list after each repetition so you'll be prepared for the next directive.

Pre-game warm-up. Choose a behavior your dog readily offers that is not yet on cue. Repeat the behavior several times with a click and treat for each repetition.

Start the game. Start with a click, followed by a jackpot of ten treats.

Prepare for the next repetition. While your dog is eating, check the next instruction, or have your helper call it out.

Follow the planned instructions. When your dog performs the behavior, mark and reward (or not) as instructed. Have your helper give you each following instruction before or as your dog offers the behavior again, and reward (or not) accordingly after your dog performs the behavior.

Progress through the game. Mark and reward (or not) according to each instruction, with the following exceptions:

- **Outstanding performance.** If your dog performs particularly well, that is, you love that behavior, click and treat (1 treat) regardless of the instruction. This is one of the main advantages of this game—your dog's performance of the behavior can radically improve. When that happens, mark and reward it!

- **Weak performance.** On the other hand, if the behavior weakens substantially or your dog stops offering it altogether, stop the game momentarily. Jumpstart the behavior and reinforce each of the next four or five consecutive repetitions with a click and one treat (1:1 schedule). Then return to the game.

Thorndike's Law (yet again). Notice what your dog does *after* each reinforcement. Keep in mind that the consequence of the previous behavior is what influences the following one. For instance, see what the next behavior is *after* you give a jackpot, what does your dog do *after* you pet and praise rather than give a treat, *after* you play with your dog, *after* you click and don't follow it with a treat.

Learn about your dog's preferences. Also, note how your dog reacts to the various reinforcers. Does he seem to like a specific reinforcer or not? This information can be useful for future training sessions.

Consider Shaping Rule #9. Your dog will likely offer a variety of other behaviors. Do not mark those, unless you wish to "put them in the bank," or you decide to switch the behavior you want to work on.

If you decide to switch to a different behavior, discontinue the game and reinforce the new behavior on a 1:1 continuous schedule.

Ending the game. Try to end on a good note. If the behavior deteriorates as you progress through the game, get it back before you stop training.

Although each dog is an individual and your dog may be atypical, here are some of the more common reactions. After a jackpot, the dog often offers a *different* behavior or a variation to the behavior you've been working on. After a click with no treat the dog often offers a *stronger* variation of the behavior. It's as if he's saying, "Hey! You forgot something! Don't you know you're supposed to give me a treat when you click?! Didn't you see me do *this*?!?"

Another fascinating aspect of this game is the opportunity it provides to learn how your dog truly feels about the reinforcers we typically think of as high value. They don't always have a high value to your dog.

> ### My Crossover Journal
> When I introduce this game to participants at a seminar, I ask for a volunteer to demonstrate it. Nearly universally, when the instruction is "pet and praise" the dog will actively move away from the owner with an annoyed expression that clearly says, "Knock it off! Stop touching me and get on with it!" Virtually every volunteer is surprised to learn that her dog really isn't interested in verbal praise and petting—at least not now. It isn't that dogs don't love being petted; of course most do...at the right time. What the dog is saying is that in a training context, petting is a low-value reward.

After playing the game, consider what you've learned about how your dog can perform this behavior. If you saw improved responses, you know how well your dog can do. In your future training sessions, these are the repetitions you will mark and reinforce, letting your dog know what you will reward as the finished behavior.

Congratulations! You've strengthened the behavior and shaped it to the precise parameters that meet your goal, and you're ready for the next step—adding the cue.

Step 4. Name it! Adding the cue

At last! You're ready to tell your dog what to do, to give a cue—a word, hand signal, facial expression, movement, whistle, finger snap, hand clap, finger point, or any other prompt that says, "Perform (behavior)." Once learned, the cue represents an opportunity for the dog to earn a reward, giving notice that a reward may be available if he performs the behavior associated with the cue.

Assessing readiness

The first three steps of this process have been about getting a "cue-worthy" behavior—one you're satisfied with and ready to name. But the behavior itself is only one criterion for adding the cue. The other important condition is that your dog performs the behavior predictably and reliably so you can connect the cue to the behavior.

Predictable and reliable means you can count on the *very next behavior* your dog offers being the one you want to name. Gary Wilkes uses as his test a willingness to bet money, with a 95% certainty of winning, that the dog will perform the behavior within the next five seconds. For example, your dog lies down. You click and offer a treat so the dog gets up, eats the treat and lies down. Click, treat. What is he likely do after eating the treat? Chances are good he'll lie down again. If you are willing to put up $20 with 95% certainty that the next thing your dog will do is lie down again, you are ready to add the cue.

Be honest in assessing your dog's readiness. It does not hurt to put it off for a few minutes of practice, or even for a day or two. It's better to wait and improve the dog's response, than to hurry the cue and later regret having given a name to an unreliable behavior or an unpredictable response.

> ## Crossover Cornerstone #6
> ### The behavior you name is the behavior you get.
> Once you link a cue to a behavior, that's the behavior your dog will perform for that cue. This means that attaching a cue to a less-than-desirable behavior will elicit that behavior…on cue. Since prior methods often include ways to "fix" behavior—to improve a behavior after it's on command—it's not unusual for a crossover trainer to add the cue too soon, before the behavior is as you want it. Additionally, the speed with which a clicker-trained dog will offer the behavior on his own without any prompts is something crossover trainers are unused to, and may create the erroneous impression that the behavior is ready for the cue. You may find that you've "named" a behavior and then you want to fix it—make it faster, straighter, more emphatic, and the like. No problem. Think of the better, improved response as a *new behavior*. Shape the new behavior, then give it a *new* cue. You can still use the old cue, but it will trigger the old behavior. Once you've named it; you've got it.

When to cue: It's the "antecedent"

Remember Antecedent, Behavior, Consequence from earlier in the book? The cue is the antecedent, the prompt, and now is the time to insert it, right before the dog performs the behavior. Simply say the cue word when you know your dog is about to offer the behavior. How do you know? Right after your dog has performed the behavior and eaten the treat, the chances are excellent she will perform the behavior again. Why? Because you have been marking and rewarding that behavior.

Notice the timing is to insert the cue *before the behavior*, not during, and not after. Some trainers recommend giving the cue *as the dog is performing* the behavior. Others recommend repeating the cue *after the behavior* is completed: "Sit…good sit." Here's the skinny on each of these.

During the behavior

One school of thought holds that you should begin by saying the cue while the dog is *in the performance of the behavior*, that is, while he is bending his knees into a sit, say, "sit," or as he's in the process of lying down, say, "down." Over time you begin to say the cue earlier in the action until ultimately you say it *before* the behavior starts.

You can certainly do it this way, but there's no advantage to it. Ultimately the cue will not prompt the response until the dog has learned the association *before he begins* the action. In other words, time spent saying the cue *while the behavior is in process* in the belief the dog is learning the cue-behavior association, is simply time wasted. How do we know? Pavlov said so.

Intending to study salivary gland responses, scientist Ivan Pavlov performed many experiments with dogs as his subject. Noticing that the dog's salivary response started at the mere sight of food, Pavlov experimented with pairing different external stimuli such as the sound of a bell with the presentation of food. He found that after enough repetitions, the sound of the bell (a cue) would trigger salivation even if no food was present. Bell → food → salivation soon became bell → salivation. The sound became a cue for the presentation of food, triggering the salivary response even in the absence of food.

To test different associations, Pavlov sounded the bell *while* the dog was eating. He found that no matter how many times he repeated bell-ringing while eating, the sound alone did not trigger salivation. In other words, giving the cue *during the performance* of the behavior did not result in an associated response to the cue.

After the behavior

Pavlov also tried sounding the bell after the dog ate. Again, no matter how many times this was repeated, no association was formed between the bell and food, so that the sound alone caused salivation. This means that no matter how many times a trainer repeats the cue *after the performance* of a behavior, it is not helpful in teaching the cue.

What about saying the cue just to remind the dog what he did, or praise him for having done it, such as saying "...good sit?" In this case, "good" is an adjective that modifies "sit," but dogs don't understand qualifiers like good, better, best. Telling a dog it was a "good" sit is as meaningless as telling him it was an "okay," "ho hum," or "crummy" sit.

More importantly, the cue word does not define a *position*; it is a *prompt for performance of a behavior*. So repeating the cue after the behavior is actually giving a new cue. The trainer may intend "good sit" to praise the position rather than the action, but to the dog, it's a call to action. On being told "good...sit" many dogs reposition themselves and sit again.

Say it before

The only experiment in which Pavlov's dogs learned the association between the bell and food so the sound triggered salivation, was when it was rung *before* presentation of the food—not during, not after.

The lesson: *Learning the cue takes place when you give the cue just before the dog performs the behavior.*

How to add the cue

Here are the steps to follow in teaching the cue:

- **Give the cue *just before your dog begins to perform* the behavior.** When you are certain your dog is about to perform the behavior, say the cue. Click the behavior and give the reward, then give the cue once again when you believe the dog is going to repeat the behavior. Continue with this sequence of cue → behavior/mark → reward/eat...cue...

- **Say the cue word or give the cue signal just once.** Repeating the cue or combining a word and signal will create a compound-cue association such as "sit-sit-sit" or "sit"/signal. The result might be, for example, that to cue your dog to lie down, you'll need to motion toward the floor *and* say "down."

- **Once you introduce a cue, stop clicking that behavior unless you have given the cue and your dog responds.** During a training session, your dog will offer behaviors you have previously rewarded. Once you have introduced the cue for the behavior, do not click when your dog offers that behavior unless you have cued it first. This is an important point—it is what teaches your dog to listen for a cue rather than simply offering various, random behaviors. More on this in the next chapter.

It takes repetition to make the association

Until your dog has performed sufficient repetitions to make the association between the cue and the behavior, a cue is simply a meaningless sound or signal. A crossover trainer's experience with command-based training may create the impression that the dog is responding to the cue from the beginning. She's not—her action is simply to follow a lure or be placed in position, without which there's no behavior. Responding to a cue requires that the dog learns to associate the cue with her *voluntary* action, that is, what she does on her own, absent any other prompts.

Regardless of training method, it takes many repetitions for a dog to associate the cue with the behavior, and more importantly, for the cue to trigger that behavior. How many repetitions? Let's look at what some methods recommend.

My previous command-based training method (in the book *Training Your Dog*), had three steps (or sequences) to train sit. We recommended training for five days at each step, practicing two or three times a day, with five repetitions per practice session. That's 50-75 repetitions per step, for a total of 150-225 repetitions before we would expect the dog to respond to a "sit" command on his own.

In training the first sequence of down, the Koehler Method recommends downing the dog 10-15 times per session for five days—50-75 repetitions before moving to the next step. The next sequence involves correcting the dog down however many times it takes until he does it "willingly, at least 25 consecutive times" without needing a correction. Again, loads of repetitions before the dog is expected to know what "down" means.

With lure-reward training, where the luring motion morphs into a signal cue, some behaviors such as sit and down have just the one step; consequently fewer repetitions are needed before the dog will respond to the motion cue. Transitioning from a hand motion to a verbal cue, on the other hand, will require the same number of repetitions to learn the word cue association as with any training method. How many? Once the dog understands the behavior to perform, it takes between 20 and 50 repetitions for the dog to learn the cue-behavior association.

One of the huge advantages to clicker training is the lack of reliance on prompts. Since the cue association is made with the dog's *voluntary* behavior, it happens much more quickly. Once the behavior is predictable, it takes 20 to 50 repetitions of the cue, followed by the behavior, mark, and reward for the association to form, that is, for the cue to "trigger" the behavior. If this still sounds like a lengthy procedure, it's not. Even taking a break after every five to ten repetitions, most dogs will offer the behavior at a high enough rate that you can repeat a behavior 30 times in five to ten minutes…or less.

Consider this, for example, when introducing the cue "sit." Your dog sits predictably, without hesitation, so you're ready to add the cue. Your dog sits; you click, then drop a treat a short distance away. Your dog gets up to get the treat, eats it, turns toward you, and is about to sit again. You say, "sit." She sits…click… drop a treat…eat… say "sit"…she sits …click…treat…eat …say "sit"… It likely took you as long to read that description as it takes to repeat the cue-behavior sequence several times.

When you start this process, don't mistakenly believe that your dog "understands" the cue just because she performs the behavior right after you give it. Until your dog has formed the association between cue and behavior, the reason she offers the behavior has nothing to do with the cue. Rather it has everything to do with your rewarding it. Thorndike again—reinforced behavior will be repeated. Your dog performs the behavior right after the cue simply because you've rewarded it before, and she expects it to be rewarded once again.

Even once the dog has formed the association, the cue simply means there's an opportunity to earn reinforcement by performing the behavior associated with this cue. In other words it says: *You know what to do. Do it; it will likely be worth your while.*

Cue a predictable behavior

You can add cues to your dog's repertoire by cueing behaviors that you know your dog is about to perform, just as I trained Mayday to bow on cue simply by signaling "bow" every time I let him out of his crate and he stretched. Cannon learned "go downstairs" when I said it each time he approached the steps into the yard. He had to learn the context of *other* stairs, but that was easy, too. Whenever he was about to descend any staircase, I gave the cue. He quickly learned to generalize "go downstairs" to mean any steps.

Do it, do it right, do it now

What if you give the cue and your dog doesn't do it, is really slow to respond, or offers a different behavior than what you asked for? There's a simple solution. Teach your dog that she has a small **window of opportunity** within which to respond, called the **limited hold**, in order to get a reward. If she responds while the window of opportunity is open, she gets a click and treat. If she doesn't respond, is slow, or offers a different behavior, the window closes and she loses the chance to earn a reward at that time. Here are three simple steps to teach this:

1. **The mark and the consequence.** Say the cue and give your dog a short time frame within which to respond, say two seconds. If he doesn't perform the behavior within that time frame, give your dog a **lost opportunity marker (LOM)** such as "oops," "nope," "sorry," or "too bad," that says the window is shut. After saying your LOM, turn your head to look away briefly for just a second or two, look back at your dog, and repeat the cue. When he responds, click,

then reward. This step is simply to introduce the LOM. *Repeat this sequence just three times—no more.* After introducing the LOM three times, you're ready for the next step.

Shari cues "down." When Siku does not respond, Shari gives her LOM and looks away. Note how Siku's focus changes, alerting to the LOM and the consequence—loss of opportunity and loss of Shari's attention. Next, Shari gave the cue again. Siku responded to the cue and Shari marked with "yes" and rewarded with a smile and verbal praise.

2. **You get just one chance to get it right the first time.** Start as you did in Step 1. Give the cue, and if your dog doesn't respond, say your LOM, turn your head away, look back, and repeat the cue. From now on, however, when you give the *second* cue, you *do not click and treat*. Rather, mark your dog's compliance with a verbal marker "yes" followed by verbal praise. The message is, "What you did was good, but not great…not good enough to earn a click and treat."

> ## "Lost Opportunity" versus "No Reward" Marker: Different markers mean different things
>
> Some trainers use the term "**no reward marker**" or **NRM**. I refer to it as a lost opportunity marker (LOM) for several reasons. "NRM" is used interchangeably for two different things: one, the lost opportunity, and second, during shaping when the trainer wants the dog to offer a different behavior. This may seem like a fine point, but there is a difference between the LOM (negative punishment) and a marker that asks the dog to keep working, just try something different. The latter is a "**cue for variable behavior**" or **CVB**. Too many initials? Just be clear about the difference between a lost opportunity due to an incorrect or slow response (P-) versus a request to try something different altogether (a cue that asks for another behavior), such as "try again."

3. **You get another chance to do it right the first time.** Immediately following "yes" and praise, give your dog *another opportunity to respond correctly to earn a click and treat*. Say the cue, and if your dog responds, click and treat. If he doesn't, repeat as in Step 2. By consistently marking and rewarding the second opportunity with just a verbal marker and verbal praise, your dog will quickly learn that the best rewards are available only when he responds quickly and correctly to the *first cue*.

Following the repetition in which Siku got just verbal praise, Shari gave Siku another chance to get it right the first time. Siku responded to the cue immediately, earning a click and treat. Note that Shari tosses the treat to re-set the behavior. She could also have held it so Siku sat up in the same spot.

To recap the limited hold (window of opportunity):

- Cue ➤ Unacceptable response ➤ LOM
- 2nd cue ➤ Response ➤ "Yes" and praise.
- Reset the behavior
- New 1st cue ➤ Response ➤ Click and treat

[handwritten margin note: To teach LOM: LOM Reune–C/T 3 times only.]

Spiffying up a known behavior

Crossover trainers often ask if it's necessary to re-train commands their crossover dog already knows. The good news—it isn't. You can and should utilize any behaviors you've trained and want your dog to perform. It doesn't matter what method you've come from, you worked hard to achieve results. You earned them, use them.

On the other hand, there may be behaviors your dog has been taught that you want to improve. Consider each behavior individually. If you are happy with the speed, accuracy, and/or precision of your dog's response, great! But if your vision of the ideal performance is different from the reality, you can spiffy it up.

Train the "improvement" as a new behavior. To your dog, it is. Let's say you want to change how your dog lies down from sit-then-lie-down into a fold-back-down-from-a-stand. Even though we think of both behaviors as the same *position*, remember to your dog a behavior isn't a position, it's an *action*. Getting to a down by folding back from a stand is a completely different action from sit-then-lie-down.

To train an improved behavior, start the shaping process as for any *new* behavior. Once you've shaped the new and improved behavior, attach the new cue to it just as you would for any other behavior. Remember the cue triggers the specific action your dog learns to associate with it, so using your old cue will elicit "the same ol', same ol'."

(handwritten margin note, rotated: "Looking Away & Back up")

> ## Cues as rewards
>
> When you give your dog a cue for a learned behavior, one with a history of reinforcement, the *cue itself* is reinforcement. The cue to jump a jump, retrieve a ball, even a cue for something as simple as "sit," not only is the activity rewarding, but the cue is, too. Here's the bad news—when your dog is jumping up on a visitor, and you say, "Sit!" that cue reinforced jumping up. But the news isn't only bad since now that you know this, you can change how you handle such situations. (See Chapter 10.)

Changing or adding cues

Another aspect of spiffying up a behavior is changing a cue, such as from a voice cue to a hand signal, or vice versa, or when you discover an unintended association that you need to eliminate.

My Crossover Journal

Mayday loved agility. It didn't take too many repetitions for me to notice that when I gave him the cue to enter the weave poles, Mayday hesitated and a confused look momentarily flashed across his face. My "Aha!" was realizing that the cue "weave" resembled "Leave it," a cue that meant "don't do it" or "move away from that." Changing his weave pole cue to "poles" eliminated his confusion.

Or perhaps you need to eliminate a verbal cue/body language association. Doris was training her dog for obedience competition. When giving the recall cue, she unconsciously bobbed her head as she said "Come!" a double-command that could earn a non-qualifying score. I had her concentrate on holding her head still. The first time Doris called her dog, nothing happened, since the learned cue was a compound head signal and voice command. Doris had to train a "new" cue to replace the head bob/"come" cue.

Here's how to change a cue word or signal. Say the new cue word, or give the new signal, pause briefly, then say/give the old cue. The dog performs the behavior, click and reward. It will take approximately the same number of repetitions (20-50) for the dog to learn the new association as it takes to learn a cue from scratch.

After a certain number of repetitions, your dog will begin to *anticipate* the old cue before you give it. Anticipation means your dog performs the behavior after the new and before you give the old. At that point, randomly give the old cue, ultimately eliminating it altogether:

Introduce the "new" cue:
New cue (pause) → Old cue → Behavior → Click

"New" cue triggers behavior:
New cue → Dog anticipates old cue, performs behavior → Click

My Crossover Journal
Wendy was training Jonah, a yellow Lab who had had some prior
compulsion training. One of the owner's goals was to have Jonah
respond to a voice cue to lie down rather than needing to pull on his collar to
get him down. Wendy discovered that even the smallest pressure on his collar
resulted in Jonah hitting the deck, instantly lying down. It was simply a matter
of new cue/old cue: "down" followed by a quick touch to his collar, and Jonah was
soon lying down on the voice cue only.

Test the cue

Whether you've taught a new behavior, changed or added a cue, a simple test will let
you know if your dog has learned the association between the cue and the behavior.
Test your dog's response to the cue "cold turkey." Give the cue when you're not "in
training." Just try it. At a time that your dog is just hanging out, not highly distracted,
give the cue. For example, while you're watching TV, get your dog's attention—no
food, no nose-tease, no warm-up—and ask for the behavior. If she performs it, great!
You're ready to move on to next step, to build reliability, precision, and speed to the
behaviors you want your dog to learn.

Attaching cues—the steps so far

1. **The behavior.** Your dog offers the specific behavior without hesi-
    tation.

2. **Predictable.** You like the behavior, and are 95% certain he will
    perform it within the next five seconds.

3. **Add the cue.** Say the cue just prior to your dog performing the
    behavior.

4. **Non-performance.** When you say the cue and your dog does
    not perform the behavior, mark non-compliance with an LOM
    followed by another opportunity. (If this happens repeatedly, re-
    evaluate. Your dog may not have been ready for the cue.)

5. **No cue, no click, no reinforcement.** Once you've started adding
    the cue, stop marking or reinforcing un-cued, spontaneous offer-
    ings of that behavior.

6. **Sufficient repetitions.** Practice the sequence: cue ➤ behavior/
    mark ➤ reward 20-50 times for the dog to make the association
    between the cue and the behavior.

7. **Test it.** Test the cue cold turkey and see what happens. If your dog
    responds, you're on your way.

8. **Congratulations!...but there's more.** In the next chapter, you'll
    learn how to teach your dog to wait for, differentiate between, and
    respond to specific cues.

Common questions about the four steps to a trained behavior

My dog's behavior is just not progressing. We seem stuck. What can I do to get a better response?

There are several possible reasons for lack of progress:

- **Examine what you're clicking.** The behavior you see is the behavior you trained. When you mark the same level of a behavior without raising your standards or requirements, you solidify that level. Click it and he'll offer it, over and over. Put it on cue, and you've got it trained on cue.

  Solution: Work on a new, different, improved behavior, click.

- **Something is reinforcing your dog's "stuck" behavior, intentionally or unintentionally.** Rewards don't come only from you; they may be innate, or from something else in the environment.

  Solution: Examine what might be reinforcing your dog and either eliminate it or make your reward the better one.

My dog's response has deteriorated. He used to respond quickly, but he's gotten slower, and now takes so long. Why and what should I do?

There are several possible causes for deterioration of a behavior after you add the cue:

- **You added the cue too soon.** This is one of the most common problems cross-over trainers encounter. Adding the cue while a behavior is still in the "experimental" stage, when your dog isn't sure what's being clicked and is still testing the premise, means for example, that if he offers a slower response and you click, you've reinforced slower. Do this a few times, and you've trained a slower response.

  Solution: Eliminate the cue; improve the behavior; add the cue. If the cue triggers the deteriorated response, change to a new cue.

- **Clicking poor repetitions.** This usually goes with, "Well, at least he did it." Right, but if you click a slow sit, for example, that's what your dog will give you.

  Solution: Click only the best repetitions. Or return to Step 3 and introduce some variability to get better responses to click and reward. *Add variets*

- **Rewarding a sub-standard "two-fer."** When you automatically click a second response, even when it is not as good as the first response, you're marking and reinforcing the deteriorated performance.

  Solution: Rather than asking for a two-fer and clicking the second response regardless of quality, click the best of the best, and withhold a click (vary the reinforcement schedule) if the response is not as good.

- **Clicking even if your dog pauses after the cue.** You give the cue; your dog waits…and waits…then performs the behavior, and you click. What have you clicked? You get it. It's called long **latency**—a slow response after the cue.

Solution: Create a "window of opportunity" (page 158). Still slow? Review your training steps.

He's fine until we go someplace new or there's a distraction. Then I have no control. I thought I was generalizing, but it didn't work. How come?

The next chapter takes your dog's training to the next level, increasing reliability in a variety of circumstances. Until you've undertaken these next steps, you're expecting more than your dog is ready for. That is both unfair to your dog and frustrating for you.

Read on…You're well on your way.

Chapter 9

BUILDING RELIABILITY, PRECISION, AND SPEED

My Crossover Journal
Ian Dunbar posits that when given a command, even one as common as "sit," most dogs simply guess. At one of his seminars, in Ian's inimitable way, he challenged us to return home and test this assumption by asking for a sit in a non-typical environment—lie on the floor and position our dogs to sit on our heads. Never being one to shirk a challenge, when I got home I stood my 180 pound English Mastiff, Calisto, in a show stance, and crawled under her. As I looked up at her huge rear end, I decided that I could just as easily test Ian's point if Calisto sat on my chest instead of my head. She did sit. Fortunately, being an extremely bright dog, she did not put her full weight on me. But Ian is not wrong—regardless of training method, most dogs just guess.

Calisto, my Mastiff, knew what "sit" meant, even when it meant sitting on top of me.

When I first crossed over to clicker training, several of my class instructors who were competing in obedience chose to stop teaching for me rather than train their own dogs with clicker training. They didn't believe clicker training could give them the precise performances they desired for an Obedience Trial Championship (OTCH). Although I felt they were wrong, I didn't have the experience or track record to refute their opinions.

Like these instructors, many potential crossover trainers have reservations about clicker training's reliability, uncertain that clicker trained dogs will be "obedient." Some trainers dabble with clicker training, but don't go beyond "playing" with behaviors. Others will allow, intellectually at least, that a trainer *may* be able to train to the highest degree of precision to earn an OTCH, but they either think it will take far too long, or they don't know how to get there.

Reliable, dependable, precise: "Obedient"

The belief that when the chips are down, clicker trained dogs are not reliable is not just wrong, it is silly. Untrained dogs are unreliable; poorly trained dogs are unreliable; partially trained dogs are unreliable. The problem lies not with the method used to train behaviors, but with the trainer's commitment to completing the process, regardless of method.

> ### It's too darn much fun!
> It is not unusual for clicker trainers to work with their dogs on a whole bunch of behaviors that are never put on cue, simply enjoying watching their dogs think, reason, and figure things out. Taking just a few, important behaviors through to a reliable performance, trainers and their dogs have fun training together without "completing the process" with each behavior. And that's fine! You don't have to take every behavior through to the end, but it's important to know how to do so when you want to.

At seminars, I meet many trainers, including clicker trainers, who simply do not know what "completing the process" entails. Without knowing how to achieve a reliable, dependable performance, trainers either can't do it, or fall back into their comfort zone—their old method(s).

One common misconception is that clicker trainers handle non-compliance by simply trying again, giving the dog another chance. For many crossover trainers—especially those seeking a highly reliable performance such as for a service dog, or for competitive events—giving the dog another chance to perform a behavior is simply not good enough.

So crossover trainers want to know if clicker training can take a dog to a high enough level of compliance for the average pet owner. And can it take a dog to a high enough level of compliance and precision for the competitive trainer? How about for the service dog trainer? The answer for all is, "Yes!" As with any training method, it is simply a question of the trainer's abilities and commitment to getting the desired level of reliability.

167

Rewarding 2nd, 3rd guesses → don't teach the dog to recognize the cue

What is reliable?

There are two aspects to reliability; two characteristics trainers generally think of when visualizing an "obedient" dog:

- First, the dog responds correctly to a cue, offering the predictable, desired behavior.

- Second, the dog's response is resistant to distractions. The behavior happens no matter what, even if you ask your dog to sit on your head.

Adding the cue is the first important step in this process, but the job is not done. As Ian Dunbar asserts, in many cases when you cue a behavior, the dog is simply guessing what behavior will earn a reward. The dog's first guess is often correct because humans are predictable—we usually cue behaviors in the same context or in the same order. For instance, first we ask for "sit," followed by "down." Or when we want the dog to do something to earn a reward such as getting to eat his dinner, we ask for the same behavior each time, "sit." Try asking for "spin," "back-up," or "bang-you're-dead," and the dog will…sit. Sit is the **default behavior** for most dogs, the first one they offer no matter what—and the one they'll try when they're not sure what you are looking for.

How can you tell if your dog is guessing? Guessing looks like this—cue "down." Your dog sits and pauses briefly. When nothing happens (no mark, no praise), he tries the next likely behavior that has earned praise in the past, he lies down. "Good boy!" rewards the guess, but it doesn't teach the dog to recognize the cue.

Teaching your dog to stop guessing, that is, to focus on, wait for, listen to, and respond correctly to cues, is the next step in clicker training. The scientific term is **stimulus control**.

I'm here!

Achieving stimulus (cue) control

There are three aspects to teaching your dog to listen for, recognize, and respond to specific cues. Let's examine each point.

Step 1. Your dog recognizes a cue that triggers the behavior you want

This is the work you accomplished in Chapter 8. You've trained the behavior the way you want it, attached the cue, and your dog has performed enough repetitions to make the connection between the behavior and the cue. You've tested this association, giving the cue when you're not "in training" and your dog successfully responded. Great! You're on your way to cue control, and ready for the next step.

Next step

Step 2. No cue…no behavior (and no reward)

As mentioned in the previous chapter, as soon as you start attaching a cue to a behavior, don't reward that behavior unless you have given the cue. Not even a word of praise if you didn't cue it first. The operative part of "stimulus control" is "control," being able to direct your dog's behavior with words, signals, and various other prompts.

Some dogs become a behavioral whirling dervish, rapidly offering spontaneous behaviors the moment you pick up a clicker. Although less common with crossover dogs, it may still happen with yours. While helpful for shaping new behaviors, such activity can feel frenzied and out-of-control. By not rewarding a behavior you've put on cue unless you ask for it, you reduce such random, spontaneous performances. If you randomly reinforce spontaneous, non-cued responses, you will encourage the "whirling dervish" performance.

Through repetition, your dog will learn:

- Respond to a cue = a click and treat
- Unsolicited performance of an on-cue behavior = no click and treat, or any other reinforcement

But my fear is that she'll stop offering (trying) behaviors which is necessary for shaping

Randomly reinforcing spontaneous, un-cued behaviors can create a whirling dervish.

Wait till I tell you

An important part of the process for achieving cue control is teaching your dog to wait for the cue before performing the behavior. When teaching your dog to wait, if she fails to respond to the cue, give your Lost Opportunity Marker (LOM) such as "oops," and cue again. Remember, the repetition that immediately follows the LOM is your dog's *second chance* to respond, and earns just "yes" and verbal praise. Then give your dog another chance to get it right the *first time*, and when she responds, click and treat.

2nd chance winners → yes
Good girl
(No food)

Here are the steps to teaching "wait for a cue":

1. Cue the behavior, click and reward. Immediately repeat this two more times for a total of three repetitions in succession.

2. After the third repetition, pause three seconds without giving the cue. The chances are your dog will offer the behavior spontaneously. Either:

    •   Don't react—no click, no praise, nothing.

    •   Or mark it with your LOM, communicating to your dog your *uncued action won't earn a reward*

    Pause 5-10 seconds, then if your dog is still waiting for you to click, re-set the behavior, but do not praise.

3. Next, just before you think your dog is going to perform the behavior again, give the cue, click the response and reward.

4. Repeat #2, pausing three to five seconds without giving the cue.

5. Repeat #3, giving the cue just before your dog is about to perform, click, reward.

6. Take a short break.

7. From this point, alternate between #2 and #3. Watch for your dog to hesitate after a cued trial, that is, watch for any delay indicating that your dog is *beginning to wait for a cue*. When you see such a pause, give the cue. Giving the cue reinforces *wait-for-the-cue*; jackpot (remember, jackpots reward behaviors that you've cued!), and take a break.

8. After the break, continue with this pattern.

While this process teaches your dog to wait for a cue, the next step teaches your dog to differentiate between cues, to listen to the *specific* cue.

Step 3. The behavior you cue is the behavior you get

This progression teaches your dog to actively pay attention to your cues—no guessing and no other intervening behavior. When you cue "down," your dog lies down. She doesn't sit and hesitate, she doesn't spin, jump up, or stand there staring at you—she lies down.

This important aspect demonstrates that your thinking dog is focused and responding to the cue, rather than offering a variety of behaviors from which you may pick one to click. For the sake of simplicity, whether your cue is a word, sound, or signal, I call it "listening."

When your dog is listening, you can give known cues in any order and she will respond properly to each without guessing or even pausing. The listening dog is focused, paying attention so she is able to recognize and differentiate between different cues, performing the specific behavior you asked for.

Once your dog has learned to listen to and respond to each specific cue, it is easier to add new ones. The more cues your dog knows, the faster she learns new ones. Here's how to teach your dog to listen. Have fun with this!

Listening drill: An exercise to teach cue discrimination

1. **Start with cues for three or more behaviors.** Use any three cues, such as "sit," "stand," and "down." (These behaviors represent six actions: sit from stand, sit up from down, stand from sit, stand from down, down from stand, down from sit.)

2. **Mix your cues.** Give cues randomly in no set order or design.

3. **Use a random reinforcement schedule.** Click and reward on a random schedule.

4. **Keep records.** Track and record the number of correct and incorrect responses. Your goal is at least 80% accuracy—no more than two errors out of ten behaviors.

5. **Errors.** An error is no response to the cue, the wrong response (a different behavior), needing a second command, or a slower response than your dog has been performing previously. **Note:** If your dog repeatedly fails to respond to a cue, makes several errors with one cue, or stops responding altogether, discontinue this exercise, isolate the problematic behavior, and work on it separately. Once you've gotten the behavior back and practiced it, re-insert the cue into your dog's repertoire of behaviors.

Here's an example of how this might go:

Down, *click and re-set the behavior*

Sit…down…sit-up, *click*

Stand…down, *click*

Take a break. Then start from the beginning again, and continue with the next few.

Stand, *click*

Down, *click*

Stand…sit…stand, *click*

Sit…stand…down…sit-up…down, *click*

Take a break. Then start from here and continue through the entire list from beginning to end.

Sit-up…down…sit-up…down…stand, *click*

Sit, *click*

> ## Sit from stand versus sit-up from down
> The action sit-up-from-down, involves the dogs front legs pushing the dog's front end upward into a sit. This action is different from folding his rear legs into a sit—the action we call "sit." Since the cue triggers *an action* rather than defining a position, It makes sense to call sit-up-from-down a different name. It's not necessary to have a separate cue, but it is something to consider. I use a hand signal, or "sit up."

Fluent, flowing, effortless...and trained

The adage "Practice makes perfect" is not entirely accurate. Practicing a flawed golf swing won't lower your handicap and practicing the wrong notes of a musical composition won't win a scholarship to Julliard. The adage should be: *Perfect* practice makes perfect.

Consider what it takes for a concert pianist to learn to play fluently. Take "The Flight of the Bumblebee," a musical piece known for its frantic tempo. Picture the pianist's fingers flying up and down the keyboard, precisely, rapidly, at a fevered pitch. Aside from years of lessons, how would a pianist learn and practice this particular piece? It would make sense to start slowly, accurately learning the notes, then with further practice, increasing the tempo. With virtually any skill, it is helpful to practice it accurately to eliminate errors, learning to perform correctly at a slower pace, then building speed to your ultimate goal.

The same holds true for building your crossover dog's responses to cues. Start slowly, and build speed with practice. Why build speed? Because as with "The Flight of the Bumblebee," speed equates with **fluency**.

> ## Three elements of behavioral fluency
>
> Behavioral fluency means "mastery," or what in dog training terms might be called "obedience." While a more accurate (and politically correct) term would be "reliable" rather than "obedient," the result is a consistent, responsive performance with predictable, desirable results. More importantly, fluent behaviors are less likely to be affected by changes in location, setting, or distractions. The three elements of behavioral fluency are:
>
> - **Short latency.** There is little or no delay between the cue and response. The dog responds promptly and without pause.
>
> - **Accuracy of response.** The cue solicits the desired, correct response.
>
> - **Speed of performance.** The behavior is performed swiftly, with confidence, without hesitation.

Consider learning a foreign language. Starting with a few words, with practice you can carry on a simple conversation. Still tentative, you're not yet able to think in the language or have an in-depth conversation, and if something distracts you, you're even less able to talk. You're not yet fluent. Fluency is immediate, effortless, quick, smooth, without hesitation, and with few errors.

Behavioral scientist Ogden Lindsley's work with "Precision Teaching" demonstrates that a fluent performance is less subject to distraction, and more easily adapts to new situations, even in the absence of new instruction. Doesn't that sound like what you want for your dog's trained behavior? And you can get it!

When your dog responds effortlessly, accurately, and transitions from one cued behavior to the next without hesitation, his behavior is fluent. As if that's not enough, the icing on this cake is that fluent behavior is resistant to distractions. Yippee! By George, we've got it! Here's how you start.

Building speed: Speed Trials, the road to success

Speed Trials both build your dog's fluency and are an excellent way to incorporate new behaviors into your dog's behavioral repertoire in an observable, measurable, and reinforcing (for you) way. Once your dog knows the cue, and performs it in any order of behaviors (in the "Listening drill"), build speed with a Speed Trial.

Starting with any three or four on-cue behaviors, have your dog randomly perform as many repetitions as possible in a set time frame. Start slowly, and with practice over time, speed up the tempo to increase the number of behaviors performed in that time frame. All you need are paper and pencil, treats, and a clock with a second hand:

1. **Time trial.** Set a time for the trial, say 20 seconds. From start to finish, you will be cuing behaviors *without reinforcement* until the end of the time trial. Some crossover dogs may get discouraged quickly and will stop offering behaviors, so you may need to start with a shorter time frame and build from there, gradually lengthening your time trial.

2. **Goal.** The goal is for your dog to perform as many behaviors in the time frame as possible. You'll give rapid-fire cues, in random order one after the other, without pausing to click, mark, praise, or reward. For instance, you might cue: "Touch, down, sit-up, stand, touch, touch, spin, spin, sit, down, stand…"

3. **Reinforcing behaviors.** Don't reinforce any behavior until the end of the Speed Trial—no click, no treat, no verbal mark, or verbal praise. Praising takes time. At the end of the trial you can mark and jackpot, but during the time trial say nothing other than giving cues.

4. **Frequency of behavior.** In your set time frame, count the number of behaviors your dog performs, both correct responses and errors. If you don't have a helper, count the correct responses on one hand, and errors on the other. An error is:

    -   No response.
    -   A wrong response.
    -   A behavior that needed an additional cue.   2nd TM

5. **Accuracy.** Correct responses must be…*correct*. That is, they have to fit your goal behavior. For instance, if you cue a down and your dog doesn't go all the way down, that is an incorrect performance. If you cue a hand touch and your dog doesn't actually make contact, that is incorrect.

6. **Keep records.** At the end of each trial, mark down the number of correct and incorrect responses, and note the behaviors that were incorrect. If your dog's accuracy drops below 80%, practice the problem behavior(s) separately. Perform at least 20 trials to chart your progress. Chart 9-1 is a sample form you can use.

7. **Deterioration.** If and when a behavior deteriorates, discontinue the Speed Trial to isolate and work on that behavior. Then introduce a second behavior and

practice alternating randomly as with the listening drill. Finally, re-introduce the behavior into a Speed Trial.

8. **Build speed.** As you practice, your dog's responses will get faster. Over time, you will be able to drill your dog's cues rapid-fire with instant responses. How exciting. Your dog's behavior is *fluent*!

Increase your dog's repertoire. Whenever your dog learns a new cue, once he knows it and "listens" for it, practice it in a Speed Trial, first with just one or two others, then with more cued behaviors. Build speed within your dog's entire repertoire of cued behaviors.

Speed Trial Record Sheet

Cued Behaviors								
1	2	3	4	5	6	7	8	9
Day	Date	Count time	# Possible	# Correct	# Errors	% Correct	Response Rate	Notes
S								
M								
T								
W								
T								
F								
S								
S								
M								
T								
W								
T								
F								
S								

Chart 9-1. In each column across record the following: (2) the date, (3) length of time for the trial, (4) the number of cues, that is, the maximum number of times your dog could have responded correctly, (5) the number of times your dog did respond correctly, and (6) the number of errors. To determine (7), the percent correct, divide column 5 by column 4. Your goal for column (7) is 80% or better. (8) To determine the average time it takes your dog to perform a correct response, divide column 3 by column 5. Your goal is for this number to decrease, meaning your dog's correct responses get faster. In column (9) note the behaviors with more errors, and anything else that might influence the Speed Trial such as location or distractions.

Here, there, and everywhere

The final step to having a reliably trained dog is ensuring that he will respond every-where you want or need him to. Building your dog's immunity to distractions takes commitment, attention, and time—time well-spent.

When a dog doesn't respond properly, some crossover trainers may fall back into old patterns, even returning to their previous method. To preclude this, the final step of your clicker training transition is understanding how to get full reliability, including what to do if your dog doesn't respond to a cue.

"Bad" dog…not!

Why would a dog be non-responsive to a cue? Is he being "bad?" Does he make a conscious decision, thinking to himself, "I know what to do, but I *won't do it*." What is in it for the dog to be "bad?" When you think about it, really not much. Rather than being bad, what he's being is…a dog.

Dogs learn to make choices that make them happy, choices that result in reinforce-ment or avoid discomfort. So when a "trained" dog is "disobedient" examine why. Why didn't your dog respond to your cue in this environment at this moment?

As with my former instructors, I have met trainers who equate "disobedience" virtually exclusively with the "wrong" training method. They are convinced that their approach will eliminate errors, but such an opinion completely ignores reality. Dogs (like humans!) do make mistakes. All-positive training is imperfect, as is correction-based training. No method guarantees perfection because there are often good, rational, understandable reasons for a dog's non-compliance.

At her advanced clicker training seminar, Kathy Sdao compares a dog's obedience to cues using a human analogy—traffic light "rules." According to the rules of "traffic light obedience," green commands "Go!" and red says "Stop!" The light color triggers us to either accelerate or brake. Unless, that is, we have reason to "disobey." Here are a few examples of reasons and situations that may prevent traffic light compliance with analogous reasons a trained dog might fail to come when called, often misinterpreted as "disobedience":

- **Inattention, a momentary distraction.** Perhaps the driver was changing a CD, checking the rearview mirror, or talking on the phone and didn't see the light change.

  Dog equivalent: Something attracted the dog's attention at the precise moment you gave the cue. In a ring situation, perhaps the wind blew a tent flap or a ker-fuffle outside the ring attracted the dog's attention. Unpredictable distractions happen in real-life, too. The difference is in the real world, we simply repeat the cue without the consequence of a non-qualifying score.

- **A mechanical/physical problem.** The accelerator didn't respond; the car stalled.

  Dog equivalent: Something interrupts compliance. What if, on his way toward you, your dog is stung by a bee? Or suddenly gets a stomach cramp, twists his toe or suffers some other transitory, physical discomfort that takes his mind off your cue? Chances are you might not even know it happened. This category includes the dog reacting slowly because he is simply not physically capable of a faster response.

- **Unable to comply.** The car in front of you stalls or a child suddenly dashes in front of your car.

  Dog equivalent: Something prevents your dog from complying. Dogs are not the best problem solvers, so when they find themselves behind a wall, barrier, or other obstruction, they may not know how to move around it to get to you. For example, I went to the back door to call my Vizsla, Tisza, in from the yard. She was nowhere to be seen. She had gone through a break in the fence, and hearing me call, was standing on the other side of the gate, unable to get back into the yard.

- **Danger.** You see a car on the cross street that clearly isn't slowing to a stop barreling toward the intersection. If you move, you know you'll be hit, so you ignore both the green light and the drivers behind you leaning on their horns.

  Dog equivalent: Something the dog perceives as dangerous prevents her response. Perhaps, in order to get to you, your dog has to pass by another dog that is clearly, unmistakably sending an evil eye message, "Don't you dare come one step closer." Unless you can see the other dog's expression, you are most likely unaware that something is stopping your dog.

- **Overriding instinct.** You're a young, healthy, unattached man sitting at a red light. Standing on the corner is a bevy of attractive women. The light turns green…but you wouldn't know it.

  Dog equivalent: Any powerful, hard-wired instinct that kicks in. When walking my dogs in the woods, if my Basset Hound, Katie, picked up a scent, I knew I had a very small window of opportunity to get her attention. Once she was on the trail it was fruitless to call her. Her instincts were so strong, she literally could not hear me.

Once Katie was on a scent trail, nothing would interrupt her.

- **Insufficient practice.** You're driving a standard shift, stopped at the top of a steep hill with a car right on your rear. You're not very skilled yet and you know you're going to roll back when you take your foot off the brake.

  Dog equivalent: Your dog is in a situation beyond her abilities. She hasn't had sufficient practice and training to comply under the circumstances.

- **An overriding cue.** You hear a siren, a sound that takes precedence over the green light. You wait to see where it's coming from so you won't interfere with the emergency vehicle.

  Dog equivalent: A different cue takes precedence, conflicting with your cue. For example, you say the word "come" but your vocal inflection, angry facial expression, and hostile body language say "Uh oh…"

- **Conflicting motivation.** A pedestrian is waiting to cross. Motivated by courtesy, you waive her across, delaying acceleration.

  Dog equivalent: You've got a food treat that's usually a good reward, but not when it is more reinforcing to chase a squirrel.

- **Unpleasant association.** Your destination is undesirable so you are slow to move. You're on your way to the dentist for a root canal, and you're taking your sweet time.

  Dog equivalent: The dog associates arriving as undesirable. Perhaps in the past she was called only to be put directly into her crate, to have her nails trimmed, or on arrival was yelled at for destructive chewing or a housetraining lapse.

- **Location association.** In the past you had an accident at this intersection, so you're extremely cautious before moving.

  Dog equivalent: The dog has associated something unpleasant with the location.

- **Unclear cue.** The sun is hitting the traffic lights in such a way that makes it difficult to see them.

  Dog equivalent: For some reason, the dog isn't sure what you cued.

- **An intangible.** You don't know the reason, but there is one. Whatever the reason, *it isn't the dog's fault.*

While non-response to a green light may earn an impatient honk from the drivers behind you, disobeying a red light can be dangerous, or result in punishment—a ticket. Yet even with a red light, we rarely have 100% compliance. Certainly most of us have sped up at a yellow light, knowing it will likely turn red before we make it through the intersection. Or maybe in the middle of the night, when we're sitting at a red light all alone, no other cars in sight, no headlights visible—surely it's OK to disobey it then. Or we've been sitting at a light for an interminable time, and it becomes clear that the light is broken.

Even with the imperative, absolute nature of a red light, 100% compliance is the exception. How, then, can we expect perfection of our dogs? Truthfully, we can reasonably expect 75-80% compliance. It isn't that we must accept "disobedience" (non-compliance). Rather, when faced with non-compliance, consider the reason.

A dog doesn't "disobey" for no good reason any more than we'd sit at a green light just for the heck of it. Whatever the reason for a dog's non-compliance, one thing is certain. It is not the dog's responsibility to work through the factors that increase reliability. *Don't blame the dog.* Training your dog to a high expectation of reliability is up to you—and you can do it!

Instincts versus training: don't blame the dog!

The stronger the instinct, the more training it will take to override it. For instance, it takes exceptional training to expect a Basset Hound in hot pursuit of a rabbit to stop what she's doing and come when called. It's not that the dog is "bad." Rather, her instincts take precedence over all her senses, including hearing. She literally does not hear you call her.

When faced with a situation where instincts may override training you have three options:

1. **Manage your dog**—Don't put the dog in a position to engage in the instinctive activity. For example, don't take your dog off leash.

2. **Save your breath**—If the dog is already engaged in the instinctive activity, don't give a cue that your dog will ignore. Doing so reinforces ignoring you, sending the message that compliance is optional.

3. **Learn from it**—Make a mental note of the distraction and use it for your training.

Sometimes an instinct may be so strong that no amount of positive reinforcement training will overcome the dog's hard wiring (see Chapter 10). Above all, it is not the dog's fault when an instinctive behavior is stronger than his or her training. Don't blame the dog!

Building immunity to distractions

There are virtually an unlimited number of things that can and will attract your dog's attention. Attractions have different relative values, or levels of distractibility. Some are easily ignored, while others are nigh on impossible to pass up. Being able to hold a stay while you clap your hands and jump up and down in front of your dog doesn't automatically transfer to staying when the doorbell rings, a far greater attraction.

To train your dog through different degrees of distractions, it helps to have an overview of their relative attraction value. Consider everything you can think of that might be even remotely interesting, attractive, or distracting to your dog. Make a list of activities, situations, places, objects, sights, sounds, odors, toys, animals, people, and the like. Chart 9-2 contains a sample list to get you started. Your list will be fluid—add new things whenever you think of them, or when you and your dog encounter them.

Once you've compiled a list, rank each item on a scale from one to ten with one being worth an ear flick or a glance, and ten being virtually impossible to ignore. Next, reorganize your list in groupings by degrees of distraction.

Set up training sessions with a variety of distractions, keeping track of how your dog does with each. Work through the lower degrees, gradually making your way up through higher distractibility. The more you practice, the better your dog will be. It takes more than just a time or two around a distraction level before you can reasonably expect compliance, so be prepared to spend time on this.

A reasonable goal is ten correct responses with each of five distractions before increasing difficulty to a higher level. When faced with non-compliance, you can increase your dog's responsiveness by working further away from that distraction. In most cases, distance makes it easier for the dog. As your dog's compliance builds, move closer.

Sounds	Watch/See/Be near	Sniff
• Potato chip bag	• Leaves blowing	• A tree
• Doorbell	• A cat standing still	• The ground
• Knock on door	• A cat walking	• The dog park
• Garage door opening	• A cat running away	• A fire hydrant
• Person calling "Hello!"	• A dog standing still	• A cat box
• Telephone	• A dog walking	• Other _____
• Car keys	• A dog running	**Object/Items**
• Kitchen cabinet door	• A dog barking	• A favorite toy
• Dog biscuit box	• Dogs playing in distance	• Food bowl
• Other _____	• Dogs playing close by	• Clicker
Activities	• Child eating	• Bait bag
• Run on the beach	• Child on a bike stationary	• Leash/collar/harness
• Play with other dogs	• Child riding a bike	• Car keys
• Chase a stick	• Child playing quietly	• Your dog-walking coat
• Chase a Frisbee®	• Children playing noisily	• Your dog's winter coat
• Chase a squirrel	• Children wrestling	• Training bag
• Go swimming	• Children running quietly	• Other _____
• Retrieve from water	• Children running screaming	**Other**
• Play with the hose	• A squirrel on the ground	• _____
• Play chase me	• A squirrel in a tree	• _____
• Go for a ride	• Other _____	• _____
• Other _____	• Other _____	• _____

Chart 9-2. A sample list of your dog's attractions and distractions.

Vary the rewards you offer your dog, using reinforcements with a high relative value, especially as you get to the higher degree distractions. *When possible, the best reward is to give your dog access to the attraction.* For example, if he's been giving you great attention while the kids play ball, mark his good behavior, then release him, and have the kids throw the ball for him.

When you find yourself faced with a higher ranked distraction than your dog is ready for, here are your choices:

- Use the distraction as an opportunity to train, moving sufficiently far away so your dog is able to focus on you and your cues.

- Keep your dog on a leash or long line so you have physical control without needing to rely on your dog's response to a cue.

- Don't give your dog a cue. Doing so may well set him up to fail, which is at best frustrating to you and at worst gives your dog the opportunity to practice ignoring you. Rather than "test" to see if he'll respond to you, assume he won't. For example, if playing with other dogs has a distraction value of nine or 10, and you have only worked through distractions valued five to six, unless you're using it as an opportunity to train, don't call your dog when he's engaged in play.

Eliminate the clicker and reduce food treats

Crossover trainers run the gamut from pet owners to highly competitive dog sports enthusiasts to service dog trainers and everything in between. Virtually all want the assurance that they can have a responsive dog without needing to carry a clicker and food treats. And they can!

Sometimes a competition-oriented trainer will tell me they don't want to clicker train because you can't use a clicker or food treats in competition. This is quite true. Likewise you can't use luring or collar corrections. You can't holler, "Ach!" or give your dog a time-out in the competitive arena. As I wrote earlier, if you're still relying on *any* method's techniques and tools, you're not ready to compete.

The fact is that transitioning from using a clicker and carrying food treats takes less time than it does to reduce reliance on most other training tools. For example, a method that relies on training with a leash and collar can take months to gain off-leash responsiveness. An approach that utilizes luring can take time to reduce and eliminate the related body language. It is possible to eliminate a clicker in no time at all. The transition from using a clicker to having a reliable dog without it, and without carrying treats is straightforward and as easy as saying "yes."

Verbal marker

Having established a verbal marker for those times when you don't have a clicker or when you don't need the precision of a click (see Chapter 5), eliminating the clicker is as simple as saying "yes" to mark the dog's successful compliance, then following it with a reward. That's it.

When I work with a dog owner who is adamant about not wanting to use clicker training, I simply have them use a verbal marker, then reward. I teach them the principles of clicker training without a clicker, and don't mention the "C" word. With the dogs my training staff and I work with in our boarding-training and daycare-training programs, we both click and use a verbal marker. Since we're training dogs for their owners, and once trained the owners take over, it is both unnecessary and impractical to try to teach the owners to use a clicker. Whatever their reasons for having their dogs professionally trained—be it time constraints, family issues, physical disabilities, or another reason—the owners don't need to learn how to click. They just say "yes."

Once you've transitioned away from marking behavior with a click, no matter how infrequently you may use it, a clicker is still the best tool for shaping new behavior. When you want to train something new, dust off your clicker and have fun.

Reducing food treats

Fading food treats—gradually reducing then eliminating them—is not difficult unless your dog has learned an association of Food = Respond, No food = Don't respond (and hold out for food). If you have created this association, review the information on "Reward associations" in Chapter 6.

Having used a random schedule of reinforcement with a variety of different rewards, some of which may be even better than food treats, you're well on your way. Verbal praise is reinforcing for most dogs, and don't forget the Premack Principle, giving the dog the opportunity to engage in a high value activity.

If your dog is food-focused, and you need to desensitize him to the presence of food, build distance from food by having the food treats off your body and in a container a short distance away, then across the room, then in a different room. After you mark a behavior, run with your dog to the bowl—a rewarding game in itself—and give him a treat. Once your dog recognizes that food rewards don't have to be visible or even in the same room to be available, random reinforcement will keep your dog's responses sharp.

Reducing the frequency of food treats doesn't mean never using one. You'll maintain a high level of responsiveness by occasionally rewarding with something your dog really loves.

Praise—a marker-reward combination

Once your dog is trained, an event marker becomes less essential. Since the marker is no longer needed for learning—to mark a reward-worthy behavior—you can transition to simply using verbal praise to both mark and reinforce compliance. It's important to differentiate between the marker and the reward in the learning stages, but once your dog is trained, verbal praise can serve as both. If your dog's performance deteriorates, simply separate the two. Mark the behavior, and then reward it with something of higher value than verbal praise.

To keep your dog's enjoyment and responsiveness high, surprise your dog from time-to-time with a really good reward, like finding the Hamburger Tree (see page 68). Think of other ways to amaze and surprise your dog with a wonderful reward. *Your* reward is your dog's reliable performance—a win-win for both of you.

III

PART III: Brass Tacks

One must learn by doing the thing, for though you think
you know it, you have no certainty until you try.

—Aristotle

Overview

From basic manners to competitive dog sports, to solving problems and eliminating undesirable behavior with clicker training, the following chapters put it all together. You'll find specific ideas, suggestions, and guidelines for everything from planning a training session to ways to strengthen behavior, building reliability around distractions, and training virtually any behavior you want your dog to perform. To paraphrase Aristotle—the way to learn clicker training is to clicker train. Have fun with it!

Chapter 10

PUNISHMENT, CORRECTIONS, AND THE CROSSOVER TRAINER

My Crossover Journal
There were a few inches of fresh, powdery snow on the ground
the day that Hobbes, a four-year-old Springer Spaniel I had just
adopted, met Shura, my five-year-old, 160 pound English Mastiff. Clearly exhib-
iting a death wish, Hobbes raced up to Shura, hackles raised, teeth bared, snarl-
ing, and barking aggressively. Soundlessly, without the slightest bit of aggression,
Shura simply knocked Hobbes down and lay on top of him. As snow spewed out
from under her, we could hear Hobbes' outrage and indignation muffled by Shu-
ra's massive body. Calmly keeping him imprisoned, she adeptly used her forelegs
to block his attempts to extricate himself. Once his fury was spent, she simply
stood up. Hobbes shook himself off—and for the rest of their many years together,
showed Shura nothing but the greatest respect. Not just toward Shura—Hobbes'
aggressive attitude toward all dogs changed that day.

Undesirable behavior exists. Dogs do "bad" things—not because they are bad, but because they are *dogs*. What is perfectly normal behavior to a dog may be disadvantageous and undesirable to the owner. As much as we may want to focus on good behavior, we cannot ignore the other side of the coin. Dogs invariably do some things we don't like.

The central theme of clicker training is using an event marker and positive reinforcement to teach behaviors we want the dog to perform, but this focus does not always address behaviors we *don't* want. Like me, many crossover trainers come from methods that involve "correcting" problem behaviors using non-clicker solutions. Virtually every training method offers techniques and recommendations to address these behaviors. Often the solution lies in positive reinforcement training, but sometimes it may not.

The information in this chapter is for crossover trainers to learn how clicker training can change undesirable behavior and to make well-reasoned choices between your previously-successful techniques, and choosing an approach consistent with clicker training.

Living as closely as we do with our dogs—sharing our homes, our sofas and beds, our food, our family, our fun—sure as shootin' the time will come when something the dog does conflicts with what his human wants. While it would be wonderful if we never had to deal with a dog's undesirable behavior, that's not realistic. Dogs are dogs.

Dogs are opportunists. If the dog has the opportunity to do something that feels good, tastes good, or is fun, he will. Given this self-serving character (and living with us 24/7), dogs have regular opportunities to engage in activities and do things we don't want them to do.

Much of the time, an owner simply reacts to her dog's misbehavior by firmly saying, *"Off!"* to the dog that's jumping up, or hollering, *"Quiet!"* at the barking dog. Such reactions don't improve behavior. Rather than being reactive—responding to what the dog is already doing—what is needed is an effective, proactive strategy to address the undesirable behavior before it starts—to control, circumvent, reduce, or eliminate it altogether. There are four specific areas to consider in fulfilling our job as a dog's best friend, trainer, and ally.

1. **Management**—to prevent the dog from doing something wrong.
2. **Training**—to put the dog in a position to do what is right.
3. **Direct intervention**—to modify the dog's undesirable behavior, if that becomes necessary.
4. **Understanding**—providing the thinking dog with the awareness, insight, and ability to make right choices.

Management

Management is a strategy that *prevents* the dog from engaging in an activity or performing a behavior that would be disadvantageous, damaging, or dangerous. Critical to any approach to problem resolution, management prevents the dog from "practicing" undesirable behaviors. It stops the dog engaging in the behavior, and thereby intermittently receiving whatever rewards the behavior might produce.

Remember Thorndike's Law about consequences (good and bad) affecting behavior. The goal of management is to prevent the dog experiencing good consequences (from his point of view) by doing bad things (from our viewpoint). Management alone is not training, however, and doesn't involve learning.

The two aspects of management that stop a dog from "getting into trouble" are: (1) managing the dog; and (2) managing the environment, or "dog proofing." When no one is able to supervise or train, safe confinement in a dog-proof room, area, or crate prevents a dog getting into trouble. *A dog can wreak havoc in less time than it takes for a quick shower. If you can't watch him, confine him.*

In the absence of a management plan, success with any strategy for behavior modification is difficult, if not impossible.

My Crossover Journal
A woman living on a fenced, three-acre property with both land-scaped areas and woods consulted us for help training her adoles-cent Labrador Retriever not to chew wood. At the top of her "forbidden items" list was her outdoor furniture, but the list also included shrubs, tree branches, even twigs and sticks that had fallen on the ground. She was unwilling to go out with her dog, would not watch him through a window, didn't want to put up a smaller enclosure to confine him, put him on a line, or do anything we said would be necessary to limit his activities while he was being trained. Since she refused all management suggestions, insisting on giving the dog unfettered access to what she didn't want him to do, we could not help her.

Environmental management prevents your dog getting into things she shouldn't.

Training

I am first and foremost a dog trainer. Even when helping people address and eliminate their dogs' behavior problems, my focus is on training—teaching the dog the behaviors the owner wants. Training is often enough to eliminate undesirable behavior, but even when training isn't enough by itself, it forms the foundation for other solutions. There are several aspects to training to affect undesirable behavior:

- **Unlearning**—teaching the dog that it is no longer advantageous to engage in a behavior that used to be reinforced.

- **Training manners**—laying the foundation for all good behavior.

- **Training an alternative "good" behavior**—teaching the dog what to do "right" in place of the "wrong."

Unlearning

Let's start with "unlearning" or changing the dog's perspective—a training principle known as **extinction**. Some problem behaviors respond well, and will extinguish by simply being ignored. This approach will not work for all behaviors (see "Self-reinforcing behaviors" below), but it works with behaviors that meet three criteria:

1. The behavior has a reinforcement history—it has been rewarded in the past.

2. Reinforcement is completely eliminated.

3. There is 100% consistency.

Behaviors that fit the "ignorable" category are those for which we are able to control the reinforcement, such as begging for food or pestering for attention. Begging is reinforced when the dog gets a treat. Eliminating all reinforcement means that no matter what the dog does, he will never get even a morsel of food in response to begging. Management is a critical component, with everyone in the family on-board and committed to eliminating it.

By totally ignoring any and all persistent, annoying, demanding behavior, begging will diminish, then extinguish. However, if the dog gets the smallest scrap of food in response to begging—even a crumb dropped accidentally—the behavior will be stronger and more persistent than ever. It takes 100% consistency, or the behavior is randomly reinforced, making it more resilient.

The same strategy can work with pestering, a behavior that is reinforced by attention and petting.

My Crossover Journal

A student described how she trained her dog, Ivy, that when she was done petting, Ivy should not pester her for more. Susan said, "All done," and folded her arms. Ivy nuzzled her elbow which Susan ignored. As the nuzzling got stronger, Susan held her arms closer. Ivy pawed at her; when that didn't work, she jumped up on Susan and pulled on her sleeve. Ivy escalated her persistent, obnoxious pestering, until Susan climbed up on the sofa and turned her back, ignoring Ivy. Unable to gain Susan's attention, Ivy finally gave up. The next time Susan said, "All done," Ivy tried to get Susan to pet her, but gave up much sooner. Each subsequent time she tried, Ivy's efforts were less prolonged until ultimately "All done" meant all done.

Self-reinforcing behaviors

Unlearning by ignoring a behavior will not work with a behavior that is innate, instinctive, and hard-wired—that is "self-reinforcing." The reward is intrinsic, and better than any consequence you might provide. A terrier that is digging after a woodchuck or chasing a chipmunk will be undeterred by either the promise of a treat, or the threat of a time-out. A hound in hot pursuit of a fox will return home with a huge smile, despite having run through painful thorns and brambles. To a sporting dog, scenting birds is manna from Heaven, far greater than any treat you may have in your pocket. Ignoring such behaviors, hoping they go away on their own is useless—the dog gets the best possible reward from the behavior itself.

Don't misunderstand. It isn't that you can't have a trained dog in environments that trigger his instincts. You can, but not by using *this* strategy. Ignoring instinctive behavior won't work to eliminate it. Reinforcement comes from the behavior itself.

Training manners—the foundation for everything

Laying a foundation of good behavior is the most important element in modifying undesirable behavior. Trained dogs are well-behaved, not because they know what "good" behavior is, but because we teach the responses we want and influence the dog's activities, limiting them to actions or non-actions we like and reinforce. By training polite behavior (manners) we reward the behavior we like, while avoiding situations or preventing the dog learning the bad stuff.

Manners-training provides two important things:

- **A foundation of good behaviors to call upon.** Whatever approach you may choose for dealing with undesirable behavior, manners-training provides alternative, "rewardable" behaviors. Teaching good behavior is critical both to the elimination of problem behavior as well establishing a healthy relationship with your dog.
- **Control over your dog's behavior when you're with him.** *When you're with him.* It is important to recognize, however, that until the dog has generalized good behavior, someone needs to be there to hold sway over his activities. *When left to his own devices, the dog's behavior is what it is—he is a dog.*

Training does not automatically mean *self*-control in the absence of *person*-control, that comes later. First, let's explore what manners-training means.

Manners do's versus don'ts

Ask most owners what they want their dog to do when greeting Grandma, for instance, and they'll say, "I don't want him to jump on her." It is natural to express what we "want" as the *absence* of a behavior, as a "don't." Don't beg food at the table, don't go in the trash, don't get on the couch, and the like.

Trying to train a "don't"—the absence of behavior—leaves the dog open to all sorts of alternative possibilities. Don't jump on Grandma? How about sniffing her impolitely? Or running under her skirt? How about if I bark at her? Get the picture? You cannot train a "don't." But you can train a "do"—a concrete, realizable, doable behavior that the dog will learn to offer because it's better (more reinforcing) than jumping on Grandma. Further, viewing a behavior as something to get rid of pits trainer-against-behavior. To teach "Don't jump on Grandma" means attacking the behavior with an unpleasant consequence. Many crossover trainers are familiar with approaches that "attack" jumping behavior such as a knee to the chest, stepping on the dog's rear feet, giving a collar correction, or holding tight to his front feet. Attacking "don't bark" means yelling, "Quiet!" Attacking pulling means giving a leash correction—each distinctly un-clicker.

Crossover trainers find that clicker training offers a profoundly different perspective. As the old song goes, clicker trainers *Accentuate the positive, eliminate the negative, latch on to the affirmative, and don't mess with Mister In-between.* Rather than view a behavior as a "don't"—the "bad" to be gotten rid of—clicker training focuses on a glimmer of "the good," builds upon, fosters, and reinforces it.

Replace *don'ts* by visualizing the behavior you *do* want. Do greet guests while standing or sitting politely, do relax on your bed during dinner, do walk by my side on a loose leash. Since many crossover trainers come from methods that "fix" bad behavior, this change in perspective may take deliberative attention. It may not come naturally, but is well worth the effort. One of the most significant differences between clicker training and other approaches is that by focusing on the do's, we can often achieve the behavior we want without needing to employ undesirable consequences.

Teach an alternative (good) behavior

Dogs don't inherently know what "the right" behavior is, but when *you* know what you want, you can train it. Replacing the "don'ts" of your dog's behavior with "do's" is called training **incompatible behaviors**—incompatible because the dog cannot perform more than one behavior at a time. When he is offering the right behavior, he cannot be engaged in the wrong one. A dog cannot sit while simultaneously jumping on Grandma. Sitting is *incompatible* with jumping on guests (or sniffing them, pulling their clothes, or nipping them).

By visualizing what you want your dog to do, you can train desirable, incompatible behaviors. Figure 10-1 is an overview of a few easy-to-train behaviors incompatible with many common complaints.

"Good" behaviors to replace the "bad"

Undesirable Behavior	Incompatible Behavior(s)
Jumping on guests	Sit, stand, lie on your bed when the doorbell rings
Running away	Come when called, stay
Pulling on leash	Walk politely on a loose leash, heel
Barking for attention	Settle, quiet behavior (mouth closed), get/hold a toy
Menacing the mailman	Get/hold a toy, settle
Taking food from the kids	Lie down, sit, settle, get/hold a toy, leave it (back away or turn away)
Resource retention (guarding an object)	Bring object, drop it, or give it up willingly

Figure 10-1. Common complaints about a dog's behavior, and some corresponding incompatible behaviors.

> ## To teach "quiet" to a dog barking in his crate
>
> Here's an approach to training the incompatible behavior—"quiet" for a dog barking in his crate. Stay nearby out of sight, and wait for a few seconds of quiet. Mark it with "yes" as you enter the room, and immediately open the crate, rewarding quiet with freedom. Gradually increase the time your dog remains quiet (yo-yo between short and longer) before you mark, enter, and let him out of the crate.
>
> It is important, too, to reward your dog *before he starts barking* in the first place. Consider that if you reinforce him for quiet only *after he stops barking*, he isn't learning to be in his crate *without barking at all*.

Training an incompatible behavior begins in a teachable environment—away from whatever triggers the behavior. While you're in the process of training the "good" behavior, use management strategies so your dog doesn't continue to practice the "bad" one.

For example, to train an incompatible behavior to jumping on people (one of the most common complaints we hear) select the behavior you want your dog to do. Stand or sit, for example, both work well for polite greetings. As with training any affirmative behavior, the first step is "get the behavior." Click when he's standing with all four feet on the floor, or when he sits. To increase his commitment to remain in position, jump up and down, wave your arms, and click before your dog's feet leave the floor. By performing actions that entice jumping, and clicking before he jumps, your dog learns the good behavior and gets rewarded for it.

Becke stands politely without even attempting to jump up as Denise helps her learn to ignore enticements, and Lynn Marie marks and rewards Becke's good behavior.

Replace the bad with the good

Once your dog has learned the incompatible behavior, the final step is to practice it in the "real life" environment that triggers the problem behavior. But such real life situations usually occur randomly without warning (you never know when a door-to-door salesman will knock). To control the training session so you are able to focus completely on your dog, set-up simulated, real-life circumstances to practice and reward your dog's "good" behavior.

To create "real-life" for polite greeting, for example, once you've trained sit or stand still when you and your family approach, invite friends over to help. Prepare them, explaining that you'll be focusing on your dog and may even have to close the door on them while you attend to her training.

It generally takes three or four set-up training sessions for most dogs to satisfactorily offer the incompatible behavior in the problem-triggering context. In the meantime use management to prevent your dog practicing the "bad" behavior. This may sound like a long process, but it can happen quite quickly. Your thinking dog will quickly learn to choose the good behavior.

My Crossover Journal

Students in a class to teach clicker training to crossover dogs from other methods were given an assignment. Their homework was to identify a behavior they didn't like, and clicker train an incompatible behavior. The next week, Joan, the owner of an active, two-year-old Rhodesian Ridgeback, reported her progress. "My husband and I have an in-home business," she began, "and Marti typically jumps on our clients as they come through our garden gate. We have to keep her shut away, which we hate to do, so my plan was to click four-on-the-floor—a stand—to replace jumping up. It went so well, we actually had a client this week that said Marti is "mellow." "You see Marti," she said, pointing to her active dog. "She's never been accused of being 'mellow' in her life! We are thrilled!"

Reinforce what you like

Once your dog knows the "good" behavior, it's important to let him know that you appreciate it. The adage, "Let sleeping dogs lie" does a disservice to dogs being good. It implies that if your dog isn't doing something wrong, ignore him. But when you've trained an incompatible behavior, you need to let your dog know that he is doing something right. Don't ignore "right" behavior. Let your dog know you appreciate his good effort! For example, Shari, one of our trainers, adopted an adolescent Lab mix, Mazzie, who had some behaviors that needed addressing. The worst was that Mazzie would rush over and leap on anyone who came to Shari's office door. Having worked on replacing Mazzie's jumping behavior, now when someone comes to her door, Shari smiles at Mazzie, who understands that the smile—a reinforcement to her—is for choosing the "right" behavior. Shari's smile says, "I see you being good. Thank you!"

The combination of management, manners training, teaching and reinforcing an incompatible behavior takes care of many problem behaviors...but not all. If these strategies don't do the trick, the next approach is direct intervention—teaching the dog that engaging in the target behavior results in an undesirable consequence.

I won't ask anything.
I answer only if he asks.

Direct intervention

There are behaviors for which management, ignoring, or training don't do the trick. It is important for the crossover trainer to know how to effectively use direct intervention for behaviors that are not addressed by other strategies. While two of the four behavior quadrants (the way dogs learn) include the word "punishment," many trainers resist even considering its use. Remember, in behavioral terms "punishment," or the just-slightly-less distasteful euphemism "aversives," simply means a disincentive that reduces or eliminates a behavior.

It would be wonderful to wave a magic wand over undesirable behavior, but life isn't Fantasy Land. Trainers need information—*an understanding of the concepts and results of consequences in all four quadrants, each one of which affects behavior.* Making informed decisions about employing both reinforcement and punishment within the framework of clicker training makes the crossover trainer the best trainer, the best friend, and the best advocate for her dog she can be.

Punishment is not a bad word

It was on an Internet clicker list shortly after I crossed over that I first encountered the controversy about "punishment" when one prolific contributor wrote, "Let's call a spade a spade. Aversives have to inflict pain to be effective." Misconceptions about punishment are exemplified in this assertion "aversives have to inflict pain."

This commonly-held perspective is both wrong and stifling to the flow of information and knowledge. Whether or not a consequence is aversive has nothing to do with *our feelings.* It's all about the dog's perspective. To affect behavior, an aversive simply has to be undesirable to the dog—a disincentive. It is not necessary that it be painful.

My Crossover Journal
Julie took her one year old Springer spaniel, Jagger, for a run in a field. To avoid his linking "come when called" with the end of fun—an association that could eradicate his willing recall—Julie called him, gave him a big reward, then released him to run again. Everything went well until it was time to leave. She called him, and as Jagger eagerly ran toward her, Julie pulled his leash out of her pocket. Jagger stopped dead in his tracks, turned, and bounded across the field, ignoring her repeated calls.

In this context, the leash is an aversive that represents "end of run." However neither the sight of the leash, nor the consequence it represents inflicts pain. Far from needing to be painful to affect behavior, a punisher is simply something the dog does not want within the specific context.

What is *punishment* in one context, may well be *reinforcement* in another. Before leaving the house for their outing, the sight of Jagger's leash triggered excitement and glee—the same leash, two different reactions. So how can a trainer figure out what is and is not punishment?

Seeing Julie holding his leash, Jagger took off. In this context, his leash represents "punishment."

Punishment versus reinforcement—bad versus good?

As with reinforcement, punishment is evaluated after the fact, solely by its success in having modified the behavior.

- When a behavior increases, the consequence that followed the behavior is an incentive called "reinforcement."

- When a behavior decreases, the corresponding consequence is a disincentive called "punishment."

Punishment is not defined by opinion or feelings, but by its effect. When the outcome that follows a behavior reduces the likelihood of that behavior being repeated, that outcome (the consequence) is punishment. For example, picture a dog tied to a dog-house, isolated and ignored, barking out of boredom. His owner comes out and yells at him to be quiet. After being scolded several times, the barking gets worse. The owner thinks, "Stupid dog, why doesn't he get it?" He does get it—he gets that the consequence for barking is companionship. When viewed by its impact on the behavior, the scolding—which most of us think of as punishment—was reinforcement.

Some trainers want to use only positive reinforcement in training, but positive reinforcement doesn't have a squeaky clean rap sheet either. As with this example of the barking dog, reinforcement (from the dog's perspective) can increase *undesirable* behavior. Consider the affect of petting the growling dog or—as we've had clients try—throwing a box of dog biscuits at their pestering dog to keep him busy so "at least he's quiet for awhile."

As these examples illustrate neither punishment nor reinforcement *per se* is harmful to dogs or to our relationship with them. Rather, it is failing to fully grasp how both good and bad consequences affect behavior that opens us up to making errors that may adversely impact our dogs and our relationships. To avoid the pitfalls, to employ both good and bad consequences intelligently, fairly, humanely, and successfully, trainers need knowledge—facts, not feelings.

My Crossover Journal

Hobbes, the Springer Spaniel, was diagnosed by a veterinary behaviorist as having "idiopathic aggression," and scheduled for euthanasia. Being an insane dog trainer, I loved the dog, so when his owners offered him to me, Hobbes became mine. Especially dangerous if he had something in his mouth, he had a hair-trigger bite response, and no bite inhibition—Hobbes bit suddenly and damagingly hard. Over time, I had built his trust sufficiently that I could carefully take things from him, but when I wasn't there, the house rule—which at the time included the office—was that if Hobbes has something, get a treat and trade.

Shortly after Myrian started working for me, I was out at a training lesson when Hobbes came into her office carrying a shoe. Myrian got up, went to the kennel where the biscuits were kept, and traded biscuit-for-shoe. A little while later she heard Hobbes go upstairs, and then reappear with the other shoe in his mouth. He paused briefly in her office doorway, and as soon as she looked up, led the way to the kennel. Still holding the shoe, he put his feet on the counter, and patiently waited for his biscuit.

Hobbes learned to bring shoes to exchange for treats.

Unintentional punishment—affecting "good" behavior

Here's Thorndike again. Since consequences rule behavior (for good or ill), consider a consequence from your dog's point-of-view. If what follows the dog's behavior is undesireable, she's less likely to offer that behavior again. This works in your favor for behaviors you don't like, but must also be a consideration with behaviors you *do* like. Without being aware, it is easy to inadvertently punish good behavior.

Consider, for example, the consequence that follows "come when called" if you immediately shut your dog in a crate and leave for work. "Come" was "punished" by being shut away. Likewise, a dog will quickly learn "keep away" if what follows getting caught—that is, your taking hold of your dog's collar—is less-than-desirable.

Knowing they shouldn't call a dog to chastise him, some people mistakenly believe that it is OK to go to the dog, take him by the collar, and show him his transgression. Regardless of the owner's *intent*, "getting caught" was "punished" by a scolding—precisely how to teach "keep away." An aversive consequence followed "getting caught," so the behavior decreases—the dog learns to stay just out of "catching" range.

So what can you do? After all, you need be able to trim his nails, put him in his crate, or do something else he may consider undesirable. And if you can't call him or go get him...well, you can. You can separate the good response from the undesirable event. Reward the behavior by spending thirty seconds interacting pleasantly with your dog, and then introduce the *new* situation. The passage of time separates the "good" behavior—coming—from the less desirable activity, preventing its association with punishment.

Punishment just is

Punishment exists. Humans didn't invent it, nature did. Dogs rebuke each other, cats slash with their claws, horses kick, falling down hurts, fire burns. Life is not a bowl of cherries.

Perhaps mistaking being "positive" with being "permissive," some dog owners strive to save their dogs from experiencing anything unpleasant, restrictive, or even mildly disagreeable—a concept that is foreign to life itself. "Nanny" TV programs showcase the holy-terror results of an indulgent attitude toward children. With dogs, as with children, the predictable result of permissiveness is out-of-control behavior. Dogs thrive on having clear-cut boundaries for both their acceptable and unacceptable behavior—boundaries that are learned through experiencing consequences.

Our dogs' brains, much like our own, are programmed to learn important lessons from less-than-desirable consequences. Dogs are hard-wired to administer, accept, understand, and *learn from* consequences, just as in the introduction to this chapter, Hobbes learned from Shura in just one well-applied lesson.

At just a few weeks of age, through playful interaction with her siblings, a puppy learns what it feels like to be bitten by a littermate, and the consequences that result when she, herself, bites too hard. More than just helpful, *learning from consequences is critical to peaceful interaction, conflict avoidance, "civilized" behavior, avoiding injury, and evading danger.*

We don't have to touch a glowing red stove coil to know that it will burn us. Likewise, puppies learn to heed the threatening look, or respect Mom's warning growl (see "Life lessons: Learning about punishment markers" on page 202). Most puppies need just one lesson to learn that bothering the cat earns a swat on the nose. Such punishment teaches the puppy to respect the cat's warning hiss, avoiding future scratches.

Assessing and evaluating punishment

Crossover trainers generally fall into two camps when it comes to considering punishment. There are those that say, "No, never, ever! You can't make me!" and there are those that say, "Hey, I use it, and my dogs and our relationship are just fine!" Feeling the need to justify simply asking a question about punishment on an Internet training list, one member wrote, "How will I know how to avoid doing something wrong if I don't know what 'wrong' is?"

To determine what "wrong" is, a trainer needs principles by which to assess and evaluate aversive consequences. With a principle-centered approach, the trainer can make informed, rational, well-thought-out decisions about employing a punishing consequence...or not.

The four principles

There are four principles by which to assess punishment, whether positive (bad things happen) or negative (good things stop).

1. **The consequence must work.** It must affect the targeted behavior by reducing or eliminating its recurrence.

2. **It must be fair to the dog and be applied fairly.** To be fair, the dog must be able to understand what earned the consequence, and be able to avoid it in the future.

3. **The consequence must do no harm to the dog, or to the dog/owner relationship.** Do no harm to the dog means avoiding physical pain as well as emotional reactions such as anxiety or fear. The dog should not associate the punishment with the person (which can cause mistrust or fear), but rather with the *behavior that earned it.*

4. **The undesirable behavior must be easily supplanted by a desirable one.** The "bad" behavior needs to be replaced by a "good" one—one that leads to reinforcement. Further, this needs to happen quickly, with few repetitions of the undesirable consequence.

Before examining how punishment fits with clicker training, let's explore how these four principles are applied—or not—in some common, other-than-clicker training approaches used by many crossover trainers.

Many training methods use a variety of applications of positive punishment (bad things happen). Typically positive punishment techniques are applied in one of three ways.

- To train new behaviors.
- To eliminate non-compliance.
- To eradicate problem behaviors.

Here's a brief rundown of each.

Positive punishment (P+) for training new behaviors. Some compulsion-praise methods of training use collar corrections (a "check" or jerk on the collar) to teach new behaviors, punishing anything that *isn't* the desired behavior. To teach heeling, for example, the trainer corrects the dog for being out of heel position. The check punishes "not-being-at-heel." By learning to avoid the punisher, the dog learns to remain close to the handler's left side. "Stay," as well, may be taught using a collar check—if the dog moves, he gets a correction. The dog avoids moving to evade punishment.

Whether or not you would choose to use this approach (and I have used it) the techniques work. There are shortcomings, however, that don't meet the four principles.

- "Correction" implies the dog erred. When being introduced to a new behavior, the dog cannot know what is and is not an error. Without knowing what to do right, the dog can't avoid doing wrong, and getting corrected many times. Failing Principle #2, the fairness doctrine.

- The dog *must* endure punishment multiple times in many "wrong" contexts in order to learn the desired behavior. Failing Principle #4, easy and fast replacement by a desired behavior.

Some crossover trainers may be thinking, "Yes, but she didn't mention praising when the dog is in the right position. That's reinforcement for the right behavior!" Sure it is, but not until after the dog has been punished first. Failing Principle #2, it's unfair to the dog.

Positive punishment (P+) for non-compliance. Next are techniques that employ punishment for non-compliance, or "disobedience." If the dog breaks a stay, for example, he receives a collar correction, and is put back in position.

- While inconsistent with clicker training, as long as there is sufficient training foundation to teach the dog what behavior(s) can avoid the punishment consequence, it may meet the "fairness doctrine."

- This approach does, however, negatively impact the dog/owner relationship. Often the dog offers calming signals as the owner approaches to "correct" a stay—lip licking, eyes averted, head turned, rapid blinking, sniffing, yawning, and more. The dog is saying, "Please...chill-out...you're making me anxious." Repeated use of punishment for non-compliance can lead to apprehension and fear. Failing Principle #3, it is harmful to the relationship.

Positive punishment (P+) for eliminating undesirable behavior. Some training methods recommend techniques such as pointing out the result of the dog's behavior, and scolding or isolating the dog. These include such things as taping a chewed object in the dog's mouth, or filling a hole with water and sticking his nose in it to stop him digging (yes, these are techniques in published training manuals). Such punishment-after-the-fact is called **noncontingent**. Here's the report card on this approach.

- Noncontingent punishment doesn't work. Failing Principle #1, the consequence must work.

- The dog does not relate his prior behavior with punishment-after-the-fact, so it is unfair. Failing Principle #2.

- Noncontingent punishment negatively impacts the dog/owner relationship. The dog fears the owner's approach. Failing Principle #3, it harms the relationship.

- The dog can never figure out an alternative, good behavior. Failing Principle #4, being easily replaced by a desirable behavior.

- This approach creates such anxiety that it often results in even worse behaviors—failing on all counts.

Citronella and "shock" collars

There is an application of positive punishment where even some "I never use punishment" trainers reside—possibly without realizing that they are using punishment. Many "positive" trainers will use citronella or shock collars for barking, for example, or install an invisible fence that uses a shock collar for containment within an area. Whether or not you choose to use one (and I don't, for myriad reasons), there is no getting around the fact that these collars employ positive punishment. Whether or not the *trainer* considers it an aversive, if it didn't constitute punishment to the *dog*, it wouldn't influence his behavior.

Using punishment in clicker training

Clicker training uses positive reinforcement for *teaching behaviors*. The focus is on providing information with clicks so that the dog makes the *right* choice and gets reinforced. Some trainers misinterpret the absence of punishment in teaching behaviors to mean that a clicker trainer does not use *any punishment at all*. This is simply not true. To affect misbehavior, punishment is one legitimate, effective approach, as long as the punishment meets the four criteria. Applications of punishment that meet these principles are not inconsistent with clicker training.

When considering employing punishment for your dog's unacceptable behavior, keep in mind the criteria by which to judge the consequence:

- It must be effective.
- It must be fair.
- It must do no harm.
- It must quickly result in good behavior.

There's more to it than just evaluating a punishing consequence, however. Punishment is used by people—and like it or not, people make mistakes. Given that, our goal should be to avoid, as much as possible, an error that can harm the dog or our relationship with the dog. Here are six fundamental elements to explore before considering the use of punishment.

1. **Target the behavior**. The trainer has to be clear on the specific behavior that is subject to punishment—to target the behavior, not the dog.

2. **The dog's understanding**. The dog has to know what "bad" behavior has earned the punishment.

3. **How to avoid punishment**. The dog has to know, and be able to offer, a "right" behavior to avoid the punishment in the future.

4. **The consequence**. The trainer has to decide what specific punishment to use and know how to apply it.

5. **It has to be effective**. The consequence must affect *the behavior*—otherwise, it's not punishment and may even be abuse.

6. **Ethical considerations**. Trainers need to consider the ethics of any approach they choose or choose not to use. *The bad rap that punishment gets is not due to using any punishment, but rather what results from incorrectly applied or inhumane punishment.*

Fundamental 1. Target the behavior, not the dog

The biggest failure with non-clicker techniques that use punishment is that such punishment targets *the dog*, to "teach him the error of his ways." Aside from causing anxiety, the dog can associate retribution-related punishment with the owner, the location in which the punishment takes place, or with some other unrelated factor—but *not* with the dog's own behavior.

Targeting *the behavior*, on the other hand, can and does reduce objectionable behavior without such fallout. So the first consideration in deciding to use punishment is to be clear about the behavior to be addressed. This focus will also help determine the best approach, which may not involve punishment at all.

Describe the behavior, don't "label" it. Dog owners often apply labels to a dog's behavior. Labels may come with pre-determined courses of action, often inappropriate for what the dog is, in fact, doing. A careful description of the dog's actions may lead you to an approach other than punishment. For example, two commonly applied labels are "dominant" and "separation anxiety."

When you label a behavior as "anxiety"—a mental state, an emotion—the pre-determined course of action may well be drug treatment. Labeling the dog as "dominant"— which assumes an intent on the part of the dog—presumes that the dog wants to be the King. To keep the dog from assuming the throne, from achieving his objective, the only course of action is for the owner to be more dominating than the dog—to keep the dog "in his place." But can we honestly assess a dog's emotional state or his intent? All we know, for sure, is what we see and what the dog does—his behavior.

Most of the time, what a dog labeled with separation anxiety is actually *doing* (the behavior) is "destructive chewing when no one is home." Rather, the most common reasons for destructive chewing are boredom, adolescent teething, or an outlet for tension resulting from the owner's prior angry responses. It has become a habit, because no one is there to tell him that it's wrong. When you describe *the behavior* as "chewing when left alone," the most logical approach is prevention. Prevent access to chewables through *management*—crate the dog, use a doggy daycare, and the like.

Behaviors labeled as "dominance" are many and varied, but what does "dominance" actually look like? What is the dominant dog doing? How about the behavior "rushing out the door first?" Does the dog rush outside because he wants to be Alpha, or because he wants to go out? Wanting to go outside has nothing to do with any imagined hierarchical relationship. Treatment for this behavior? *Training!* Teach "sit and wait."

What about "growling when he has something in his mouth?" Surely that's dominance, isn't it? When he growls, is it because his intention is to be in charge? Isn't it more likely that he growls because it's successful—he gets to keep what he has? The *behavior*—resource guarding—should be dealt with, not by addressing an imagined intent and thereby setting up an adversarial relationship, but by *training*—teaching an incompatible behavior such as "give it to me." Treating "dominance" with greater domination is antithetical to a cooperative relationship.

So the important first step in eliminating undesirable behavior is *to identify just what the dog is doing, the specific behavior to be addressed, and establishing the best approach*. If you have determined that punishment is the appropriate course to take, the next step is to ensure that your dog knows what that undesirable behavior is.

Fundamental 2. The dog's understanding—wrong versus right

To use a non-dog-training analogy, I hate hearing a complaint from a client. On the other hand, if we are doing something wrong in my business, we can't fix it if we don't know about it. So I am, in fact, grateful when a client lets me know we've got a problem. It's the same for your dog. He can't avoid doing something wrong if he doesn't know it's wrong, and he can't replace wrong behavior with right unless he understands that, too.

Timing is everything. Dogs live in the *now*. They can't fathom "last week" or "plan for the future." It's not that they don't have memories—they have excellent memories—but they don't make temporal associations such as, "Last week, when I was really good, Mom took me to the park. I'll be really good today, so maybe she'll take me again." Nor do they think, "I'm getting scolded for eating that cookie I stole from the baby thirty seconds ago."

Because of the immediacy of the dog's focus, to affect a behavior the consequence must be tied to the behavior. What makes the reinforcement marker—the click—so powerful in positive reinforcement training is that it says, *"That precise behavior just earned you a reward. Do it again, and you'll get another one."* Consider, then, how compelling it is to let the dog know exactly what he just did that earned punishment—what he needs to avoid doing in the future! To tell the dog that the behavior of this moment is subject to punishment, enter the marker for punishment.

"Yes" for good, "Nope" for bad. The marker for punishment zeros in on the undesirable behavior, telling the dog that the behavior he is engaging in *right now* has earned the consequence. A **punishment marker (PM)** can be a verbal utterance such as "Nope," "Ach," or "Stop;" or a sound such as a buzzer, a motion sensor alarm, or the like.

Just as the "Yes" marker is unemotional, so should your punishment marker be unemotional. Don't holler *"NO!!!!"* as in, "Bad dog! Shame on you!" The PM is not the punishment, it simply highlights the punishment-worthy behavior. As reinforcement follows the click, so, too, does punishment come after the PM.

The PM provides the critical information that connects the dog's behavior with the consequence. Once the dog makes that connection, rapid improvement most often follows. The dog knows what behavior to avoid doing to avert the consequence.

Dogs are not stupid. Consider why a dog would continue to engage in a behavior that he knows is disadvantageous. The answer is, he wouldn't! So when punishment doesn't change the dog's behavior, we need to examine why. There are two main reasons a dog continues performing a behavior that has earned punishment:

- **There's something in it for the dog.** There's more reinforcement to be gained from the behavior, than whatever consequence you think of as punishment. (Covered later in "Pick your punishment" on page 205.)
- **The dog hasn't connected the behavior with the consequence.** He doesn't get that what he's doing earned the punishment.

A thinking dog will quickly learn to avoid punishment (change his behavior) if he simply understands what he has done to earn it. It is incumbent upon us, therefore, to provide this information. Applying punishment without the dog being able to recognize precisely what behavior earned that punishment is not just ineffective, it is unfair and unethical.

Say "no" to a "no vocabulary"

Select and apply one punishment marker for all undesirable behaviors. If your dog is doing something punishment-worthy, it earns your one, universal PM. A "no vocabulary" such as "no sniff," "no bark," "no bite," "no jump," "no dig," or "no (fill in the blank)" lacks helpful information. A "no (behavior)" is as meaningless as is the cue-after-praise, "good sit." Identifying a behavior with "no" makes two presumptions. First, that the dog understands "no" means "don't do (this behavior),"—which he may. However, the second presumption is that he understands that the behavior he's engaged in is called "sniff," "bark," "bite," "dig," or "jump." Unless you've taught your dog a word association for that behavior, he has no clue what the "no" modifies. Further, how fair is it to ask a dog—a species that investigates his environment through his nose, just as we do with our eyes—to stop sniffing?

Again, picture *do* rather than *don't*. For example, the behavior most people want when they say, "no sniff" is "walk with your head up." Train the incompatible behavior "walk with your head up" and give it the cue, "heel." When you don't care if your dog investigates the ground, use a different cue such as, "let's go."

Teach your dog positively reinforced, incompatible behaviors, and drop the "no's."

Fundamental 3. How to avoid punishment—this is what you can do right instead

Having identified for the dog the punishment-earning behavior, we need to make sure that he knows how to avoid it—that he knows a "good" behavior to choose. Choosing to do right not only replaces the undesirable behavior, but the ultimate goal is for the dog to choose right behavior without engaging in "wrong" ones.

The joy of preventing punishment. Wouldn't it be nice if we could avoid unpleasantness? Remember how you felt when your mother gave you "the raised-eyebrow look?" You knew you needed to not do what you were about to do…or else. Most likely, you stopped and reconsidered your actions—you didn't need to experience "or else."

Knowing that something bad is lurking around a corner, we would avoid turning that corner. So would your dog. When we give our dogs information that helps them safely interact with their environment with as little conflict as possible—so they don't "turn the corner into danger"—we are acting in their best interest, helping them avoid aversive consequences, stress, and anxiety. But it gets even better.

With clicker training, you will not only find that minimal punishment is sufficient to eliminate undesirable behavior, but that you have the opportunity to eliminate bad behavior *without using any punishment at all*. Once the dog makes the connection between the PM and a resulting consequence, the PM—much like Mom's raised eyebrow—tells the dog, "The behavior you are about to engage in is 'dangerous'." The further message is, "If you don't engage in that behavior, you'll avoid danger—nothing bad will happen." Consider the reinforcement of not only making the right choice and avoiding punishment, but getting a reward for choosing the right behavior to boot.

Think about this win-win situation—how clean and elegant it is to use a punishment marker as an opportunity for the dog to earn reinforcement. By giving the dog the opportunity to *choose the good behavior* on his own, we not only put him in a position to control himself, but we don't need to use punishment. How great is that?!

Life lessons—learning about punishment markers

Just as we recognize the meaning of the "raised-eyebrow look," puppies learn critical "life lessons" from Mom. For example, during the weaning process, if the puppy bites Mom with his needle-sharp teeth, she gives him a warning look or growl. At first he ignores the warning because it has no significance, no frame of reference. But Mom follows the warning with the lesson, "Pay attention to 'the look' or 'growl'—it's a punishment marker for the behavior you were engaging in. The tag I'm about to give you is the consequence for hurting me." Generally all it takes is one or two such events for a puppy to forever recognize and respond to a warning.

Learning this lesson enables a dog to avoid conflict with another dog, rarely needing the consequence of a bite. The look or growl—the PM— is sufficient to change the dog's behavior, thereby avoiding danger.

We, too, are the beneficiaries of this early learning. Because dogs understand the significance of a punishment marker, they are well-able to learn *our* PMs. Once learned, the association gives a mere sound the ability to affect behavior. Thank you, Mom!

A puppy learns punishment markers from his Mom.

Both manners-training and teaching incompatible behaviors help build the critical foundation to put the dog in position to "do right." But sometimes foundation training alone is not enough to eliminate undesirable behavior. What may be required to finish the job is putting the two together—reinforcing the "good" and punishing the "bad." By creating a dichotomy between the good and bad behaviors—Behavior "A" earns reinforcement, Behavior "B" earns punishment—the dog learns to choose "A," the good, desirable, reinforceable behavior. Sounds too simple? It is just that simple! You'll see.

Fundamental 4. The consequence—what and how to apply punishment

Having examined what the dog is doing (the behavior), how to let the dog know what behavior is disadvantageous (the PM), and what the dog needs to know (foundation manners, training an incompatible behavior), next is what the trainer needs to know.

- The differences between negative and positive punishment.
- Selecting the least aversive consequence to get the job done.
    - The right consequence for the dog.
    - The right consequence for the behavior.
- Timing punishment properly.
- Preparation—setting it up for success.
- Application—the right way to do it.
- Aftermath—what follows the punishing consequence.

The two applications of punishing consequences are negative (good things stop) and positive (bad things happen). Table 10-2 contains a list of some specific consequences consistent with clicker training, and some that aren't.

You lose—the power of negative punishment. For most dogs, negative punishment (you lose, good things stop) is all that is needed to eliminate wayward ways. Even a crossover dog that is used to collar corrections (P+) can be profoundly affected by negative punishment.

Negative punishment includes withholding or removing something the dog wants, preventing him from accessing or participating in something he likes, and removing him from something he enjoys. Here's a sampling of ways to use negative punishment with:

- A treat—put it away or give it to another dog

- A toy—take it briefly or put it away

- Your attention—turn your head or turn away or ignore your dog or pay attention to another dog or remove yourself, leave.

- An activity—stop the activity or remove the dog

- A time-out—put the dog on a down or in a crate or in another room.

For how long? For most negative punishment, a few seconds to let it sink in is enough. For a bigger infraction—say one that requires your dog to be removed from the activity or put in his crate—do a slow count to ten. If you have to repeat the time-out, give it 30 seconds to a minute. This doesn't mean you can't leave your dog crated longer, for instance if you yourself need a break, but a longer time-out is not likely to have more impact on the behavior than a short one. Table 10-3 has specific recommendations for using negative punishment.

Applying positive punishment. Some behaviors may require, and will respond well to the application of a positive punisher such as a sharp utterance. One of the many (wonderful) surprises I've discovered since crossing over is that the more training a dog has with a behavior marker and positive reinforcement, the less the dog requires any positive punishment, rarely needing more than a mild warning that has been associated with a punishment marker (see "Understanding" on page 200). Where I used to say *"AH ACH!!!"* I now need to utter just a soft "uh." While this is definitely the case with dogs that are clicker trained from scratch, it becomes the case with many crossover dogs as well.

Examples of punishers

Consistent with clicker training	Inconsistent with clicker training (All are P+)
<ul><li>Remove attention (P-)<ul><li>Turn head</li><li>Turn away</li><li>Walk away, leave</li></ul></li><li>Withhold/remove food (P-)</li><li>Withhold/remove other reinforcement (P-)</li><li>Withhold/remove access (P-)</li><li>"Time out" (P-)<ul><li>Lie down (ignore)</li><li>Put in crate</li></ul></li><li>Remove from area (P-)</li><li>End the activity (P-)</li><li>Brief verbal utterance (P+)</li><li>Water spritz (P+)</li></ul>	<ul><li>Yelling, chastising, prolonged scolding</li><li>Scruff shake</li><li>Muzzle hold</li><li>Fingers or fist in mouth</li><li>Ear pinch</li><li>Hit dog with throw chain, shake can, etc.</li><li>Frighten or startle dog with noise maker</li><li>Corporal punishment (hit, slap, etc.)</li><li>Collar corrections</li><li>Hanging or elevating</li><li>Knee to chest</li><li>Step on feet</li><li>"Alpha roll" or any physical domination</li><li>Repeatedly punishing without results</li></ul>

Table 10-2. This partial list includes punishments that are consistent and inconsistent with clicker training.

My Crossover Journal
Mayday, my crossover dog, was often lying under my desk while I returned phone calls. If I needed to advise a client to say "Ah! Ah!" even though Mayday was clearly not doing anything wrong at the time, he would invariably get up and leave my office, going to lie under Myrian's desk. No matter how softly I said it, he left. I simply couldn't say it out loud—I had to spell it. Fortunately, Mayday couldn't spell.

It has to be effective—pick your punishment

Choose the least aversive consequence that will get the job done. You don't need an axe to swat a fly. If one consequence doesn't work—doesn't affect the behavior—re-evaluate and try another (see the "Rule of Three" on page 214).

To affect behavior, the consequence must be meaningful *to the dog*. It doesn't matter how *you* feel about the punishment—what matters is how your *dog* views it. "Meaningful" doesn't mean harsh, frightening, or painful; it means significant, objectionable—enough to be a disincentive.

Ineffective use of punishment, that is, employing a consequence that is not a sufficient disincentive, can be worse than doing nothing at all, resulting in one or more of the following.

- The behavior doesn't improve.

- An "ignorable" consequence may actually reinforce the behavior, intensifying it—making it more difficult to eliminate.

- Gradually building intensity in small increments can lead to the dog building a tolerance, or becoming desensitized to the consequence.

- Building a tolerance to negative punishment may require switching from negative to positive punishment to affect the behavior. Lack of success may strengthen the crossover trainer's belief in, and reliance on prior techniques inconsistent with clicker training.

- Lack of improvement frustrates the trainer, whose emotional reaction can negatively impact the dog, the relationship, and the dog's reaction to the punishing consequence. For example, if the trainer angrily storms out of the room, the resulting time-out may actually be a relief to the dog (negative reinforcement).

As with reinforcement, there's no one punishment that applies universally. The table below includes some considerations to take into account when choosing a consequence. Note that mark means punishment mark (PM) here.

Table 10-3. When, what, and how to apply punishment

The behavior	What to do and when
Jumping up	**Best**: Mark the intention behavior—muscles tensing, prior to take-off.
	Good: Mark the execution—while the dog is in mid-air, or has just landed on you.
	Too late: After the dog is back on the floor. Gravity took care of that; your timing was late.
	The punishment: Turn away, turning your back to your dog.
	Reinforce sit or stand before the dog jumps.
Counter surfing	**Best**: Mark the dog thinking about investigating the countertop
	Good: Mark the take-off before the dog has a chance to sniff the countertop.
	Too late: Once the dog's feet are on the counter, especially if the dog has eaten something—even a crumb.
	The punishment: Time-out—put the dog on a down, in a crate, or in another room.
	Reinforce look away, move away, or sit.

The behavior	What to do and when
Taking food from a child or off a table	**Best**: Mark the moment he notices the food. **Good**: Mark as he focuses on or moves toward the food. **Too late**: After he's tasted it; he's gotten a reward. **The punishment**: Time-out (as above) **Reinforce** looking away, moving away, choosing to avoid the food, or any cued behavior.
Chasing	**Best**: Mark the moment the dog's muscles tense, the moment he begins to move toward the object-of-interest. **Too late**: Anything after "don't even think about it" is too late. **The punishment**: Time-out (as above). **Reinforce** looking away, watching calmly, choosing to stay put—to not chase, or any cued behavior.
Inappropriate barking	**Best**: Mark any related utterance—even a whimper. **Good**: Mark the first bark. **Too late**: Waiting until after the dog has really mouthed off. **The punishment**: Time-out—put the dog on a down, in a crate, or in another room. **Reinforce** quiet—whatever activity the dog is engaging in without barking, or any cued behavior.
Inappropriate attention-seeking behavior	**Best**: Mark the first sign of attention-seeking—nudge, paw, bark, etc. **Good**: Mark after one or two repetitions of the behavior. **Too late**: After prolonged, persistent attention-seeking behavior. **The punishment**: Removal of your attention, time-out. **Reinforce** other-directed behavior, chewing a bone, lying down, etc.
Nipping in "play"	**Best**: Mark the moment the dog's tooth touches skin. **Too late**: Continuing an activity after your dog's tooth has grazed you, at best reinforces "carelessness." This is one time to react to random occurrences—if a tooth touches you, mark it. Game over. **The punishment**: End of activity, loss of attention, leave, or time-out. **Reinforce** Playing the game is reinforcing. As long as he plays by "the rules"—that is, no tooth on skin—the game is on.

If the owner is oblivious to what his dog is about to do, chastising the dog after he's taken the treat is too late to be effective.

Elements that influence the effect of punishment. All dogs are not equal—neither are all consequences. The impact and effectiveness of a chosen punishment depends on a variety of factors. These examples are offered as starting points to consider when choosing a consequence.

- **The dog.** The effectiveness of a consequence depends on the dog's temperament, personality, likes, and dislikes. For example, time-out is punishment for a dog that craves personal contact, but is less effective for a dog that is disinterested in companionship. Likewise, a non-food-motivated dog, won't care if you eat the treat.

- **The behavior.** The more reinforcing the behavior itself, the more meaningful the punishment needs to be—meaningful, not painful.

- **The environment.** Consider the reinforcement the dog is getting from the environment itself. Would he rather be elsewhere? Is there something in the environment that is reinforcing no matter what punishment you apply? Consider whether it is punishment to give a dog a time-out in a fenced yard where he can sniff, explore, roll in the grass, or play with another dog.

- **The moment.** This includes both the dog's and the trainer's mental state, and transitory, serendipitous, or accidental events that happen "in the moment."

- **The dog's history.** Including his upbringing, training, reinforcement history, and punishment history. The dog's past can impact the effect of different consequences. For example, a pet shop dog (not well-socialized, accustomed to living in a crate) may well be *happy* with a time-out—it may not constitute punishment.

Spontaneous versus recurring behavior. How the trainer applies punishment depends on whether the problem behavior just happens—is spontaneous—or is a recurring, repeated transgression.

- **Spontaneous events.** A serendipitous happening. Hobbes attacking Shura was a spontaneous event. Reacting at the moment with a spontaneous reprimand, a significant consequence (as Shura did with Hobbes), let the dog know that this behavior shouldn't be repeated. For the most part, reacting spontaneously to something the dog does at the moment is enough to nip the behavior in the bud. If the spontaneous reprimand doesn't affect the behavior, or if the behavior is reinforced, it will recur, putting it into the next category.

- **Recurring behaviors.** These behaviors recur within a specific context. Once you know the context, you can predict and re-create it, being prepared to deal with the undesirable behavior.

My Crossover Journal
Wendy was caring for my dog Cannon, an adolescent Beardie. Excited to see her, he jumped up, his head sharply striking her chin. Her pain-induced, reflexive reaction was a shocked, "HEY!" Cannon hit the deck and slunk away. It took minutes for Wendy to coax him out of the corner. As to the memorability of the incident, Cannon has never again tried to jump on Wendy, nor is he afraid of her or shows any reluctance in greeting or being with her. His association was with jumping up—perfect, spontaneous timing.

Act...don't react. Even though recurring behaviors are often predictable—taking place in a specific, foreseeable context—most of the time we don't react until after the behavior has run its course. For example, when the dog jumps on company, most people holler, "Don't jump! No! Off! Get down!" Then when the dog is back on the floor (gravity having played its role) embarrassed about the dog's behavior, the owner scolds him, takes him by the collar, and puts him in his crate. This reaction doesn't constitute punishment. It doesn't reduce or eliminate jumping on guests. The next time the doorbell rings, the dog is right there, ready to jump on whoever walks in.

Removal (negative punishment) is an effective tool, but the typical way in which a time-out or other punishing consequence is applied makes it ineffective for several reasons.

- **There was no connection with the dog's behavior.** No event marker (PM) connected the behavior with the event that followed it.

- **The undesirable behavior was reinforced.** Jumping on guests earns stroking and attention, plus whatever self-reinforcing rewards are at play.

- **The behavior was persistent.** Even if the dog did connect the punishment with the behavior, it wasn't until after he had jumped repeatedly, an event that has likely happened many times.

- **The punishment was not sufficient to overcome the reward**. Consider, for example, counter-surfing in Table 10-3 on page 206. If the trainer reacts when the dog is already on the counter eating something tasty, the consequence is unlikely to overshadow that food reward. On the other hand, if the trainer is prepared to mark and punish "thinking about jumping on the counter" there is no compensating reinforcement for the bad behavior.

The way to tackle behaviors you want to eliminate from your dog's repertoire is... tackle them. Act on them at the moment they start, not after they're over.

Scouts and dog trainers—"be prepared." As with training an incompatible behavior, waiting for random occurrences to apply consequences often puts you in a position of reacting after the dog "misbehaves." Just as importantly, intermittent punishment means the behavior is being intermittently reinforced—strengthening it.

Reactive punishment is not just ill-timed, it is often fraught with owner frustration and anger. Never punish in anger—that is a relationship-destroyer!

The purpose of punishment is constructive, not destructive—to help the dog learn what behavior is disadvantageous, and what to do instead. To teach this, you must be mentally and physically prepared before the dog engages in the behavior.

Plan your "real life" situation. Gather props, invite and prepare any helpers, and arrange the environment. For example, you may want to have a crate nearby for easy access to a time-out, or anything else that will facilitate your punishment-training session.

Point out the behavior...punishment follows. With your plan in place, visualize how it will likely go. Picture how your dog looks as she begins to engage in the objectionable behavior—the first subtle sign of her intention to act. That's what you will mark. Consider how you will mark it; what punishment you'll apply; how you'll apply it; and what you will do before, during, and after the punishment.

Here's how you might tackle jumping on you when you come home.

- **You're prepared**. Be ready to mark your dog's behavior before you open the door to greet her. You open the door, and as soon as you note your dog's *intention* to jump—gathering her muscles, preparing to take off...

- **Mark it with your PM**. Time the PM to correspond with *the behavior*, not with the punishment.

- **After you mark, pause briefly**. The PM provides important information—that behavior is what earned this punishment. As with a click and treat, a *brief* time separation is needed between the PM and the punishment. This "time-stands-still" moment allows the marker to sink in so your dog makes the connection between the behavior and the consequence. Applying punishment simultaneously with the marker, without any pause, diminishes the significance and power of the PM.

- **Follow through with the punishment**. Turn away, turning your back to your dog. The consequence is loss of your attention and applying that consequence is important—the PM is the marker, not the punishment. Until your dog recognizes that punishment follows the PM, the marker has no meaning on its own.

- **Remain calm and unemotional**. Anger is unnecessary and counterproductive. It interferes with learning. Then cue a good behavior, click and reward. (See "After punishment, then what?" on page 212.)

Positive punishment—painless and effective. Some long-standing behaviors are resistant to negative punishment. An option to consider is using positive punishment (bad things happen). Employed appropriately, gently, humanely, and effectively, something as simple and painless as a squirt of water can profoundly influence behavior, often eliminating long-standing, obnoxious activities with just one or two applications.

Since many crossover trainers come from methods that employ other forms of positive punishment, it is important to understand both the application and the effectiveness of this gentle punisher. Without this knowledge, if negative punishment is ineffective, a crossover trainer may revert to a previous, more physically punitive method to deal with undesirable behaviors.

Surprising to many crossover trainers, a spritz of water from a water pistol or trigger spray bottle set on stream, can have a powerful impact. The rules to using this technique are the same as with negative punishment:

- Mark the punishment-earning behavior with the PM.
- Pause briefly and then apply the punisher. Spray directly at the dog's face, rapid-fire squirts. More often than not, four or five spritzes are all it takes for the dog to turn his head to the side as if to say, "OK…I get it."
- After you squirt, stop, pause to let the consequence sink in.
- Then cue a good behavior, click and reward.

Dog owners sometimes tell us that they have tried squirting the dog, but it didn't work. These are the most common reasons why it may not have been effective:

- Failure to use a behavior marker—The dog can't change what he isn't aware of.
- The spray is set on mist, not stream—Misting isn't sufficient disincentive for much of anything.
- Squirting just once or twice—Again, this is not sufficient disincentive. If the punishment is "ignorable," the dog will build a tolerance.
- Failing to set it up; being unprepared—Reacting with intermittent punishment means intermittent reinforcement, strengthening behavior.
- Using the spray bottle as a threat, brandishing it with an implied "or else"— Used this way, the water bottle becomes a cue for "avoid this behavior." In the absence of the cue, the behavior remains unchanged.
- If on seeing the spray bottle the dog stops the unwanted behavior, not following-through with punishment—Over time, the PM, the spray bottle and the punisher lose their impact.

- Assuming a Lab (or other water-loving dog) likes being sprayed—Even to a Labrador Retriever, the rapid-fire squirts are often sufficient to punish behavior when the behavior is marked with a PM.

- Not following the "Rule of Three" (page 214).—Continual use of ineffective punishment leads to undesirable fallout, often resulting in worse behaviors.

If you choose to use positive punishment, select the least aversive consequence that will be effective, and apply it correctly, or don't use it at all.

After punishment, then what? Whatever the punishment, once it's over, it's over. There's no additional value to be gained from either prolonging the time frame or demonstrating continued dissatisfaction. In fact, doing so may damage your relationship.

As described in the introduction to this chapter, when Shura let Hobbes up, she simply stood there, letting the event sink in. Picture a mother dog disciplining a puppy. She growls (her PM), then follows it with the consequence—a quick, snapping tag—swift, brief, memorable, and over. She provided information and made her point. There's no guilt, no blame, no recrimination, no holding a grudge—and no apology…just information and consequence.

It is precisely the same when we humans apply punishment. You gain nothing by showing your dog your frustration or annoyance. Once you've eaten the treat, the message has been sent. Once your dog has been removed from an activity for a time-out, punishment is over.

Now do something "good." Follow the punisher with an opportunity to earn a click and treat. You can do this either by giving the dog a cue for a known behavior such as "sit," or give him another opportunity to *get it right*—to perform the desired behavior without the error that earned punishment. This juxtaposition of Behavior "A" earning punishment, followed by an opportunity to earn reinforcement with Behavior "B" provides the important contrast between good and bad. Learning this distinction is what teaches the dog to make "right" choices—to think.

My Crossover Journal

Mayday loved knocking bars off agility jumps. It wasn't that he couldn't clear them—he could clear a two foot ring gate with room to spare, so a 16" jump was a piece of cake. He simply enjoyed barreling through bars like a bull in a china shop. We tried heavier, sand-filled bars, but it made no difference. He just liked knocking them off. Negative punishment was the solution. When running a course, the first time Mayday knocked a bar, I marked it with "Nope." The consequence was stop, lie down, and wait while I re-set the bar. Then I gave him another chance to get it right. If he cleared the jump, his reward was to continue running the agility course. If he knocked the bar a second time, I marked it with "Nope" and we left the course. After everyone else in class had their turn, we'd try again. After just three repetitions of this punishment, Mayday stopped knocking bars.

Mayday delighted in knocking bars off the agility jumps.

Fundamental 5. Did it work? Evaluate punishment's effectiveness

Benjamin Franklin said, "The definition of insanity is doing the same thing over and over and expecting different results." Since punishment is defined by its affect on behavior (results) if the dog's behavior doesn't change, the consequence isn't punishment. Before simply continuing to apply an ineffective consequence, stop and consider possible reasons why it's not working. Here are the likely possibilities.

- **Timing your PM**. Does your PM mark *the behavior?* For example, to mark jumping up, the PM is comes before or as the dog takes off, not once he's back on the floor.

- **Delivery of the punisher**. The punishment should be delivered after, not simultaneously with the marker. As with the timing of click…and…treat, the timing is PM…then…apply the consequence.

- **Effectiveness**. Just because *you* think the consequence is undesirable, doesn't make it aversive to the dog. Punishment has nothing to do with *our view or feelings*. Consequences are defined solely by their effect. If your dog doesn't like agility, a time-out for barking on the agility course would not be undesirable. Rather, leaving the course would likely reinforce barking.

- **Sufficient intensity**. Remember, a consequence must be less desirable than whatever the dog gets out of engaging in the behavior (see "Pick your punishment" on page 205). The good news is that for most dogs, a time-out, withholding a reward, or loss of opportunity is significant.

- **Correct, consistent application**. After the marker, apply the punishment. Don't just threaten—follow through with the consequence *until the job is done*. Quite often this is where trainers fail, giving up before the behavior has been dealt with.

- **Unintentional reinforcement**. When a behavior doesn't improve, there may be some reinforcement you're not aware of. Just because you're not *intentionally* reinforcing a behavior, doesn't mean that *something* isn't. Consider what the dog might be getting out of the behavior—whether from you, your reaction, from the environment, the activity, or the dog's hard-wiring.

Crossover Cornerstone #7

The Rule of Three: If three applications of a consequence do not affect the behavior, stop, reexamine, and reevaluate.

As with Benjamin Franklin's definition of insanity, continuing to use an ineffective consequence not only does no good, it causes trainer frustration, and even anger, possibly damaging the relationship. Further, an ineffective consequence undermines the significance of the punishment marker, ultimately rendering it meaningless. If there is no change in the dog's behavior after three applications of a chosen punishment, discontinue using it and reevaluate.

Spontaneous recovery and extinction bursts. You've done it! You've addressed a behavior, employed an undesirable consequence, and the behavior has all but disappeared…that is, until it shows up again. The return of a previously addressed behavior is not unusual and it doesn't spell failure! In fact, you've almost achieved total victory—you simply need to finish the job. Behaviors that return, generally do so in one of two ways:

- Spontaneous recovery
- Extinction burst

My Crossover Journal

In Rally Obedience, the dog and handler team move through a course of stations, each with a sign for an exercise the team performs. Bruce's dog Cody, a Shetland Sheepdog, would start barking if Bruce showed any indecision as they approached a sign. At even the slightest hesitation, Cody would start telling Bruce off. To address the behavior, Bruce marked Cody's first bark, had him lie down and turned away briefly. If Cody barked again, Bruce took him off the course. Cody's barking had diminished so much that Bruce ignored it when Cody uttered a tiny little woof—a "woofle." That one, unpunished vocalization was enough to start the behavior all over again. It took several practice sessions, marking even the smallest utterance with total consistency, until Cody stopped barking on the Rally course.

Spontaneous recovery is the reappearance of the behavior, usually in a milder form. However, the milder behavior is still *the behavior*. Deal with it once and for all, and you're likely done. Cody the Sheltie's woofle was spontaneous recovery. If Bruce had punished the woofle just as he had Cody's bark, it would likely have ended the barking once and for all. By ignoring the woof—after all, it was nothing like his loud bark—Bruce had to once again give Cody time-outs, paying attention to and marking any vocalization.

The other way a seemingly-extinguished behavior will reappear is in an extinction burst. This is the bad behavior's last gasp. It is not a dying breath, however—it is a compelling typhoon. Far more dramatic than spontaneous recovery, with an extinction burst the behavior reemerges with a vengeance, usually accompanied by other unrelated, and often worse, behaviors. When a trainer is not prepared for an extinction burst, he often gives up, thinking, "I've failed. Everything I've been doing is for nothing." Not so! You're almost done!

When you see an extinction burst, mark the behavior as you have been doing, and employ the same consequence. It has worked; after all, the behavior had gotten so much better, it was almost gone. If you don't punish the behavior—if you give in to the extinction burst—not only will the behavior return, but it will be stronger, far more durable, and difficult to eliminate.

Take, for example, attention-barking. You've marked the undesirable behavior, and given the dog a time-out. The behavior has all but disappeared, until you see the extinction burst. Not just a woof or two, but furious, loud, frustration barking, accompanied by new behaviors—jumping, pawing, perhaps even nipping at you. Keep your composure, don't get angry. Follow through just as you have been. Mark the behavior with your PM and calmly escort your dog to his time-out spot.

Be prepared for an extinction burst. The alternative, giving in, not only reinforces the original behavior, it reinforces the more insistent behavior, along with—are you ready for this?—*reinforcing persistence, that is, keep trying this bad behavior*. That's the last thing you want your dog to learn! Follow through consistently, and you will soon see the end of the behavior. Your efforts will be well-rewarded.

Fundamental 6. Ethical considerations

No discussion of punishing consequences would be complete without considering the ethics of punishment. Each trainer must decide for him or herself what techniques fit their personal philosophy.

My own philosophy is laid out in Chapter 1. In my pre-clicker incarnations I used a wide variety of aversive techniques that I would not use today. Unquestionably, as a crossover trainer, I've undergone a philosophical shift, but it is much more than that. *What I have learned through clicker training is that, without exception, there are other, better, more elegant ways to achieve the same results. We no longer need to employ techniques that were commonplace in our pre-clicker methods, with no consequent decline in responsiveness, drop in precision, or decrease in "obedience."*

A discussion of ethics must, however, include the ethics of discussion—the ethics of talking about, learning about, and thinking about using punishment. Several years ago, the author of an online dog training course asked for copies of my class training manuals to consider them for their recommended reading list. He later told me that they would not be listed because they included information on how to use a water pistol for positive punishment. The implication was that merely *reading about* using positive punishment (no matter how gentle) is unethical, unacceptable, and abusive. If a manual, 99% of which is devoted to positive reinforcement training, was excluded because of reference to the application of a spritz of water, I could only conclude that the students were not learning anything at all about positive punishment—except for *don't even consider it*. Whether or not a trainer chooses to use positive punishment, *learning about it* doesn't mean *using it*.

In our increasingly politically correct world, it is challenging to find and engage in polite discourse with opposing points-of-view. Nowhere is this point more evident than in discussions between people who want to use only positive reinforcement, and those they think of as "punishers." Rejecting information about punishment out-of-hand does a disservice to the flow of information, and to an individual's ability to assess what is best for her dog. To quote from Steven Lindsay in the *Handbook of Applied Dog Behavior, Volume I*, "The aim of punishment is to eliminate the use of punishment in the future. Instead of extreme positions, accusatory innuendo, moralizing, and half-truths, what is needed is a balanced and informed attitude regarding the practical use, misuse and abuse of punishment." He goes on to say, "Many critics of punishment … [believe] that the heartfelt repetition of a falsehood is enough to make it true."

Many crossover trainers come from backgrounds like mine—backgrounds that include collar checks and other applications of positive punishment. What we know from our experience is simple—punishment works. The other thing we know from our experience is that using punishment is not something either participant—at either end of the leash—enjoys. Given a choice, humane trainers do not choose positive punishment over effective alternatives. But pragmatism and practical considerations have a place in this discussion, and the discussion itself must not be deemed unethical.

Ethical considerations must be based on more than feelings. I would love to never have to say "No!" to a dog (P+). But I do. I would love to have dogs not only recognize where their advantage lies, but have their advantage match mine. But it doesn't always.

Just as we choose techniques for training positive responses based on a humane, "dog advocacy" position, so should we understand *reducing behaviors* from the same dog advocacy position. Informed choices must take into consideration not just the ethics of using punishment, but the potentially greater consequences for a dog when an owner doesn't know how to deal with and eliminate problem behavior. Ignorance is not bliss.

Dogs are not "born trained," nor do we humans instinctively know how to effectively deal with a dog's bad behavior. Misconceptions, misinformation, and misapplications abound. Often following a training book, or advice from a breeder or veterinarian, owners may treat "bad" dogs badly. They may be abused, abandoned, brought to a shelter, or killed. How does a person get useful information about properly dealing with behavior issues, including the effective and proper use of punishment, if trainers who understand the concepts, won't discuss them?

One of my mentors once advised me that the loudest protests come from the person on the verge of change. He opined that the most vociferous arguments are made in the struggle to become convinced. Put another way, might an argument in favor of using collar corrections, for example, be an "extinction burst?" The mere possibility means we should invite discussion rather than stifle it. We cannot educate unless we stop being judgmental and engage in civil dialogue.

The road to understanding both practical considerations as well as ethical standards is to *talk about them*. To make well-reasoned choices between previously-successful techniques or using clicker training, people need information, not the suppression of discourse. When discussion of punishment on an Internet clicker training list, was cut-off by the list Moderator, a list member who is a "layman," a client, not a trainer, wrote:

> *When only one portion of an approach is explained (not used, explained) the whole picture of why to use the approach you chose is lost. Trainers who won't discuss P+ or R- in a comprehensive discussion of Operant Conditioning confuse me and run the risk of making their clients feel "lacking" or "not too bright," undermining the client/trainer relationship. I want my trainer to explain all aspects so I can think them through, and truly integrate the information. I want my trainer to do for me what they want me to do for my dog: make it clear, have respectful communication that shows me the way to show it to my dog. When trainers present only one part, positive reinforcement, they do a disservice to the people they are working with and the dogs they are helping to train. How can a client think through their own behavior without the knowledge to think about it? Otherwise the client's own action and behavior is lost in the process. If trainers want people to "see" that dogs can think and learn then they must approach their clients as if "they" can think and learn.*

Knowledge is power

Knowledgeable trainers wisely use the concepts of how all consequences affect behavior, applying them intelligently, kindly, humanely, and effectively. It is through the sharing of knowledge, experience, philosophy, and ethics that crossover trainers are able to make well-reasoned, well-informed choices in evaluating prior-used techniques or clicker training solutions. Armed with information, crossover trainers are able to consider the dog, the quality of life, and the alternatives before either using or rejecting a technique, making ethical decisions about management, training, and the application of consequences—with knowledge and understanding of concepts and of dogs—for the dog's sake.

It is my profound hope that through studying, practicing, and learning all aspects of clicker training, crossover trainers will experience this gratifying, joyful partnership—thoughtful trainers and thinking dogs.

A Note to Professional Trainers

As professional trainers, we are often faced with life-and-death decisions, and must evaluate choices and solutions considering what is best for the dog. Often this includes determining whether or not to consider positive punishment. In evaluating options, these are the criteria we use before considering anything beyond the aversives discussed in this chapter.

- First, other options for modifying the dog's behavior have either been exhausted or are inappropriate.

- Next, the dog's behavior is dangerous to the dog. That is, the dog is in danger of injury or death as a result of his actions, or may be euthanized because of them.

- The dog's behavior poses a danger to others.
- The dog's behavior requires immediate and permanent change...or else...

Regardless of which "camp" your background is—no positive punishment, or judicious use of it—those of us who train dogs for a living, and are often the last stop before death, must weigh the consequences of refusing to consider positive punishment. Rather, we must know how to use it fairly, effectively, and humanely. The alternative may well be far worse.

You are reading this book for a reason. I believe that you are, as I am, always looking for ways to grow and better ways to train, to better serve your clients—canine and human. I've been where you are. I've gone through periods of depression thinking, "If only I knew then what I know now..." I long ago let go of any residual guilt in recognition that the techniques I used previously were the best that I knew.

Looking forward, as you explore, play with, and hopefully embrace clicker training, opening yourself to the possibilities it presents, you will discover its power and brilliance. You, the dogs you train, your training practice, and your clients will all be the better for it.

Chapter 11
ENGAGING YOUR DOG

"Back in the day," the first training book I followed was *The Koehler Method of Dog Training*. I read the instructions, studied the drawings, trained my dog, and consulted the book to correct my technique or learn the next step. This was the recipe-driven approach I followed with my own dogs and in my first few years as a dog trainer. My next training incarnation, also followed a set recipe—put your right hand here, left there, and perform (blank). Most training books tell you what to do and what procedures to follow, using a formula with step-by-step instructions for teaching foundation behaviors like sit, lie down, stay, heel, and come. Even clicker training books tend to offer one or more suggestions (usually lure or shape) for training these behaviors with a clicker.

The drawback to having instructions etched in stone (or printed in black and white) is that the information is both limited and limiting. Without additional, follow-up instructions, the trainer doesn't know how to progress beyond the specific, delineated steps—which is decidedly un-clicker. Further, such instructions generally don't address the pitfalls…and yes, there are pitfalls. Trainers trying to follow a set of directions may find themselves either unable to achieve their goal within the confines of the instructions, or may encounter a training problem which the book doesn't address.

So now here we are at the point in a training book where logic dictates I delineate just how to clicker train your dog—the nitty-gritty of the method. But there is no nitty-gritty in clicker training, there is no set plan to follow. Clicker training is to dog training, what improvisation is to performing for an audience—we have no script. We, the performers (trainers), rely on our knowledge, experience, talent, and ingenuity. Clicker training is an adventure, not a recipe.

The very power of clicker training is its flexibility, inventiveness, non-conformity to formulas, adaptability, and the freedom to experiment. This very latitude makes me reluctant to lay down specific procedures. I fear, should my recommendations not work, that the crossover trainer will give up and return to the more comfortable, familiar method. Yet without having specific guidelines or instructions, some crossover trainers may do just that anyway.

With this dilemma in mind, I offer these last two chapters with suggestions about designing, starting and ending training sessions, evaluating and adapting training to your dog's individual work ethic, and ideas to help you achieve your goals. Follow them or not…but play, enjoy, try, make mistakes, try again, and learn, together with your dog. Don't be afraid. You won't hurt your dog or harm your relationship. Honest!

Different perspectives for different goals

Different trainers approach training dogs from different perspectives, with a variety of goals for both long-term objectives, as well as for an individual training session. These differences, along with the diversity of our dogs themselves, affect how each of us approaches training. Clicker training fits beautifully with this diversity. With clicker training there is no "one right way" either for a specific order of training, for training any individual behavior, for any one training session, or for tackling a learning opportunity. Start anywhere, train anything, at any time. So let's explore some different approaches to training sessions themselves.

In both of my previous, pre-clicker incarnations, training took place in a planned, formalized session. Gather equipment and props such as leash, training collar, reinforcers (tug toy, treats, and the like), get the dog, go to the training area, and then start. The props, as well as the context told the dog, "The trainer is in." While this same contextual association exists with clicker training, being a clicker trainer means taking advantage of consequences all the time. Any moment may present a learning opportunity. The following are some different contexts that constitute "in training," and how each may fit with your goals and schedule.

Dogs easily learn contexts of being "in training" and not.

By behavior session. This is a traditional, more structured, "typical" approach. Set a time, plan a session, get your dog in a distraction-free, training environment where you control the setting, work on a behavior, followed by another behavior, then another.

By behavior. In your training environment, you may choose to work on just one behavior or related behaviors such as target stick training. Or you may choose to work on just one thing, for example, building distance or resistance to distractions on stays.

By training sequence. You might work on behaviors that are still in the early shaping stages and need a controlled, training environment. Practice nearly-finished behaviors sequenced into your dog's repertoire for fluency, and work on still other behaviors that are ready to be added into a Speed Trial. Or take your dog to the park to work on another set of behaviors in a new, distracting context.

By engaging your dog. My personal favorite, take any brief opportunity to tune into something you might accomplish at any given moment. Possible with clicker training as with no other approach I'm aware of, you can achieve a great deal in 30 seconds of training. Not a "formal" session, rather you simply let your dog know that your attention is available, and you are prepared to reward him for engaging with you. Such "waiting for the kettle to boil" training, provides a moment for a "listening drill," a brief Speed Trial, or even starting to shape a new behavior.

Opportunistic training. Grab any opportunity. You always have at least a verbal marker ("yes") available and you always have some type of reinforcement ("good"). Be mindful of reinforcements whenever they may be available. If you're about to give your dog something of value (go outside, chase a ball, eat dinner, get off leash in the park, and the like), rather than something for nothing, take the opportunity to have her give you something in return. Take advantage of any available reinforcement.

Learning can take place under any circumstances and at any time. How and where you "train" depends on your goals, your achievements to date, and opportunities that present themselves.

Adapting to your dog

As important as taking advantage of opportunities, training will vary depending on your dog's individual learning style and type. It can be frustrating when your dog isn't cooperating, and while we are often quick to blame the method, the truth is that not all dogs react to training (by any approach) precisely the same. Just as different people have different learning styles (auditory versus visual learners, for example), a dog's individual temperament, past training history, experiences, energy level, and work ethic all play a roll in how the dog reacts to training. With this in mind, here are a few broad classifications that affect your dog's training. Dogs can fit into one or more of the following general types.

Workers. These dogs are active participants, highly motivated by the game and/or the rewards. Totally engaged, they just keep trying—working, offering behaviors. While the easiest and most fun to train, workers nonetheless require training breaks and rest periods. You may have to enforce breaks—stop your dog, offer him a drink of water, and an opportunity to clear his head. Workers can make for obsessive trainers, so be sure to teach an "off" switch. And when you introduce a cue, be very clear about not marking and reinforcing that behavior unless you ask for it (see Stimulus Control in Chapter 9).

Distracted. These dogs will focus on virtually anything that attracts them. They may be highly social, or highly reactive to sounds, scents, or movements. Training in a distraction-free environment is successful, but you must use high-value treats when introducing anything new. In new locations and when working on distraction training, proceed gradually, with a high rate of reinforcement.

Sensitive. Sensitive dogs need a connection with the trainer. I sometimes see trainers with stony, impassive expressions, focusing 100% on the task and on their dog, but unaware that their aloof, poker face is off-putting, even stressful to the dog. This may apply even more to crossover dogs, but it is true of those without prior training as well. Sensitive dogs need a smile, a soft word of encouragement, a relaxed demeanor. They need to make a connection beyond just, "Will work for food."

Short attention span. Short attention span dogs simply don't tolerate multiple repetitions, even with a high value reward. Juba, the first Rhodesian Ridgeback we clicker trained, taught us an important lesson. She would participate for one or two repetitions, then shut down. Treats weren't of great interest to her. We thought it might be that she was highly distracted, but reducing distractions didn't help. What we've learned over time is that there are dogs that seem to be the opposite of "workers." What is interesting, however, is that these dogs learn quickly. The trainer simply has to be aware to take frequent breaks and keep progressing—change the picture, change the exercise, change the motivator, and the like.

Passive. Passive dogs are reluctant to try something new. They are compliant, docile, and may be timid. This can be a result of the dog's training history (prior training suppressed the dog's initiative), or it may be the dog's basic temperament and personality. Verbal praise and quiet encouragement may be helpful, especially when first beginning clicker training (see "Treat delivery" on page 92 for ways to build enthusiasm). It is important to connect with these dogs as with the sensitive dog. Keep your early training sessions short. Stop after just one or two successes, jackpot any signs of initiative, and build from there.

Crossover. While any dog can fit the above descriptions, the crossover dog who is waiting to be told what to do can really test your patience. But stick with it. Review the information in Chapters 3 and 4 regarding the issues of crossing over.

Dogs can fall into more than one category, for example they can be "sensitive" and "passive," or be "passive" and have a "short attention span." Further, these categories are fluid and changeable. Mayday, my crossover dog, clearly changed from a "crossover" to a "worker" once he caught on to the game.

My Crossover Journal
After having worked with a variety of dogs for several days, the students in our Professional Trainers Academy were reviewing what they had learned about dealing with the different learning styles, temperaments, and work ethic of the dogs they had trained over the course of the five-day school. In assessing the categories of these dogs, imagine how pleased and proud I was when my formerly easily-distracted adolescent Beardie, Cannon, made it onto the list of the dogs the class considered to be "workers." Wahoo!

Six training steps for behaviors

The following is an overview of the steps to take a behavior from the first subtle movement through to fluency and real-life. These steps are not absolute. For example, you may choose to add the cue earlier or later, or take your dog to new locations early on. This review is an at-a-glance reminder of the general order of training, including some suggestions and helpful hints, offered as a reference for developing your training plans.

Step 1. Your objective (Chapter 5)
Clearly define and envision a mental picture of both the ultimate behavior, as well as short-range goals, broken into small, easily achievable steps with a high rate of reinforcement (ROR).

Step 2. Get the behavior started (Chapters 6 and 7)
In a distraction-free "training" environment where your dog can focus on figuring out how to make you click, whether capturing, shaping, or using a prompt such as a target or lure, there is no "one right way" to get behavior started. Just start.

Treat delivery options (page 92). Use treat delivery to put the dog in a position to easily offer the behavior, to set your dog up to repeat the behavior, to speed responses, to affect demeanor, and the like.

Handler posture or position (page 136). Consider ways your posture or position can put the dog in the optimum position to perform the behavior, or investigate if they might be impeding your dog learning the behavior on his own. If used to put the dog in a position to easily perform the behavior in the early stages of learning, handler posture or position will need to be eliminated quickly, that is, unless your posture is an integral part of the behavior.

Step 3. Move the behavior along (Chapters 5, 7, 8)
Move incrementally from the first hint of a behavior through to the dog readily and predictably offering the behavior without a prompt, and repeating it without hesitation.

Small, reachable steps. Keep the dog actively engaged and successful with easily achievable behavior clusters for a high ROR.

Repetitions (page 65). Consider how many times you'll click and treat before you change the premise or take a break. This is especially important for a crossover dog just starting clicker training. To enable you to focus on your dog, count out a specific number of treats. When the treats are gone, you know how many repetitions you've done. Or challenge yourself to achieve a specific goal by the time you've used up ten treats.

Adjust the Premise (Chapter 8). This step helps the dog determine the precise context for the behavior—that it isn't about facing you, being in the kitchen, or related to your posture. Unless, of course, it is.

Guidelines for adjusting the premise. Introduce context changes early and often, as soon as the dog offers the behavior several times. The sooner you introduce changes, the easier for the dog to zero in on the precise parameters of the behavior. *The longer you practice without changes, the harder it is for your dog to adjust to changes in the future.*

Change after several successful repetitions. Here's a good rule of thumb. After your dog has readily offered the behavior three consecutive times, change an element. When you alter a premise, relax your expectations and give your dog a chance to adjust to the change without help. If you do need to prompt, nose-tease just once or twice.

Here's a rundown of the elements to change.

- **Posture**. Your body posture—stand, sit, crouch, kneel, and lie down.
- **Orientation**. Face your dog and stand sideways—both sides. You may need to make subtle adjustments, turning slightly, then a bit more. You might try facing away from your dog, but watch your dog's reaction. He may consider turning away as disengaging, the loss of your attention—a punishment.
- **Proximity**. Adjust your distance from your dog to eliminate spatial associations, unless the behavior is related to being close to you (or to another object).
- **Locations**. A different part of the room, different rooms, and new locations. When you change location, initially relax your expectations, separating different elements, such as practicing different postures and orientations, and your dog will quickly regain his previous level of proficiency.

Increase time/distance (Chapter 8). For behaviors that involve a time frame and/or distance goal, yo-yo around your goal, sometimes increasing the challenge, and sometimes making success easier to achieve. Do not simply increase the difficulty of the behavior.

Breaks (page 66). Tell your dog when he's "off the clock," whether for just a few seconds, a longer break, or the end of the session. In planning breaks, you may find it helpful to count out five to ten treats and take a breather once they're gone. Use breaks to introduce changes to the premise—posture, position, location, etc.

Step 4. Vary the reinforcement (schedule and rewards) (Chapter 8)

Click the best of the best, withholding a click (and reward) for a less-desirable repetition. When you withhold a click, re-set the behavior by moving to a new spot, crouch, pat your leg, or clap your hands. When your dog performs the behavior again and you like that repetition, click. If you love every performance of the behavior, randomly withhold clicks, making sure there's no pattern to your clicked and non-clicked repetitions. Mix in different payoffs—don't always use food treats. If the behavior slows or your dog stops offering it, see "Losing the behavior" on page 150. Play with variability, too. See what happens when you do.

Step 5. Add the cue (Chapter 8)

Back in your distraction-free training environment, when you are sure that the next thing your dog will do is perform the behavior you've been training, and you like it, you're ready to name it. Have your dog perform the behavior, click and reward. Right after your dog eats the treat, say the cue just *before he starts* to perform the behavior again. Once you add the cue, you no longer mark and reward that behavior unless you cued it. After 20-50 repetitions the dog learns the association between the cue and the behavior. Here are the four aspects that build your dog's understanding of cues.

- **Window of opportunity (limited hold)** (page 158). To eliminate hesitation between the cue and your dog's response (short latency), give your dog a short time span (e.g., two seconds) within which to respond. If he doesn't, your lost opportunity marker (LOM) shuts the window.

- **Lost Opportunity Marker** (page 158). The LOM marks non-compliance, immediately followed by another opportunity to perform the behavior. When your dog responds to the *second* opportunity, say "yes" and reward with verbal praise only. Then give him a new "first chance." Remember the click and treat are earned only for responding to the *first cue*.

- **Test the cue** (page 163). Give the cue "cold turkey" in a non-training context.

- **Wait for the cue** (page 169). To train "wait for me to cue you," pause before giving the cue. Reinforce hesitation by giving the cue.

Step 6. Finish the job

The last step in training is to finish the job and gain fluency. This includes distractions, teaching your dog to listen, and finally, real-life situations.

Take it on the road (Chapter 9). This will increase your dog's ability to ignore distractions. When faced with an attraction more enticing than your dog's motivation to respond, move far enough away to regain your dog's focus, then move closer as your dog's responsiveness improves. If it's appropriate to do so, use the attraction as a reward.

Build your dog's behavioral repertoire (Chapter 9). Once again, we are back to your training environment. Mix cues randomly to make sure your dog is listening for and responding to the specific cues.

Listening drill (page 171). Give cues for known behaviors in random order so your dog learns to listen to the specific cue. As your dog learns new cues, mix each new behavior in with previously learned ones. Change the order in which you give cues so your dog listens rather than following a pattern. Mark and reward, randomly changing the number of behaviors before you click and treat.

Speed Trial (page 173). A speedy performance equates with fluency. Build speed by practicing learned behaviors in a Speed Trial. Click and reward only at the end of the time trial.

Real life. Back out on the road again…see how your dog does in a set-up, real-life situation. If your dog's behavior is just what you want, yahoo! You've achieved your goal. If not, go back to whatever previous step needs work, either in your training environment or with distractions, and build from there.

As with any learning (a skill, behavior, knowledge or information), "use it or lose it." To keep your dog's responsiveness high, practice what he knows. Live life, give him jobs to do, tell him how terrific he is, and enjoy your time together, the hard-earned fruits of both your labors—a well-trained, responsive, thinking dog.

Check your technique

As you work through the six training steps, from time-to-time review the fundamentals of your technique outlined in Chapter 5. Focus on the following.

- **Timing**. Be sure you are clicking the instant of the behavior you want to mark.

- **Rate of reinforcement (ROR)**. A high ROR keeps your dog motivated and working. The high frequency of clicks provides information critical for learning.

- **Success**. Break the behavior into small, easily achievable steps and sequences to keep a high ROR. Success motivates your dog (and you!).

- **Watch for pitfalls**. In the specific behaviors in the next chapter, instructions may include some common pitfalls to watch out for. Whether or not a potential problem is mentioned specifically, you'll discover a glitch on your own when your dog's behavior tells you you've erred. *The behavior you see is the behavior you trained.*

- **Food is out of sight**. Not held in your hand and not used as a visual prompt or lure.

- **Hold still when you click**. Click…then…reach for, pick up, and deliver the treat.

- **The clicker is a marker**. It is not a remote control. Keep your clicker hand still. Don't point it at or thrust it toward your dog.

- **Deliver the treat**. Do it in a way that advances your training, to re-set the behavior, effect demeanor, reward in place, toss it to increase distance, and the like.

Training sessions—start with engaging your dog

Regardless of where you train or your dog's basic type, the start of any learning session begins by getting your dog to engage, to participate in her training. Often this happens simply by picking up a clicker, an action that says, "You're on…the bar is open." One or two clicks should do it, but don't just click. Remember the click is not a "recall" or "pay attention" cue. Rather, it marks what the dog is doing at that precise moment. I've seen trainers click to get their dog's attention from something the dog is focused on. That's the trainer's *intent*, but what they are *actually marking* (and with sufficient repetitions, what they are *training*) is "pay attention to something other than me." Rather, here are some better ways to engage your dog.

- Call your dog's name and when she alerts, click and reward with a high-value treat or jackpot. Then do one of the following.

- Give your dog a cue for a simple, known behavior such as "sit," mark and reward. Repeat it once or twice.

- Or my favorite, ask for a hand touch, with or without a verbal cue. Hold out your hand (a signal cue), your dog touches it with his nose, mark, reward, repeat it, and you're good to go.

Don't spend a great deal of time engaging your dog. Simply get her attention and start training. Both you and your dog have finite limits—time limits, motivation limits (the number of treats before satiation), fresh brain cell limits (focusing and thinking are hard work for both of you), and the like. The more you repeat something unnecessarily, the less energy is available for "the new." With a limited number of repetitions available in any training session before your dog (or you) reaches her limit, make the most of them.

While her brain is fresh…and so is yours

Once you have your dog's focus, work on a new behavior, the next sequence of a behavior you've been working on, or something else challenging. Why start with the new? For two reasons:

1. Just as we learn better when we're fresh and rested, so does your dog.
2. In a longer session, you're working toward the familiar, toward something your dog already knows. This means the training session gets progressively easier, rather than progressively more difficult and stressful. This won't make a big difference in one individual session, but repeated over time, your dog will learn the pattern.

If you're fortunate enough to have a "worker" dog, you can do virtually anything in any order, but even with a highly-motivated dog with a strong work ethic, it makes sense to train something challenging when both of you are fresh and sharp.

Keep the lesson moving along with a high rate of reinforcement, providing clear steps and lots of information.

A "typical" training session—behavior-by-behavior

Now let's get specific, starting with what most people think of as a "typical" training session.

- **Plan your session**. Know just what you're going to do. Have your training plan in mind, from engaging your dog, through taking breaks, including treat delivery, and everything you can think of from starting to ending the session. Use the Six Steps review (page 223) as a reminder template for your lesson plan.

- **Gather your paraphernalia**. This includes treats, clicker, and any props needed for your plan.

- **Get your dog and start training**. Put your dog in a familiar context where he recognizes the clicker, the bait bag, the location, and anything else that constitutes "in training."

227

- **Focus your dog**. Engage him in training.
- **Start with "the new."** Work on a new behavior, the next step of a behavior-in-progress, or a new sequence.
- **Move to the familiar**. Review previously learned behaviors, perhaps practicing with a change in the context, review a listening drill, add distractions, and the like.
- **End your session**.

Sample training plan

Here's an example of a training plan for working on "stay." (See instructions on page 261.) You will likely revise your plan as you train, but have one in mind (or written) considering how you think training will progress before you start. If things don't go according to your plan, take a break to re-evaluate and plan your next steps.

- **Prior training (your starting point)**. Dog sits on cue. Click delayed five seconds (no "stay" cue).
- **Objectives for this session**. Introduce the cue "stay." Begin building distance, distractions, and duration on sit-stay.
- **Goals**. Cue: "stay." Distance goal: 2 feet away. Distractions: Food offered on open palm, 2 feet from dog. Dog stays when food is placed on floor 2 feet from dog. Duration: 5 seconds with distraction, 10 seconds without distractions, standing 2 feet away from dog.
- **Training location**. Distraction-free.
- **Props**. Bait bag, loads of treats.

Training plan for "Stay"

- **Markers to use**. "Yes" for success, "nope" (or "oops") marks errors.
- **What if**. If dog starts to get up or lie down, mark the first sign of movement with "nope," and remove the treat. Sit dog and try again.
- **Start session**. At the beginning of the session, engage dog with 2 hand touches, "yes" and treat. Then follow the numbers.

    1. Cue "sit," mark with "yes," drop treat so dog has to get up.
    2. Sit, pause 3 seconds, mark, drop treat so dog gets up.
    3. Sit ("good," quiet verbal praise only), cue "stay," pause 2 seconds, "yes" and treat in place. (Dog may get up or remain sitting.)
    4. Build duration. If dog is standing, sit (praise with "good"). "Stay," pause 6 seconds, "yes" and treat in place. Repeat six times, yo-yoing around 10 second time frame (e.g., 5-seconds, 10, 5, 14, 6, 15). Click and jackpot last repetition.
    5. Take a break. (Cue "take a break.")
    6. Build distance. Engage dog after the break. "Sit" (quiet verbal praise), "stay," take one step back (~2' away). Pause 2 seconds, "yes" and treat.

Repeat—re-sit (if necessary, with "good"), "stay," step back one step, pause 4 seconds, "yes" and treat. Repeat five times (~2' away), yo-yo-ing around five-seconds. (6-seconds, 4, 8, 2, 5). Click and jackpot last repetition.

7. "Take a break," offer dog water. (Assess the session so far to determine what to do next. Options: continue "stay" or work on a different behavior.) If continuing with stay, go to 8.

8. Introduce distraction. Engage dog. "Sit" (verbal praise), "stay," take one step back (~2' away), hold hand with treats by side, open hand to show dog treats.

   - If dog moves, "nope," close hand. Re-sit and repeat.
   - Count to three, "yes" and treat (dog may get up to take treats from offering hand).
   - If dog doesn't get up on "yes," introduce release cue such as "OK" and treat.

   Repeat, and begin lowering hand toward floor.

   - Continue this until treats are on the floor. Pause, mark, release.
   - If dog gets up, block treats so dog can't get them.
   - Repeat, yo-yoing time frame around a five second goal (5, 2, 8, 4, 6), jackpot after last click.

9. "Take a break."

10. Change location. Repeat #6-8 in new location (easier sequence).

11. Give dog a break.

12. Change behavior—move to the familiar. Work on a different behavior (previously learned, or behavior in progress) such as attention on name.

13. End with success. Cue "all done," and jackpot.

When finished, assess the session. Count and log number of repetitions of each sequence, including how many times dog responded successfully to "stay" cue. Note anything else relevant.

Overview of behaviors

Having the freedom and flexibility to experiment means you and your dog can achieve behaviors you never even imagined possible. Because there is no set formula, either for a specific behavior, or even for what behaviors to train in what order, you can start your dog's clicker training with any behavior.

Consider training a behavior listed in one of the following general categories, one that is detailed in the next chapter with specific guidelines, or start by choosing from a virtually limitless range of behaviors dogs can perform (see Appendix C for a list of over 200 behaviors). Have fun teaching both useful and amusing behaviors. Any training you do enhances your knowledge, your dog's creativity, and engages your dog's brain. Here is a review of the major training categories with just a sampling of some behaviors in each (some fit more than one category). Those with an asterisk* are detailed in Chapter 12.

- **Shaping behavior**. Start with any movement, then build the behavior.
  - Down*
  - "Settle"*
  - Ring the bell to go out* (Pictorial)
  - Retrieve
  - Ride a skateboard
  - Agility obstacles
- **Target training**. Use an object as a target, directing your dog with a finger or target stick, using your body as the target, having your dog target a location to go to, and the like.
  - Heeling*
  - Finish*
  - Loose leash walking*
  - Ring the bell*
  - Recall* (Hand touch)
  - Settle*
  - Directed retrieve
  - Change directions in agility
  - Skateboard
  - Go-out
  - Crawl
  - Spin, twirl, roll over
- **Chain behaviors**. Build a series of behaviors forward from the start or backward from the last behavior in the chain, the one that earns the reward. The cue starts the chain, and each link leads to the next.
  - The cue "Settle" triggers go to your bed, lie down, and remain there until released.*
  - Finish—the cue triggers move to my left side and sit at heel.*
  - Retrieve over the High Jump in Open Obedience. The cue triggers the release from stay, followed by going to and clearing the jump, picking up the dumbbell, holding it to return over the jump, and sitting in front of the handler.
  - Agility weave poles. The cue starts a homogenous chain of weaving that continues through to the last pole.

- **Capture behavior**. This is especially helpful for behaviors your dog offers spontaneously that may be difficult to shape, for behaviors you can reasonably predict, and when you can set your dog up for a predictable performance.
    - Sit (an easy one to capture for most dogs)*
    - Stay*
    - Recall*
    - Bow (stretch)
    - Shake-off
    - Sneeze
    - Yawn

- **Be creative**. In one of her seminars, Kathy Sdao does a demonstration of "give me something different." She clicks a behavior, then a different behavior, then a different one, and so on. The Flat Coat Retriever (a worker breed) she uses for this demonstration quickly figures out that any previously-offered behavior will not be rewarded, so she comes up with something new.

    In her book *Lads Before the Wind*, Karen Pryor wrote about an experiment entitled "the creative porpoise." The game "101 things to do with a box" is derived from that research, rewarding "do something new." Encourage (and reward) creativity and inventiveness—amazing things can happen!

Experiment. Be not afraid! Clicker training is not only fun and exciting, it's forgiving. It can also be humbling. When we don't get the behavior we're looking for—either the dog isn't getting it, or is offering a "wrong" behavior—it is the human partner that is on the wrong track. You can learn just as much from a failed behavior as you do from a successful one. Perhaps best of all, your dog won't know you've failed, and wouldn't blame you even if he did.

The sky's the limit

I started this chapter with a disclaimer—the difficulty involved in giving specific directions for learning clicker training. One of the most exciting factors when I first crossed over was that clicker training provides skills beyond a list of "how to's." Clicker training provides a way for me to teach my students to be dog "teachers"—not just how to train the specific behaviors I cover in class, but to understand *how to educate their dogs*. With my prior methods, every behavior followed a specific formula for any individual exercise, but other than teaching specific behaviors such as sit, down, and come, it was difficult to teach my students how to teach their dogs how to behave. To learn new behaviors or perfect their skills, students needed more lessons, more recipes. Not so with clicker training.

Remember the adage in the Introduction, "Give a man a fish, you feed him for a day; teach a man to fish, you feed him for a lifetime." Clicker training provides more than a trained dog—it teaches an understanding of how the dog learns and how to teach them to behave the way we want them to. With an understanding of the key concepts, recognizing how consequences affect behavior and how to control those consequences, and your understanding of the principles of shaping behavior, you are now prepared to fully explore the possibilities that clicker training presents—you don't need a "how to" manual of instructions.

You and your dog are limited only by your imagination. The more you teach your dog, the more you will learn, the more easily your dog will learn, and the more you can teach your dog. This is the way to an exciting new phase in your life with your dog. This is the path to a thinking dog.

Chapter 12
PUTTING IT ALL TOGETHER

It's come down to this…the final chapter, providing examples that put it all together. The following behaviors are expressly selected to demonstrate specific aspects of clicker training, focusing on skills that apply to these and other behaviors as well. For example, once you understand how to use (and fade) targets, you can apply this knowledge to a wide variety of behaviors. Once you become reasonably proficient at shaping, you can use your skills to train virtually any behavior. Whatever your individual goals, whether or not they include training the following behaviors, these skills apply to anything you want to accomplish.

Here's an overview of the various behavior types and the skills and concepts each represents, beginning with key foundation behaviors. As you practice clicker training with your dog, whether using these behaviors or others, Appendix B has a video exercise you may find helpful to assess and improve your skills with your dog.

Foundation behaviors

Hand target (includes other target training) (Page 237)
Objective: Your dog touches his nose to your hand. One of my favorite behaviors, we use this for engaging the dog's focus, and as the foundation for a wide variety of behaviors. As the first behavior to teach, and as a behavior your crossover dog may not already be trained to do, the instructions focus on a number of concepts.

- Using and quickly fading a food lure.
- Target training.
- Treat delivery options from getting a behavior started to advancing your training.
- Providing a foundation for many other behaviors (Recall, Finish, Attention and more).
- Increasing distance.
- Varying the reinforcement schedule.
- Adding a cue.

- Using the Window of Opportunity.
- Using the Lost Opportunity Marker (LOM).
- Teaching your dog to wait for the cue.
- Taking it on the road.
- Adding a new behavior into your dog's repertoire.
- Teaching your dog to listen.
- Using a new behavior in a Speed Trial.
- Introducing other targets.
- Fading targets.

Recall (Page 244)

Objective: Your dog comes when you call. The behavior dog owners tell us they want more than any other, this behavior is an extension of the Hand Target. In addition to the skills noted above, it includes the following.

- Introducing a hand signal cue.
- Attaching a voice cue.
- Changing cues.
- Building distance.
- A systematic approach to training with distractions.
- Varying the reinforcers.
- "Fixing" a previously-learned behavior (come when called).
- Handling non-compliance.
- Using distractions as rewards.
- Assessing your dog's level of training.
- Turning "errors" into opportunities.

"Settle" (Page 248)

Objective: Your dog goes to his bed, lies down, and stays there until released. This behavior is used as an example in Chapter 7. You'll find it helpful to review it with the 20 "Rules of shaping." This behavior is included to demonstrate the following skills.

- Shaping.
- Using handler position as a lure to speed learning.
- Changing the premise.
- Treat delivery to advance training in different contexts.
- Using differential reinforcement.
- Using a high rate of reinforcement (ROR).
- Building distance, duration, and changing context.
- Chaining.

- Using interim cues.
- Adding the cue.
- Using the Lost Opportunity Marker (LOM).

Down (Page 253)

Objective: Your dog lies down on cue, or alternatively, as a link in the chained behavior "settle." These instructions include several options for lying down and references for when one approach is better than another. It demonstrates the following skills.

- Clearly defining the trainer's goals and the dog's goal behavior.
- Shaping.
- Using and fading a food lure.
- Selecting cues.
- Changing cues.
- Communicating with more than one click.
- Using the Window of Opportunity to speed the response.

Sit (Page 258)

Objective: On your cue "sit," your dog will assume a sit. This behavior demonstrates the following skills.

- Capturing a behavior.
- Using and fading a food lure.
- Changing context early and often.
- Adding the cue.
- Using the Window of Opportunity.

Stay (Page 259)

Objective: On your cue "stay," your dog will remain in position until you click or release, included to demonstrate the following skills.

- Clearly defining the goal behavior.
- Using a cue from the start of a behavior.
- Using a voice marker ("yes").
- Adding a different behavior (and cue) to an already learned behavior (sit).
- Systematically adding distractions.
- Building distance (yo-yoing).
- Building duration (yo-yoing).
- Using a Lost Opportunity Marker (LOM).
- Using negative punishment (P-).

Loose leash walking (LLW) (Page 263)
Objective: Your dog will walk politely on a loose leash without pulling. This behavior demonstrates the following skills.

- Defining the behavior.
- Considering the dog's perspective versus the human's.
- Building distractions, distance, and duration.
- Understanding the importance of consistency.
- Recognizing, controlling, and using environmental reinforcements.
- Using a high rate of reinforcement (ROR).

Competition-oriented behaviors

To demonstrate using clicker training for competitive events such as Obedience or Rally, the following behaviors are offered as examples. Even if you are not interested in competition, these behaviors illustrate additional helpful skills. Again, they are just one possible way to achieve these goals.

Heel (Page 270)
Objective: Heel position is walking at your left side, with "the area from the dog's head to the dog's shoulder…in line with [your] left hip." We visualize this behavior as the dog walking with her head up. It demonstrates the following skills.

- The importance of clearly defining the goal behavior.
- Using a target stick.
- Fading the target.
- Building distance and duration.
- The importance of ROR.
- Avoiding post-performance pause.
- Separating individual elements of the goal behavior.
- Fading food treats.

The finish (Go to heel) (Page 274)
Objective: Called the "finish" because it completes several exercises in obedience competition, on your cue, your dog moves from in front of you to your left side and sits in heel position. Another "target" behavior, it is included to demonstrate the following skills.

- Another behavior chain—starting with the last behavior in the chain.
- Introducing, using, and eliminating interim cues.
- Using environmental aids for success.

Helpful and problem-solving—training an incompatible behavior

The final behavior is offered as an example of a helpful approach to solving a problem. It's a fun and useful behavior to teach your dog, answering the question, "How can I get my dog to let me know when he wants to go out?"

Ring a bell (Page 279)

Objective: The dog will ring a bell located by a door to the outside to alert the owner to let the dog out. The pictorial demonstrates the following skills.

- Shaping a behavior.
- Targeting with foot or nose.
- Changing location and context.
- Building distance.
- Transferring from food to non-food reinforcement.

Hand target (and other target training)

I love this behavior. We use this at my training school to start a crossover dog, and to establish a training relationship with a new dog. Targeting forms the basis of many other behaviors including using the hand target as a recall (next). Here is a step-by-step approach to teaching this.

1. **Objective.** Your dog touches his nose to your open palm.

2. **Get the behavior started.** Start with a food lure. Close your fist around a small piece of food. With your palm facing toward your dog, hold your fist in position for your dog to investigate. When he touches your fist with his nose, click, open your hand, and give your dog the treat. Repeat three times with food in your hand. Next, eliminate food in your hand. Close your empty fist and hold it in the same position. Click the moment your dog's nose touches your hand. After the click, reach for, and deliver the treat with the same hand.

   To deliver the treat, you can either give it to your dog or drop it near you so your dog stays close to you, able to easily repeat the behavior. Depending on the size of your dog, begin either sitting or standing up with your hand held directly in front of your dog, just a few inches from his nose so he can easily target your hand.

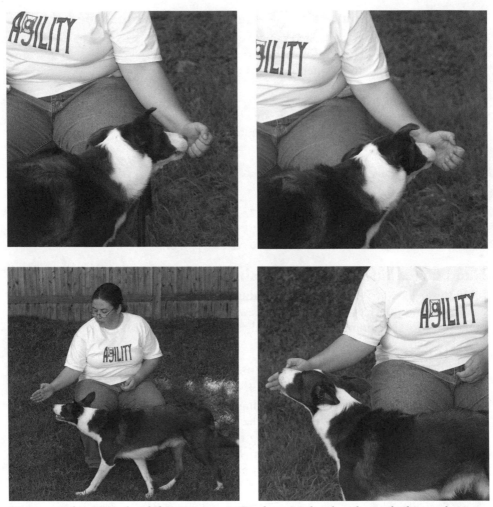

Vision touches Kris' closed fist. Kris progressively opens her hand, until ultimately Vision targets her open palm. With each progression, Kris clicks Vision's hand touch and delivers the treat.

3. **Move the behavior along**. Open your fist to expose your palm toward your dog. You may have to do this in small increments. Click the moment your dog's nose touches you. After each successful repetition, move your hand slightly—closer, farther away, in front, behind. Depending on your dog, you may need to make the changes gradual and subtle. Give your dog a breather after five to ten repetitions, taking frequent breaks, especially with a crossover dog in the first stages of clicker training.

As soon as Vision is touching the open palm, Kris moves her hand around, on both sides, changing the context so Vision has to move to target her hand, getting a click (and treat) for each touch.

After four or five consecutive repetitions, change your posture so your dog touches your hand when you're sitting, standing, crouched, or even lying down. Practice having your dog touch your hand held in different spots, from your front to your back. Have your dog turn in different directions to touch, as well as touch either hand on either side. Toss the treat in different directions so your dog comes from all sides to touch your hand.

Work in different spots around the room, in different rooms of the house, and new locations. For the first two or three repetitions in each change of location, make it easier for your dog, holding your hand closer to him, then increasing the distance.

To build distance, yo-yo the distance your dog travels to touch your hand, sometimes closer to you and sometimes a greater distance away from you. You can increase the distance your dog has to travel to touch you by tossing the treat further away after you click.

You may choose to use a verbal marker rather than a clicker at virtually any time as you progress through this behavior. You may also choose to eliminate the clicker at some point in your practice, and switch over to a verbal marker. Either works fine for the hand touch.

4. **Vary the reinforcement schedule**. Click a firm nose touch, and withhold a click if it's not a definite touch. Move your hand to a different position, for a second or third touch for one click.

5. **Add the cue**. For this particular behavior—touching your hand—you can choose a cue that means touch my hand, such as "touch," or you can use a cue that will mean "come to me." For the latter, if you have already taught your dog a recall command or cue, we recommend using a new word for the hand-touch-recall cue, such as "here." (See Recall page 244.)

Working in your training environment without distractions, when you are confident that the next thing your dog will do after eating the treat is to touch your hand, add the cue. Work close to your dog at first. To introduce the cue, first have your dog touch your hand without a cue, click and treat. After your dog eats the treat, say the cue "touch" before he touches your hand again. Click contact then treat. Continue saying the cue after your dog eats, as he turns toward you to touch your hand. Move your hand around as you continue practicing with the cue. *Once you start using the cue, do not click for touches if you didn't say the cue first*. Remember, it takes 20-50 repetitions for your dog to associate the cue with the behavior.

If your dog's response to the cue is slow, close the window of opportunity. Say your Lost Opportunity Marker (LOM) (e.g., "oops"), and move your hand so your dog can't touch it. Pause then present your hand again and cue "touch." "Yes" and praise when your dog touches your hand, then immediately cue "touch" again, and if your dog responds, click and treat. Click and treat the faster (better) responses. For more on this, see "Troubleshooting" page 242.

To teach your dog to wait for the cue, after a successful repetition, pause before giving the cue again. If your dog touches your hand, do not mark the behavior. Watch for a slight hesitation on your dog's part, then give the cue, click and treat. Repeat this sequence, reinforcing hesitation by giving the cue.

And finally, you're ready to test the cue. Outside of your training environment, when you're not in "training mode," hold out your hand and cue "touch." If she touches your hand, "yes" and reward (at least with verbal praise).

6. **Finish the job**. When you go to new locations and work around distractions, start out with your dog close to you. Practice around a variety of attractions. The hand touch is a great way to focus your dog around distractions.

Practice "touch" mixed with other behaviors, randomly mixing the order of your cues, as well as the number of behaviors you cue before you click. For example, "Touch, sit, touch, down" click and toss the treat so your dog gets up. "Sit," click. "Touch," "down" click. "Touch," "touch" click. "Sit," "touch," "down," "touch," "touch" click.

Then build speed, working on a Speed Trial with this behavior mixed in with others. Click and jackpot at the end of the Speed Trial.

Use a hand touch often in real-life. It is an easy behavior anytime you want to focus your dog or if you're going to give your dog something anyway and want to ask for a behavior first.

Check your Technique

- **Hold your hand still** without moving it toward your dog. Your dog touches you—you don't bump your dog's nose. That is unpleasant and constitutes punishment.

- **Check your clicker skills**.

  - **Timing**. Be careful not to click early, before your dog makes contact with your hand. Or late, after your dog has moved away from your hand. Click contact.

  - **Clicker hand**. Hold your clicker hand still. Don't point your clicker at your dog like a remote control, or thrust it toward your dog as you click. If it would be helpful, place your forearm against your body, so all that moves is your clicker-pressing thumb or finger.

- **Rate of reinforcement should be high**. If your dog shows no interest in touching your hand when it isn't holding food, try rubbing it with smelly cheese.

- **Hold your target hand** at your dog's head height so your dog doesn't have to stretch or jump up to touch it.

MaryBeth is holding her hand high, requiring Finlay to jump up to touch it. This is OK with a trained dog, but not when you're just starting out. Hold your hand in position so your dog can touch it easily without needing to stretch or jump up.

Troubleshooting

- **Dealing with non-compliance**. Remember to use your LOM.

- **Frequent non-compliance**. If you cue "touch" and your dog does not touch your hand, and it happens repeatedly, you may have started using the cue too soon. If so, stop saying the cue, strengthen the behavior, put it on a random schedule of reinforcement, then re-introduce the cue.

Additional recommendations for targets

Using your hand target. A hand target is helpful with a wide variety of behaviors. Teach your dog to target and follow your index finger, for example, to train behaviors and tricks such as spin (one direction), twirl (the other way), roll over, finish (go to heel), crawl, etc.

Just as with training the hand target, teaching your dog to touch your finger is a simple task. Click a finger touch and use this finger target to shape other behaviors.

Kris uses the finger target to teach Vision to spin.

LynnMarie uses her finger target to train Becke to weave under her legs for her musical freestyle routine.

Other targets. Use this same approach for teaching your dog to touch the end of a target stick, touch his nose, foot, head, shoulder or hip, to a different target such as a yogurt lid, carpet remnant, placemat, Post-it note, bell, or virtually anything else. Targets make training immensely easier, giving the dog a specific, tangible focus.

Target training has nearly limitless possibilities and applications. Use a target stick to shape a spin, train a Go-out to a target, or Drop-on-recall on one. A target is inherent to many behaviors, such as to lie down on your bed ("settle"), turn on a light, or go to an object. The bed, light switch, and object are "targets." Your side can be a target for heeling, your front for sit on a recall.

Transferring targets. Using a target such as a target stick, for example, you can focus your dog to a location, object, or other target to facilitate shaping. You might use this to teach your dog to turn on a light switch or close a door. Or you can use it to direct your dog for shaping another behavior, such as heelwork.

Fading or eliminating a target. When the target is not a component of the behavior, you will need to fade or eliminate it. The process of fading means incrementally reducing the size of the target until it can completely disappear.

Alternatively, here's another approach to more quickly doing away with a target used to draw the dog to a destination. Send your dog to the target, click, and have your dog return to you for the reward. Repeat this four or five consecutive times. After the fifth repetition, as your dog is returning to you, have a helper quietly remove the target. After your dog gets the reward, send him toward the target location once more. As he arrives at the spot where the target was previously located, click. You may need to have your helper randomly replace and remove the target once or twice when your dog isn't looking, but this process can progress quickly.

Target training "other" body parts. To teach your dog to target with her shoulder, hip, or other part of her body (not foot or nose), it can be helpful to start by applying light pressure with your hand so your dog resists the pressure slightly (activating the opposition reflex), then relax the pressure, and click the brief moment your dog leans into your hand.

Recall ("Here")

Chances are your crossover dog has had some training to come when called. If you are happy with your dog's response, congratulations! If not, read on.

Even clients that tell us they haven't done *any* training prior to coming to us, often have used the word "come." If it's been used repeatedly without any training foundation to teach the dog what to do, the dog ignores the word—creating an unhelpful association. Or worse, there may be an unpleasant association with something undesirable (like getting put in the crate, for instance). In any case, "Come!" is likely a useless or ruined cue. The solution is to train the recall as a new behavior, and attach a new cue such as "here."

Recall is a destination

Typically, the recall behavior is viewed as an action of moving to the trainer, that is, "come to me." To make it clear to your dog, it is helpful to think of the recall as a destination. *You* are the end of the trip. Consider, then, how seamless it is to teach the recall as an extension of the hand target. You're well on your way. To start, let's recap the steps you've already accomplished.

1. **Objective.** Your dog comes to you, arriving from anywhere to touch your hand.

2. **Get the behavior started.** You've trained your dog to move to you and touch your hand.

3. **Move the behavior along.** In addition to tossing the treat to build distance, increase it further by backing up away from your dog as he goes toward the treat (not as he approaches you). You've also had your dog touch your hand in different positions, and you've practiced in different locations.

4. **Vary the reinforcement**. When you're reinforcing the best of the best, consider how quickly your dog is able to come when you call under some circumstances, for instance, when it's dinnertime. Consider that as your benchmark for the best of the best.

5. **Add the recall cue, "here."** Whether or not you've first introduced the cue for "touch," you can introduce a recall hand signal, word cue, or both. The following instructions cover both the cue "here" and a recall hand signal.

Word cue—"here." You can introduce a word cue as soon as you start to build distance with the hand touch. Toss the treat away from you, and when your dog comes toward you, say "here." When your dog arrives, hold your hand out for your dog to touch. Click the touch and toss the treat to re-set the behavior. If you've already introduced "touch," you are changing the cue (see "Changing or adding cues" in Chapter 8). The sequence is:

a. New cue ("here"). When your dog turns toward you, give the new cue before the old cue.

b. Old cue ("touch"). As your dog arrives, say "touch."

c. Click touch.

In this case, it is likely that you can eliminate the old cue "touch" very quickly, as your hand held with your palm open and available for your dog to touch acts as a cue.

Hand signal—if you have not previously taught the cue "touch." You can introduce a hand signal as soon as you start to build distance. Toss the treat away from you and place your target hand at your waist. As your dog comes toward you, motion to your side as a hand signal and target. Click when your dog touches, toss the treat away from you, and return your hand to the neutral position in front of you. Repeat this motion with your target hand, as your dog heads toward you and click the touch.

Hand signal—if you have previously taught the cue "touch." Start with your hand at your waist as above. Make the same hand motion and as your dog approaches, say "touch." In this instance you are changing the cue. The sequence is:

a. New cue (the signal). When your dog turns toward you, give the new cue before the old cue.

b. Old cue ("touch"). After giving the signal, say the old cue.

c. Click touch.

To train a recall hand signal, Shari starts with her hand at her waist. She offers the new cue, the hand signal, by extending her hand out to her side, followed by the old cue, "touch."

Mazzie touches Shari's hand and gets a click for a great "recall."

This is a fun behavior to do with family members, practicing the cue while building your dog's responsiveness to others. Sit in a circle and call the dog from one person to the other, with each person marking the hand touch ("yes" or click) and rewarding. Spend a few moments reinforcing the dog, then stop petting, and have someone else call, using the cue, marking, and rewarding when the dog touches their hand.

6. **Finish the job**. This is one of the behaviors that my students and clients tell me is most important to them—and the most frustrating. The reason for their frustration is almost exclusively related to the fact that they don't invest the time training the dog to respond regardless of what else is going on. A recall when you're standing in your kitchen where your dog knows there's a good chance he'll get something for his response, bears no relationship to calling him away from a great game of chase a dog on the beach. If you want a really reliable recall, you have to invest the time. There are no two-ways about it. Using your list of distractions from page 179 start with those ranked one and two. Practice with these distractions until your dog has responded 20 times in a row without error. Keep records. After 20 consecutive successes, increase to the next two levels of distractions, and continue working through increasing levels of difficulty for your dog.

Mix up rewards and be generous, especially as you get to higher level distractions (chasing a squirrel is far more rewarding than Cheerios®). Use a food treat (a good one!), throw a ball, play tug, run backwards, or play chase-me. Make coming fun and rewarding! When possible, reward your dog with access to the distraction. For example, call your dog away from playing with other dogs, then reward him with the opportunity to play.

Duke often prefers his tug toy to treats. To vary payoffs, Denise throws this toy and plays with him—a jackpot for Duke.

Troubleshooting

- **When faced with higher ranked distractions** than your dog is ready for, try the following.

    - Keep him on a leash or long line.

    - If you let him run free, *don't call him.* Ignoring you, practices *not coming when called.*

- **Dealing with "errors."** When working around distractions, if your dog fails to come, approach slowly and unemotionally, put his leash on and, saying nothing, trot backward to where you called, "yes" and praise (no click, no treat). Take his leash off and try the same distraction, this time being closer to your dog when you call. Click and treat successful compliance, then move farther from your dog and do it again. If your second effort (closer) was also unsuccessful, you may have progressed too quickly or the distraction is ranked higher than you thought.

- **Play it safe**. If you are not sure if your dog will come to you, keep her on a long line (20-30'). If she doesn't respond when you call, go and get her (the line prevents running away). Hold the line close to her collar and guide her to where you were when you called. Say "Yes," praise, and release with "Go play!" *Do not use the line to pull your dog to you.* It is simply a management tool that prevents your dog moving away as you approach. This exercise teaches your dog that coming to you does not mean the fun is over.

"Settle"

This is a great way to learn shaping, and chaining several behaviors together. "Settle" is an example of a behavior chain, three separate behaviors performed in a sequence.

1. Go to the mat.

2. Lie down on the mat.

3. Remain there until released.

Once the behaviors are chained together, one cue will start the behavior chain, and each behavior will automatically follow the previous one.

Go to the mat

1. **Objective**. The dog goes to the mat or bed and gets onto it with all four feet.

2. **Get the behavior started**. This is a pure shaping exercise, and a good one for learning how to shape behavior. The moment you put the mat down, the chances are good that your dog will look at it. Be ready to click that first glance and you're off to the races! Click small incremental movements toward, around, and onto the mat. Remember Shaping Rule #5—accidents count. If your dog "accidentally" walks near the mat, *click!*

    Present or toss the treat away from the mat to re-set the behavior. While you may feel that it's easier to "get the behavior" by tossing the treat onto the mat, don't. It is luring with food and will not advance your training—you will still need to shape the behavior without a food lure. There is an exception, however, if your dog is reluctant to walk onto the mat. In that case, tossing a treat onto it once or twice should overcome this hesitancy, then continue shaping without the lure.

In the very beginning of shaping this behavior, where you stand can be helpful for getting the behavior started. For example, toss the treat to the side opposite to you. After eating the treat, the dog's natural inclination is to move toward you, toward the mat. Click his approach. After two or three repetitions, toss the treat to a different spot, and continue shaping.

Other than your position relative to the mat, avoid giving subtle body signals such as leaning or staring at the mat, moving around to attract the dog, and the like. This is a common pitfall for crossover trainers when they first start shaping, but such help is unhelpful. Remember, a training session is not about what your dog is doing at this moment. It's about what your dog is learning for the long run. Let your dog learn to figure it out. That's a thinking dog.

After the click, Shari tosses the treat to the opposite side. After Dax eats the treat, Shari's position draws Dax toward her, so Shari can click for approaching or touching the mat.

3. **Move the behavior along.** Click *progress*—improved responses such as touching, walking onto, and standing on the mat. Don't dwell on one behavior cluster. Stand sideways and move to different spots to help your dog zero in on the premise—it's not you—it's the mat. Move the mat to different spots, and adjust your posture and orientation early and often. You may be tempted to remain in one spot until your dog gets it. That's unhelpful. The sooner you change the premise, the faster your dog can zero in on the mat.

Do not, however, move around while your dog is working. Doing so is a distraction at best, and a lure at worst. Change your position only when your dog is going toward the treat, or after a break.

If this is your first shaping exercise, both you and your dog will need frequent breaks—for the dog to clear his mind, and for you to consider how you're doing. Tell your dog when you take a break and pick up the mat to make the task unavailable. The training session starts again when you put the mat down.

As you adjust the premise, yo-yo your distance from the mat, sometimes standing close, and sometimes further away from it. Also, toss the treat different distances from the mat, using treat delivery to vary and increase the distance your dog travels to return to *the mat.*

4. **Vary the reinforcement schedule**. Shaping (differential reinforcement) should be on an intermittent schedule—selecting improved behavior to click and reinforce. Once you have shaped your dog to have all four feet on the mat, click the best, such as returning quickly after eating the treat. When he goes directly to the mat repeatedly without any hesitation, you're ready to add the next behavior, the next link in the chain.

5. **Add the cue**. Not yet. Going to the mat is the first link in the chain of behavior. The cue will trigger the complete behavior chain once you put them together.

6. **Finish the job**. Because this is just the first element in the behavior chain, you're not ready to finish the behavior until all the elements are put together.

Check your technique

This shaped behavior is a great place to review the fundamentals of shaping.

- **Clicker timing**. Your dog's progress tells you about your timing. If the behavior progresses, you're doing fine. On the other hand, if your dog's movement onto the mat doesn't improve, your dog seems confused or shuts down, he's telling you he can't figure out what you're clicking. Examine your timing (early or late) and the clarity of your clicks.

- **Rate of reinforcement**. The more clicks, the more information, the faster your dog catches on. Make the goal of each shaping cluster readily-achievable for a high rate of reinforcement. Review the "rules" in Chapter 7.

- **Differential reinforcement**. The focus of shaping is moving incrementally closer to your goal, discontinuing to mark earlier aspects of the behavior.

  1. Break the behavior into small enough chunks for a high ROR.

  2. Do not mark (and reinforce) more than three consecutive repetitions of the same step or the behavior gets stuck.

  3. On the other hand, if your dog's improvement regresses, mark an earlier level of the behavior to keep him involved and trying. By providing helpful information, your dog will quickly progress again.

- **Other skills**. Often, beginner clicker trainers inadvertently create some common associations.

  - Holding food focuses your dog on the food, not on his behavior. Put the food away until after you click.

  - Get your bait-delivery hand out of your pocket or bait bag. Don't move to deliver the treat until *after* you click.

  - Hold your clicker hand still. Don't thrust or point the clicker at your dog.

Go to the mat and lie down

1. **Objective**. The second link in the chain, the dog goes to the mat and lies down on it. **Note**: Crossover dogs that have been trained to watch you, may actively stare at you. Envision how you want your dog to lie down on the mat, keeping in mind that this is a "relaxed" exercise, not an "attention" exercise. You don't want your dog focused on you, waiting in anticipation. If your dog is attention-trained, click when she is looking elsewhere, rather than staring at you. Watch for and mark a relaxed demeanor. You may also choose to shape "rest your head on the mat," with or without a cue.

2. **Get the behavior started**. Whether or not your dog is trained to lie down, you can easily shape this step of the behavior. This is where a clicker-trained dog truly advances your training. Once your dog readily goes to the mat, simply pause—delay your click. The chances are good that your dog will try something new when he doesn't get clicked immediately. The new behavior the dog offers is often sit, or he may even start to lie down, which enables you to start shaping "down on the mat."

   While I prefer not to use a cue at this time, if your dog already knows the cue "down," you have the option of using it as a brief interim cue. When your dog has gone onto the mat, cue "down," click, then toss the treat off the mat. After you've done this a few times, discontinue using the "down" cue, and it is likely your dog will automatically lie down when he gets onto the mat. The reason to eliminate the interim cue is because the "settle" cue you introduce later will start the behavior chain, which will include lying down with no additional cue.

   Treat placement to re-set the behavior depends on what you are shaping. If you are training "go to the mat and lie down when you get there," toss the treat off the mat after you click. If you're working on "lie down on the mat," and you want the dog to remain on the mat, place or hold the treat to reset the behavior on the mat.

After a click, there are two possible ways to deliver the treat—move the dog to a different position, or keep the dog in place. To reset Dax to "go to the mat," Shari tosses the treat off the mat. Kochi gets his reward on the mat so he stays in place to shape "lie down on the mat."

3. **Move the behavior along**. Once you have shaped "go to the mat" and "lie down on the mat," put the two together. Click lying down several times in a

row, delivering the treat in a way that keeps the dog on the mat, but has him get up to re-set the behavior. Next, toss the treat off the mat. When the dog returns to the mat, pause—don't click. Because you have worked on lying down several times, when you withhold your click, the chances are excellent your dog will lie down on the mat. Click.

Once your dog is going to the mat and lying down, you may choose to mark with "yes" rather than use a clicker. The clicker is the ideal tool for the precision of shaping, but at this point as you continue to increase the time frame, you don't need the precision of the click.

As with shaping your dog to go to the mat, change the context, moving the mat to different spots, and adjusting your posture and orientation. Yo-yo the time your dog remains down to increase it to whatever you feel you'll need for practical purposes. You can introduce a release word such as "Free" or "Okay" making sure that your dog remains in place until you release him. Once you reach 15 or 20 minutes, your dog will have the idea that this is an indefinite exercise, and he should simply remain there until released.

4. **Vary the reinforcement**. Reward the best of the best, such as going to the mat and lying down without hesitation, and the like. Since the behavior you name is the behavior you'll get, work on shaping it the way you want it before adding the cue.

5. **Add the cue**. Once your dog is readily going to the mat and lying down, you're ready to introduce the cue. Toss the treat off the mat. Say the cue as your dog turns to head back onto the mat. Wait for him to lie down, then click. As you practice with the cue, continue to yo-yo the duration your dog remains down before you click.

   Remember, once you add the cue, if your dog doesn't respond, say your LOM then try again. The "second chance" gets only "yes" and praise; not click and treat. Then give your dog another opportunity to get it right *the first time* to earn a click and treat. To test the cue, give your "settle" cue and see if your dog responds by going to his bed.

6. **Finish the job.** The complete chain: Go to the mat, lie down, and stay there until released. Continue to increase duration (you'll find more specifics with Stay). You may choose to add a cue such as "relax," meaning "You'll be there for awhile, so you may as well chill-out."

   Use the behavior in real-life situations. Consider when this behavior is most useful to you and train in that environment. If you want your dog to settle during your dinner, set it up and practice it with you sitting at the table. If you want to use it while you're relaxing on the couch, practice in that location and with that posture. Use this behavior as it fits your needs—in class, visiting friends, attending seminars, and the like. Teaching your dog to relax on a mat or bed gives you an "off" switch. Your dog will relax, and you can, too.

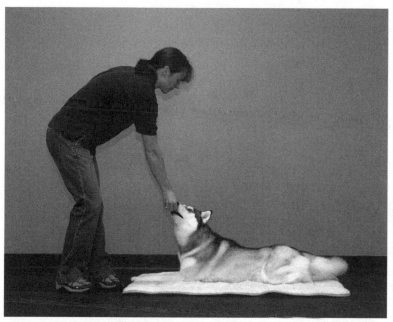

When working on increasing time on the mat, reward the dog in place, so you don't have to start over with "go to" and "lie down on" the mat.

Down

1. **Objective**. This behavior includes several options: two actions and three separate postures. The action of lying down can be either from a standing position or from a sit. How you train this behavior depends on how you envision it—as sit-then-lie-down or fold-back-down-from-a-stand. You can train either or both.

   Further, the down posture may be an active one with both rear legs tucked under, a more relaxed posture with the dog's weight shifted onto one hip, or fully relaxed, with the dog lying on her side. While these differences may be immaterial to you, knowing what you are training this behavior for can help determine which you choose. Chart 12-1 offers some suggestions.

Activity/Training	Action to Lie Down			Down Posture			
	From sit	From stand	Either	Active	On hip	On side	Any posture
Basic Manners			X				X
Grooming			X			X	
Obedience (down-stay)	X				X		
Obedience (drop on recall)		X		X			
Rally-Obedience	X	X		X			
Agility (table)		X		X			
"Settle," "Relax"			X		X	X	
"Bang you're dead			X			X	

Chart 12-1. This chart presents some options for both the action of lying down as well as the posture your dog assumes when he's down.

Dax demonstrates the difference between an "active" down with her rear legs tucked under, ready to spring up, and a "relaxed" down, lying over on one hip, rear legs extended to the side in a relaxed fashion.

2. **Get the behavior started**. Regardless how you envision the behavior, it can be either shaped, captured, or lured. The approach I like best is shaping, clicking any movement toward your goal—lowering the head, moving a foot out, a weight shift backward, sitting, sniffing—anything that leads to lying down as you envision it. Avoid getting stuck on one aspect such as head movement. Focus on the whole dog, watching for any subtle movement that can lead to lying down.

Knowing that many crossover trainers come from lure-reward backgrounds, you have my permission to lure a time or two (or three), but then stop! Your dog must learn to lie down without a prompt (lure or hand motion). After three lured repetitions, shape it. Be patient! You will get it (and so will your dog). The first few behaviors you shape are the most challenging, and the most helpful and educational for all future training.

3. **Move the behavior along**. Using differential reinforcement, shape toward your goal behavior. Use treat delivery to re-set the behavior either into a stand or into a sit. To shape the relaxed and very relaxed postures, once your dog is readily lying down, begin to click weight shifts so your dog lies over on one hip rather than with both rear legs tucked under him. Adjust context elements such as your posture, location, orientation, and the like.

4. **Vary the reinforcement schedule**. Once your dog is readily offering the behavior, begin to select and reward the best of the best.

5. **Add the cue**. When your dog readily lies down without hesitation, add the voice cue. Keep in mind that to your dog this behavior is an *action* not a *position*. Since the *action of lying down* will be triggered by the cue, if you train both sit-then-down and fold-back-down, give each a different cue.

   You may also choose to use a different cue for each posture. I use the cue "relax" to mean "shift your weight onto your hip," giving two cues, "down . . . relax." And "bang" can cue "lie on your side."

   If you already have a hand signal cue that is an off-shoot of luring, that's perfectly fine, but a voice cue can be a life-saver. The following is the sequence to train the voice cue.

   a. New cue ("down"). Say your new cue before giving the signal, the old cue.

   b. Old cue (the signal). After giving your new cue, give the signal.

   c. Click your dog for lying down.

   d. Repeat until your dog anticipates the signal, lying down on just the voice cue.

   Using the window of opportunity with your LOM will greatly speed your dog's response to this cue. Cue "down," and if your dog hesitates before responding to the cue, say your LOM. Turn your head away briefly, turn back, and cue again. Once you say your LOM, even if your dog lies down before you give another cue, ignore it. Do not mark that behavior, just get her up to re-set the behavior. Then cue "down" again, and if she responds, "yes" and praise, followed by another chance to respond to the first cue for a click and treat.

6. **Finish the job**. I consider an instantaneous response to "down" to be one of the most critical behaviors to have on voice cue. I rate it as high in importance as "come," training my dogs to lie down on a dime the instant they hear the word. I know many students that have used this in some potentially dangerous situations. Not only is it important to practice this behavior in real-life situations, but this is one of the foundation behaviors I use in every Speed Trial and Listening Drill. As with the recall, go through your list of distractions and solidify this behavior. Time spent on this may one day save your dog's life!

Troubleshooting

If your dog is reluctant to train this behavior, consider whether there might be an underlying physical reason. Structural issues such as arthritis, hip or shoulder dysplasia, or spinal problems can make lying down and getting up repeatedly uncomfortable, or even painful. Consider your dog's well-being above all else.

Double click? Maybe…sometimes…

The "rule" is mark the behavior with a single click, then treat; don't click multiple times, or mark more than one behavior before giving a treat. There can, however, be exceptions to this rule—times when you might click, then follow with another click before you've given the treat. Keeping in mind that the click marks the behavior you want the dog to perform, here's an example.

In "My Crossover Journal" on page 120 I wrote about our Training Academy students shaping Kochi to lie down. Kochi had been clicked for scratching, plus scratching is his default calming signal—the one he most often offers when he's confused. Since the shaping process involves some confusion, Kochi's tendency to scratch was a double whammy—scratching having been previously reinforced, as well as being his default stress release. Actually with Kochi, scratching is a triple whammy, because he is an agile, fast, inventive, bright dog that offers behaviors quickly. A lot of fun to shape, he challenges the trainer's timing, making it difficult to shape down without inadvertently including some facet of scratching. Enter the double click. Here's how it might go.

- Kochi sits, simultaneously raising his hind leg to scratch. Click and treat.

- While he's eating the treat, he's not scratching—click and treat.

- He eats, and starts to raise his leg, click. Hearing the click, he stops scratching, click…treat.

Can you see how this last click, the second part of a double-click marks *not* scratching? With the process started, shaping continues by marking different *non-scratching* behaviors, whether or not they lead to lying down. The point to communicate to Kochi is "We're *not* working on scratching, give me something different."

Not just for shaping "down," but for any behavior, since the click is *communication* take the opportunity to communicate helpful information with a click, even if you haven't yet delivered the payoff for the previous click. Just don't do this often.

Because Kochi had been clicked many times for scratching while being shaped to lie down, it was important to click before he scratched, getting to the point that even the slight head movement before he lifts his rear foot—the "intention"—was clicked, letting him know it isn't scratching that we're working on.

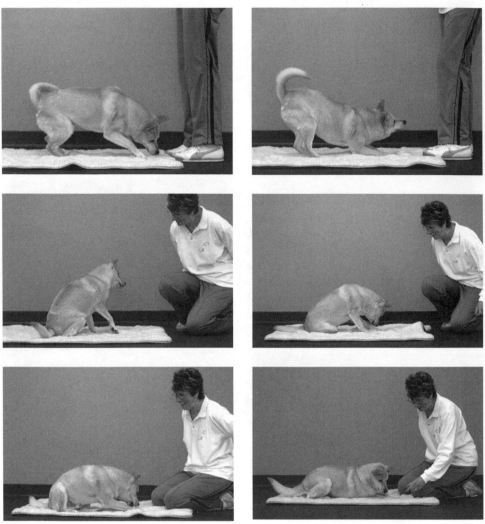

Having gotten past scratching, we began the process of shaping Kochi to lie down. I clicked any behavior that lead to lying down—sniffing the mat, lowering his front end, sitting and lifting a forepaw, and then lowering his body until...Eureka! He lies down and gets his reward in place.

Sit

1. **Objective**. Your dog will sit on cue.

2. **Get the behavior started**. Sit is generally an easy behavior to capture. Stand close to your dog and simply look at him. If he sits, click. If he doesn't, prompt him with a nose-tease. Show him a treat, then put it out of sight. Click the instant your dog sits. To re-set the behavior, drop the treat a short distance away, or present it so he stands up. If your dog does not sit, try luring briefly.

   Holding a visible treat, lure up over and slightly behind your dog's head, and hold your hand still. As your dog looks up, he'll likely sit. Click, then re-set the behavior with your treat placement. *Repeat no more than three times with food,* then lure without food. Make the same motion, this time not holding food. Click, then reach for the treat. Toss or hold it to reset the behavior. *Repeat no more than three times.*

After these six luring repetitions, your dog will offer a sit without the lure. If your dog loses focus, nose-tease to re-focus him on the availability of a reward.

3. **Move the behavior along**. Because sit is a simple behavior, and is the default behavior for many dogs, it is easy to quickly move through the Six Steps. After your dog sits two or three times, move to a different spot and do it again. Change criteria and contexts frequently. Don't dwell on practicing in any one location, or with one posture, position or orientation. Each time you adjust a criterion—location, posture, orientation—be prepared for your dog to hesitate before sitting. You may need to nose-tease to focus him on the task in the changed context, but fight the temptation to lure.

4. **Vary the reinforcement**. Click the best of the best.

5. **Add the cue**. When your dog is sitting without any hesitation, and you are willing to bet that your dog is about to sit, say "sit" just before he begins the behavior. This behavior presents a good chance to practice the window of opportunity. If your dog does not respond to the cue immediately, say your LOM, look away briefly (just a slight head turn), look back, and re-cue "sit," "yes," and praise. (If your dog sits after you say your LOM, but before you give another cue, ignore it. Simply get your dog up to re-set the behavior.) Then give your dog another chance to get it right the first time.

6. **Finish the job**. For most dogs, sit is their default behavior—the one the dog assumes first, or when he doesn't know what behavior you're looking for, and starts somewhere. You'll find it easy to have your dog sit on cue in virtually every context. But you need to practice for your dog to generalize.

Stay

Stay offers some exceptions to the "rules." First, it does not need the precision of the click—your dog either stays, or he doesn't. If he stays, "yes" marks the behavior just as well as a click. You can of course use a click if you prefer, but a verbal marker works just fine. (In the following instructions, "click" means either "yes" or click.)

Another difference in training "stay" is that, even at the start of training this behavior, you can set it up with 95% certainty that your dog will stay put. Since this level of predictability fits the criteria for attaching the cue, you can use the "stay" cue from the start of training. Using the cue, however, doesn't mean the dog knows what "stay" means until you have practiced it sufficiently.

Because stay is an exception to the rules, the order of the Six Steps is different in the following recommendations which refer to Sit-stay. The same suggestions apply to Stand-stay and Down-stay.

1. **Objective—Define "stay."** Decide what parameters of movement are acceptable to you, and be consistent. To me, stay means remain in the same location

and the same posture. Moving from sit to either stand up or lie down is not acceptable, nor is scooting forward in a sit to a different spot.

Note: When you cue "sit" to work on "stay," use verbal praise only for the sit—no click. Since click ends the behavior, your dog may stand up when you click, and you want him to remain sitting...so just use quiet, verbal praise.

2. **Get the behavior—Wait for the click**. The first step in training stay is to simply delay the click. After your dog sits, praise quietly, pause a second or two, then click. Yo-yo this delay interval around a goal of three or four seconds. Do not move your position—just delay the click.

3. **Moving the behavior along**. Again, this behavior is an exception to the "rules." You add the cue before the behavior is learned because you can create success. Now's the time.

   Sit your dog, praise (no click), say "stay" and take a small step back (one to two feet). If your dog moves (stands or lies down), mark with your LOM, then cue or lure *without a treat* back into a sit, repeat "stay," and step away again. You don't have to replace her in the same spot, just have her sit. Pause for three seconds, click and treat. Click ends the behavior so she may get up. You will save time repeating this behavior if your dog remains sitting; however, if she gets up, she still gets the treat. Simply sit her again. If she doesn't get up, reward in place.

   Throughout your training this behavior, be consistent. If you say "stay," and your dog moves, LOM, and repeat the same step until you have success.

4. **Distractions help your dog learn "stay."** Using distractions teaches your dog to *commit to staying*, helping her develop self-control, and to focus in on the premise "Stay" means stay.

   In the following progressions, at the *first sign of movement*, say your LOM marking the first subtle weight shift rather than waiting until your dog has changed posture or moved from position. Here are a few suggestions for a systematic approach to introducing distractions.

   a. Holding food in your hand, say "stay", take a step back, and with your hand by your side, open it and show your dog the food (see the "Sample training plan," page 228). If your dog starts to move, say your LOM, and close your fist. Pause, re-sit your dog if necessary, and open your hand again. Repeat this until your dog stays when you show the food in your hand, pause briefly, click and reward. Repeat, gradually lowering your hand to the floor, then put the treat on the floor. If your dog moves when the treat is on the floor, say your LOM, and *pick up the treat*. Do not let your dog get the treat unless you click or say "yes."

With Duke on a "stay," Denise shows him a treat in her open palm. The moment Duke starts to get up, Denise marks his move with her LOM, closes her fist and removes the food as negative punishment. She immediately repeats the exercise with the same distraction. This time Duke stays.

b. Build the distraction. Put more food on the floor until your dog will stay with a pile of food as you quietly praise (no release), and reward with treats from the pile. Release with "yes" or click then reward.

c. Another distraction is to say "stay," step away, two feet in front of your dog and crouch down. Say your LOM and stand up at the first sign of your dog's *intention* to respond to this enticing posture.

As a distraction to increase Finlay's commitment to stay, Marybeth crouches down—an enticing body posture.

261

d. Use "stay" at feeding times before you put your dog's dish down, gradually lowering the dish to the floor. Mark the intention to move and pick up the dish if your dog starts to get up before you release her. Dinner is her reward.

5. **Vary the reinforcement schedule and reinforcements**. You're working on a variable schedule by yo-yoing time and distance. Work on time and distance separately as described in the "Sample training plan" on page 228. Standing close to your dog, start by concentrating on time, yo-yoing around your time frame goal. Then to build distance, shorten your time frame and yo-yo around your distance goal. As your dog's stay improves, build time and distance as separate elements. Once you've trained each separate element, combine time, distance, and distractions and work in new locations. Change your posture and orientation.

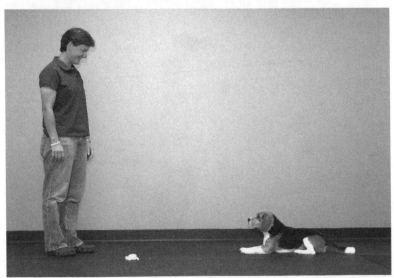

Upping the ante and increasing the difficulty for Finlay, Marybeth puts down a pile of food, then stands up. Good Beagle! When you do this, make sure you can block or cover the treats to prevent your dog getting a reward if he fails to stay.

Virtually any activity your dog enjoys can be used to reward stay. Say "stay" as you open the door, then release him to go out. Release him to play with the kids, get a cookie, chase a squirrel, retrieve a ball—you name it. The caveat is if your dog moves before you release him, you must prevent access to the reward.

6. **Finish the job.** Stay is easy to reward with the Premack Principle. Ask for a stay before releasing her to go play, perform agility, see a buddy, and the like. Use your list of distractions on page 179. When working with a new distraction, distance makes it easier to tolerate. For example, if your dog has trouble staying when the kids are playing ball, move her further away, and reward her by having the kids throw her the ball when you click. Use life situations as opportunities for training. The more you do, the more you'll build your dog's immunity to distractions.

   This is a potentially life-saving behavior. My young dog Cannon once jumped out of the car in a dangerous situation because he didn't hear (or possibly ignored) my cue. To make sure this didn't happen again, I trained new cue/old cue. I opened the door (new cue) and said "stay," repeating this sequence sufficient times that the new cue, "door open," now means "stay" without my saying a word.

   Once your dog knows that "stay" means don't move, practice it with other postures—down and stand. At first, shorten time and distance, but having laid the foundation with sit-stay, you can quickly build your dog's understanding of "stay" in any posture.

Check your technique

- If you are working on stay on-leash, do not use it to control, manipulate, or stop your dog from moving. Many training methods use leash guidance to reposition a dog, so the crossover trainer may unconsciously do so. Watch for this. Your goal is for your dog to control *himself*.

- When you lower the treat to the floor some dogs, especially those that have been lure trained, may see this as a cue to lie down. Say your LOM *the moment your dog starts to lie down*, pick up the treat, re-sit your dog, and do it again. Gradually work through this, starting over each time the dog starts to move.

Loose leash walking (LLW)

To humans, loose leash walking is all about having slack in the leash. But our dogs aren't always in control of whether or not there's tension on the leash. We're at the other end of the leash—and we're often the ones tightening up on it. We may shorten the leash at a street corner, to move past another dog, or to pull the dog away from something yucky. *So from your dog's perspective, what you want her to know isn't about the leash—it's about learning to be aware of where you are, and where she is in relation to you.*

Of course the dog is also aware of collar pressure, so as you practice this, avoid creating tension in the leash, or allowing the dog to pull, stopping, and then regaining her focus—an approach called "be a tree." By waiting until your dog feels the release of collar pressure, and reinforcing her when the tension is relieved (negative reinforcement), the dog learns to back up a step when she feels collar pressure. This can create a bungi-jump effect when what you want is, "Pay attention to where you are, and walk next to me within a three foot radius of my side." Looked at from that perspective, LLW is a targeting behavior—the dog is peripherally targeting your location.

There are many different ways to approach teaching loose leash walking. We particularly like the approach we've adapted from Turid Rugaas. The instructions refer to "click," but you can use "yes" as well.

This is another behavior where you can introduce the cue early since the behavior is predictable. Your dog moves with you when you start walking. The cue I use is "let's go."

1. **Objective—Define the behavior**. LLW is not heeling, which is walk close to your left side focused on you. With LLW the dog has a two to three foot radius by your side. He may sniff the ground and look around as long as he doesn't pull on the leash.

2. **Get the behavior started**. The first step is establishing communication, to teach your dog that there are no surprises. Introduce an "alert" noise such as a kissing or clucking sound. Make the noise and when he looks toward you, click or "yes." Repeat this several times to teach your dog to pay attention at the sound. You will use this to alert your dog before you change direction.

   Start by walking backward with your dog facing you. Click and treat with a high rate of reinforcement. If you change direction, make the alert sound, then click and treat. The figure and photo on page 265 show the direction of movement with the dog and handler facing each other. Repeat several times. Your goal is to have your dog moving easily with you, paying attention to your direction. (This is not an "attention" exercise, so she doesn't have to be focused on you or looking at your face, but to move with you, she needs to be aware of where you are.)

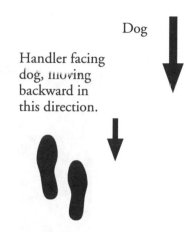

Dog

Handler facing dog, moving backward in this direction.

Marybeth walks backward to orient Journey to her, clicking and treating as she goes.

3. **Move the behavior along**. Next, start out walking backward, click and treat, then pivot to your right, turning clockwise to face in the same direction as your dog. Your dog is now on your left. The figure and photos on page 266 demonstrate this maneuver. As soon as you complete the turn, immediately click and treat, take one more step forward, click and release.

(**Note**: These instructions are for walking with your dog on your left. You may walk your dog on either side. If you prefer your dog to walk on your right, you'll need to reverse these directions.)

Handler turns to the right, clockwise, to face same direction as dog. Dog on handler's left.

Dog

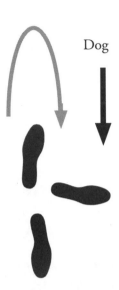

Marybeth turns clockwise to her right to move in the same direction as Journey. After she turns, he is by her left side.

You have lots of options for treat delivery with LLW. You can reward with either hand, or drop the treat on the floor, but whichever way you deliver the treat, do not use it as a lure. If you reward with your right hand, be careful not to unintentionally draw your dog across your body. After you reward, bring your hand to a neutral position so your dog is not focusing on the treat hand. If the treat bounces away from your dog, move with her toward the treat. Don't let the leash tighten as your dog goes to the treat.

Notice how both Marybeth and Shari deliver the treat without causing the dog to cross in front of them. Marybeth hands Journey the treat, and Shari puts it on the floor, each making sure that the treat is at their left.

As you build distance forward, click when your dog is walking by your side or slightly behind, but not when she is ahead of you. When she is in front, she can't see you, causing her to lead out and pull. The moment your dog starts to move out ahead of you, make your alert noise, walk backwards a few steps to reengage and reorient your dog, then turn and walk forward again. *Click only while walking forward. Backing up is simply to reorient your dog to you, so once you start moving forward with your dog, discontinue clicking her for following you as you back up.*

Practice changing direction with your dog—turning right, left and about—as a separate exercise. To change direction, alert your dog with the sound, turn, click and treat.

4. **Vary the reinforcement schedule and reinforcements**. Continue this sequence starting backward, then turning to move forward with your dog at your left, and build distance moving forward before you release. Use a high ROR as you continue yo-yoing the distance you walk with your dog. Randomly vary

267

the number of steps you take around an average target goal. Every so often, reinforce several times in rapid succession. That will keep your dog's motivation high.

It is easy to fall into a consistent pattern of walking, marking, and treating such as every fifth step. To avoid such a pattern, consciously change the number of steps you take before you click. For example, reinforce two or three times in rapid succession, then four steps, click, then two steps twice in a row, seven steps, one step, one step, three steps, and the like. Click the best of the best. Mix your rewards, using "life rewards." For example, mark, then run with your dog toward a tree. (See Troubleshooting.)

5. **Add the cue**. Say the cue each time you start to walk. You may choose to repeat the cue if you change direction, or introduce a different cue for changing direction such as "this way."

6. **Finish the job**. Practice around distractions. When you introduce something that attracts your dog, make your alert sound the moment your dog focuses on the attraction, walk backward to re-focus him, turn, and walk toward the distraction with a high ROR. The bigger the distraction, the more you'll need to re-focus your dog, and click as you move toward it.

Reminders. The time to alert your dog and begin to back up is *before the leash is taut*. Don't wait for your dog to hit the end of the leash. The time will come when your dog catches himself before the leash tightens. When you see that happen, have a party! Tell your dog how thrilled you are.

Check your technique

In addition to letting your dog know when you like his behavior (by marking when he walks with a loose leash), leash handling is your responsibility. Some people automatically and unconsciously hold the leash tight. Your dog can't learn to walk on a loose leash when you're applying tension.

- Fold the excess leash into your hand. Don't grasp the loop end of a six foot leash and have your dog five and a half feet away, or hold your hand way up in the air to take up the slack.

- If you have trouble coordinating a clicker, treats, leash, dog, walking, chewing gum, and whistling—or even just the clicker, treats and leash—use "yes" instead of the clicker. If you need still more freedom, consider a hands-free suggestion in "Create a third hand" on page 62.

Note how there is slack in the leash even when Dax is two feet away from Shari's side. This is loose-leash walking!

Troubleshooting

- By definition, LLW means there is no tension in the leash. This rule is absolute: *Your dog may not pull and be successful.* Any time your dog pulls and gets to move forward, pulling is reinforced. So from the moment you start training LLW, *any time your dog is on leash*, you are either in training, or using equipment that prevents pulling, such as a front-connection harness or head halter. Do not use a Flexi- or bungi-lead as they reward pulling.

- You have loads of opportunities to reward LLW with instinctive behaviors. The downside to environmental reinforcement, however, is that if your dog is pulling at the same time as he's sniffing and being a normal dog, *pulling is reinforced.* Anytime you allow your dog to pull successfully, you set back your training. Consistency is critical to success. No matter what your dog is doing, the moment that leash gets even a little taut, back up, re-focus your dog, and then continue on.

- Here's a good way to check whether or not your dog is pulling—or to stop you unintentionally tightening up on the leash. Make a loose loop in the leash as if you're tying a knot, but don't pull it tight. When this loop starts to tighten into a knot, you'll be aware of it. If you hate knotted leashes as much as I do (which is *a lot!*) this strategy can help you reinforce your dog when the loop is loose—and so is the leash.

Heel

Heeling, as opposed to Loose Leash Walking, is a competitive behavior used in dog sports such as Obedience and Rally-Obedience. If you train this behavior to compete with your dog, have a clear picture of what the precise behavior is that you're shaping. The following is my vision of heeling; yours may be different.

1. **Objective**. Heel position is defined by the American Kennel Club in this way: "…whether the dog is sitting, standing, lying down, or moving at heel. The dog should be at the handler's left side straight in line with the direction the handler is facing. The area from the dog's head to shoulder is to be in line with the handler's left hip. The dog should be close to, but not crowding, its handler so that the handler has freedom of motion at all times."

   Keeping this definition in mind, consider how to shape this behavior—how to get your dog to figure out how to keep "[t]he area from the dog's head to shoulder…in line with [your] left hip." I teach this as a target behavior to give the dog a focus. Without such focus, it's difficult for even a thinking dog to figure out how to align any part of his body with any part of yours.

   Further, envision the dog having her head up, muzzle parallel with the ground. When you define and train heeling to include your dog's head position, you will never ever ever need to say, "Don't sniff!"—the equivalent of someone commanding you to drive your car blindfolded.

2. **Get the behavior started**. To shape this behavior, use a target stick (TS) with a butterfly clip or a piece of duct tape.

Using a target stick with a butterfly clip is one option for teaching heel position. The clip can later be transferred to your leg or hip, then faded completely.

If you have already taught your dog to target your finger, you can easily transfer that "touch" to the clip on the TS in just four or five clicks. Hold the clip by your finger and cue "touch" once or twice, clicking and rewarding each. Then move your finger so that it is slightly behind the clip, with the clip between your dog and your finger. Cue "touch" and click as your dog is close to the clip. Remove your finger and continue working on "touch" with the clip moving it around so your dog readily touches it.

If this is your first targeting behavior, you have not previously worked on "touch," when you first present the target stick, be ready to click the merest flicker of a glance. Shape your dog to touch the clip or tape. Hold the TS so your dog's head is erect. Move the stick and repeat until your dog readily touches the clip.

3. **Move the behavior along**. The next step is to teach your dog to follow the TS. Hold the stick in your right hand, parallel to the ground, held out to your right side. The height of the stick should be such that your dog's head is level when he follows the TS. Turn slowly in place, moving the TS in a clockwise circle clicking your dog for following it as in the illustration below. Start with one step, and keeping a high ROR, gradually increase until your dog walks ten steps following the TS.

Handler turns in place as dog walks around following the stick.

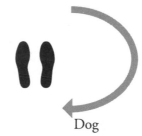

Dog

Next, with the TS in the same position and height, face your dog and begin to walk backward. Click your dog for following the TS with her head in the same position. Yo-yo the time frame (or steps) to 15 seconds. This step is critical for shaping your dog to walk with the correct head carriage—an important element of this behavior. Don't rush it.

You may find it helpful to introduce an interim cue for "walk with your head up." Later, your "heel" cue will mean "walk in heel position with your head up."

Rachael walks backward to teach Gabe to walk with his head up following the target stick. Don't rush this step.

Practice this next maneuver without your dog so you can perform it smoothly holding the TS steady before doing it with your dog. With the TS held in the same position, start out walking backward, then pivot to your right to face the same direction as your dog. As you turn, move your hand to keep the TS in position in front of your dog. Your dog is now on your left, about two feet from your side. Click the first step your dog takes walking by your left side, head up.

Once Gabe has learned the right head position, Rachael turns so he is at her left side. She starts out holding the target stick away from her body, clicking and treating Gabe for following it with his head up. Over time, she'll move the target stick closer, and then clip the butterfly clip to her pants leg at that same height.

Continue to turn and walk forward, yo-yoing distance to 20 steps forward with your dog 2 feet from your left side, following the TS. Gradually bring the TS closer to your left side while maintaining your dog's head carriage. Hold the TS steady. Continue to work on distance as you bring the dog closer.

Cody's posture and position look great next to Bruce as he heels along, following the target stick.

Once your dog is heeling next to your left side, attach the clip to the side of your pant leg at the same height as the TS, above your knee. (If your dog's head is below your knee, continue using a TS held in front of your hip, keeping it perpendicular to the ground.) Starting with a step or two, mark and reinforce this position at heel, yo-yoing to increase the distance you and your dog heel together.

Next, introduce the other elements of heeling, each shaped separately: heeling at fast and slow pace; changing pace normal to slow, slow to normal, normal to fast, fast to normal; turns, right, left, and about; plus starting and stopping.

4. **Vary the reinforcement schedule**. Using a variable schedule of reinforcement continue to yo-yo the distance you walk, the number of starts and stops you take, and the like between marking and reinforcing your dog. As with Loose Leash Walking, it is easy to fall into a consistent pattern of heeling the same number of steps, mark, and treat. To avoid such a pattern, consciously change the number of steps you take before you click. To avoid the scallop effect, reinforce several times in rapid succession.

   Here's an example of a reinforcement schedule: Reinforce two or three times in rapid succession, then four steps, click, then two steps twice in a row, seven steps, one step, one step, three steps, and the like. Click the best of the best. Just as with LLW, you can mix your food rewards with other rewards, including "life rewards." For example, mark, and then let your dog sniff the ground or throw a ball for him.

5. **Add the cue**. Once your dog is walking at heel with his head up, add the cue. If you've used an interim cue, say the new cue before the interim cue—new cue/old cue.

6. **Finish the job.** Since this approach to heeling is a competition behavior, finishing the job means taking your dog to new locations, working around increasing distractions, and working through all the changes in criteria to help your dog. When you first go to new locations, it may be helpful to return to using your target stick to help your dog focus as you build reliability around distractions.

Part of finishing the job is to eliminate food treats. Keep in mind the concept is "fade" food treats, not go cold turkey. Here's a strategy for doing so. In your familiar training area, put on your bait bag or load your pockets as usual, with another source for treats in an easily accessible container on the side. When you mark the behavior, take your dog to the container for the reward. Randomly alternate between rewarding from your bait bag and from the container. After several sessions leave your bait bag near the container and return to it to reward. When you practice in new places, put treats in strategic locations before you start to train (don't let your dog see you). Surprise your dog. Have treats in a shirt pocket, or have a helper give you a treat for your dog. The idea is that your dog never knows when (or where) he'll get a reward.

The finish (Go to heel)

Teaching the finish requires that your dog has two foundation behaviors on cue—"sit" and "touch." You will be using known cues as interim cues, as well as teaching and using other interim cues. Using interim cues means the order of the Six Steps is different.

1. **Objective.** Your dog moves from in front of you to sit at heel at your left side in heel position. Review the definition of "heel position" on page 270, and keep it in mind as you're shaping this behavior. There are two ways to get to heel from in front.

   - Finish to the right. The dog moves around you to the right in a clockwise circle to sit next to your left side.

   - Finish to the left. The dog moves to your left side, turning in a counter-clockwise circle (toward you) to sit by your left side.

   The arrows in the following figures show the direction of the dog's movement.

Finish to the right

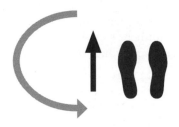

Finish to the left

Think of this as a two-step chain "move to my left" and "sit in heel position," teaching each separately, starting with the last behavior in the chain, sit at heel.

Note: In the following instructions if your dog is short, use a target stick. How short? Your dog needs to be tall enough to touch your hand without jumping up.

2. **Get the behavior—Sit at heel**. Stand next to a wall or barrier leaving just enough room so your dog is by your left side, facing straight. Facing the same direction as your dog, stand one step in front of him (about two feet). Turn your left palm toward your dog and cue "touch," cue "sit," then click and reward. Your hand position should be held so that after the touch, when he sits, he is next to you in heel position. After three or four repetitions, add a cue for "come up to heel position," such as "come-up…," then "touch," then "sit." As you practice, eliminate the "touch" cue, so your new cue is "come-up…sit," a cue you will use when teaching the finish.

   Practice until your dog is readily moving to heel position and sitting. Then begin to move away from the wall or reduce the size of the barrier. Keep your body facing ahead, shoulders straight, and maintain this posture as you move away from the wall.

Once your dog is sitting at heel, combine it with the finish—to the right and/or to the left.

MaryBeth stands about two feet in front of Finlay, leaving just enough room between herself and the barrier so he will sit straight at her side. She calls him up to heel position to touch the target stick, and then cues "sit."

Finish to the right

3. **A. Move the behavior along**. Sit your dog, and move in front of him. Hold your right hand at your side, palm toward your dog, and cue "touch." Move your hand back further and repeat "touch." Next, hold your left hand behind you, palm toward your dog and cue "touch," followed by "come-up-sit." As you practice, reduce the "touch" interim cues one-by-one, until you are using just one right hand "touch" to get your dog started, followed by "come-up-sit."

Bruce uses a target stick to move Cody from a sit in front around Bruce's right side, to a perfect sit at heel.

4. **Vary the reinforcement**. Reinforce the best of the best.

5. **Add the cue**. Once your dog is moving on the first "touch" cue, and sitting by your side on "come-up-sit," introduce a finish cue (new cue) such as "around."

    1. Cue "around," followed by "touch" on the right, and "come-up-sit" when your dog is on the left.

    2. When your dog gets up on the "around" cue, in anticipation of "touch," you can eliminate the "touch" cue. Your cues will then be "around" then "come-up-sit."

    3. Finally, cue "around," and pause before cueing "come-up-sit" to see if your dog sits automatically.

Finish to the left

3. **B. Move the behavior along**. Start as above, standing in front of your dog. Extend your left arm back, palm open, held behind your body with room for your dog to turn counter-clockwise behind you. Keep your feet stationary. If your dog needs more room than the length of your arm allows for, use a target stick. Cue "touch," then "come-up-sit."

Using her hand as a target, Michelle trains Cody to do a finish to the left, once again ending in a straight sit at heel.

4. **Vary the reinforcement**. Reinforce the best of the best.

5. **Add the cue**. After several repetitions of "touch," then "come-up-sit," introduce your finish cue (new cue) such as "swing," then cue "touch," and "come-up-sit." As with Finish to the Right, fade the additional cues.

6. **Finish the job**. Finally, for both Finish to the Right and to the Left, practice in new locations with distractions. You may need to re-introduce the interim cues, and you may need to use a barrier of some sort to ensure that your dog's position is straight by your side.

Ring a bell (go outside)

1. **Objective**. This is an approach for shaping your dog to ring a bell to ask to go out (without scratching at the door). Some owners lament that they have difficulty housetraining the dog because he doesn't ask to go out—he just "goes." Here are two possible approaches to teaching the dog to ask. In the first approach, the dog rings a bell with his nose and the second uses a foot target. I do not recommend shaping the dog to ring the hanging bell with a paw, since that will likely result in scratching the door.

Begin by shaping your dog to target the bell with his nose. Start out holding the bell stationary, holding your clicker in your other hand.

Shape any interest or interaction with the bell—starting with the merest glance.

Deliver the treat away from the bell to reset the behavior.

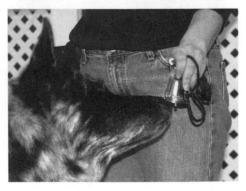

Continue shaping the dog to touch the bell strongly with his nose.

Once the dog is touching the bell, let out the string so the bell dangles.

Continue shaping the dog to touch the hanging bell.

Attach the bell to a doorknob, or hang it next to the door, and continue shaping bell touch. Shape a strong touch so the bell rings.

When the dog rings the hanging bell, click or "yes", open the door, and toss the treat outside.

Every time the dog wants to go out (or you want the dog to go out) have him ring the bell first, then reward by letting him out. He rings, mark the behavior ("yes") and let the dog out. Food reward is optional—for many dogs, going outside is better than food.

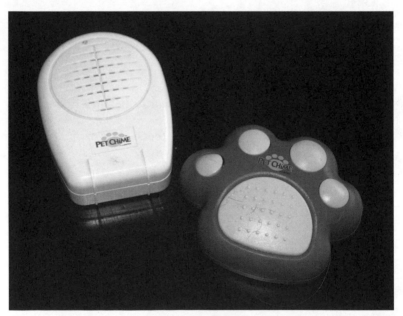

Cool Option—Lentek "Pet Chime" Wireless Remote Control Doorbell®—This clever product consists of a paw-shaped transmitter and a 2-tone receiver. With a flip of a switch, the receiver either sounds a doorbell chime or dog barking. It can be placed in another room, distant from the transmitter. The transmitter can be operated by the dog's foot, or can be mounted so the dog pushes it with his nose. More than one transmitter can be used, making it possible for the dog to "ring the bell" to ask to come in, as well as go out. Several Internet sites have this product, so check around for pricing and availability. Waaaaay cool!

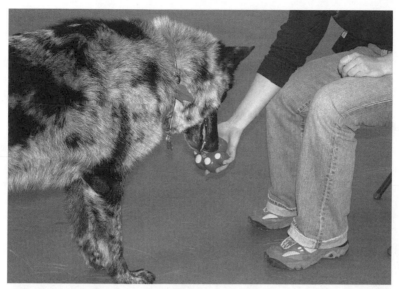

As above, shape the dog to notice and target the "paw." It's not necessary to hold it in your hand, but it's often easier to start there. Alternatively, you can start with it on the floor.

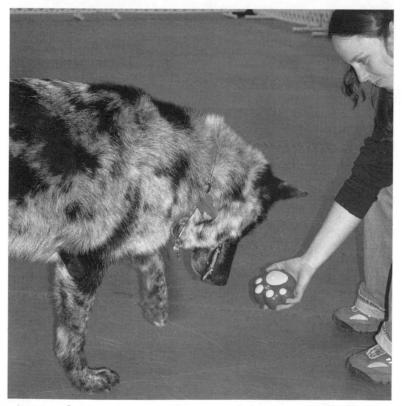

Start shaping any foot movement leading toward the dog pressing the paw with his foot.

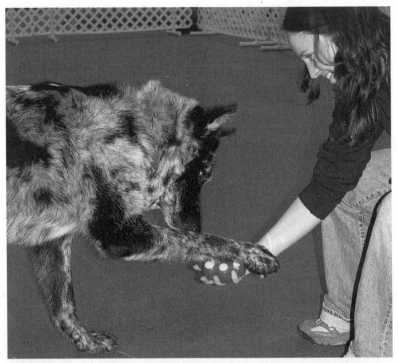

Shaping stronger, more definite touches.

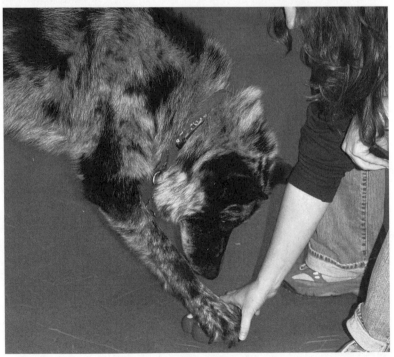

Move the target closer to the floor, continuing to shape strong touches. (Just as an aside, notice the expression on both the trainer's and the dog's faces. Can there be any doubt that clicker training is fun?!)

Move away from the target, until the dog is going to the target, and ringing the bell. Proceed as above for linking the behavior to "asking to go out."

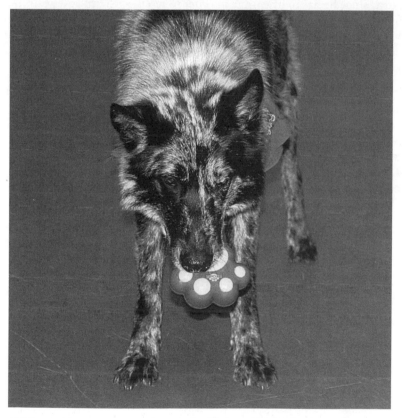

"Ma . . . Did you mean to leave this on the floor?" (You gotta love that face! Logan is a 9 year-old Shepherd, Aussie, Malamute mix—near as we can tell).

Common questions about specific training and training sessions

My dog keeps zoning out. I use a nose-tease to re-focus him, and then I get just one or two repetitions of the behavior before he's gone again and I have to nose-tease to get him back. What should I do?

Before addressing your dog's behavior, first examine why he is disengaging.

- Are you using good treats?
- Is the behavior broken into small enough chunks so your dog can easily achieve success?
- Are you clicking and reinforcing at a high rate?

If the answer to each is yes, you've trained "disengage." When you repeatedly use a nose-tease to get your dog's attention *after he disengages*, you're reinforcing "zone out and I'll bring you back." In other words, *you're* doing all the work.

To fix the behavior, don't nose tease. Wait for your dog to re-engage, click and reward the moment he does, then keep him working with a high ROR. Do this three to five times. Next, since he has to disengage in order to re-engage, and you want him to stop disengaging altogether, once he re-focuses on you, first ask for a behavior, and click that. This sends the message, "It's OK for you to zone out, but nothing good happens until you're working with me again." Be sure to give lots of reinforcement when he stays focused beyond one or two repetitions.

It may be that your dog has a short attention span or there is another reason for this behavior. Review the general types of "workers" on page 221 for further suggestions.

When we're heeling, after I reward my dog, he drops his head or lags for a few steps. Then he comes back with perfect form, we heel further, I mark and reinforce, and it happens again. What can I do so he stays in heel position after I reward him?

This is called the scallop effect (see page 147). The solution is to reinforce your dog for arriving in heel position, then immediately reinforce him for *being* in heel position, and then reinforce once more right away for *staying* in heel position. In other words, increase your rate of reinforcement, sometimes reinforcing every single step for three or four steps in a row. Randomize your reinforcement schedule, yo-yoing around your distance goal and, to avoid scalloping, every once in a while surprise your dog by reinforcing two or three times in rapid succession.

When we leave the house either to go for a walk or to train in a new place, my dog knows if I have food on me or not. He pays attention only when I have food. My inclination is to put a training collar on him and let him know there's a consequence to "goofing off," but I really want to give clicker training a good effort. Ideas?

Yes, several. First of all, don't use food as your exclusive reward. There are plenty of other reinforcers for good behavior, many even better than a food treat. Mix reinforcements, sometimes giving a treat, throwing a ball, or letting him chase a squirrel. Get your dog used to the idea that even if you have food, something better may happen. Next, surprise your dog. Before you take your dog out, put treats, toys, or balls in strategic places so you are able to reward with food or other reinforcers even when you're not "wearing" any. If you are out with a friend, have him hold your treats. When my students do run-throughs in class, I sometimes carry treats for them to reward their dog, or have them mark a behavior and then run to the table for a treat. The message is, "Just because I don't have food on me doesn't mean you won't get a reward for your good response."

I need to practice off-leash for Rally (a competitive event). My dog is outstanding on leash or if I have food. Take off the leash, or have an empty pocket, and I may or may not have him. With my former method, if I lost his attention or he left my side, I'd get him, put his leash on, and "correct" him. Without correcting him, what should I do when I lose his attention or when he leaves my side?

There are two issues, the first is fading the treats so your dog doesn't know when he'll get a reward, whether or not you're wearing a bait bag (see "Reducing food treats" on page 181). This is critical to solving this problem, since your dog is fine off-leash if he knows you have treats. Once you've systematically faded food treats if the problem persists, plan a strategy to apply a consequence.

The moment your dog *begins* to lose focus or leave your side, mark that instant with your punishment marker (PM). Calmly approach your dog, put his leash on, and without saying anything, escort him from the ring or room. Wait 30 seconds, then return and try again, starting one or two stations prior to the point at which you lost him. If you lose him again, do the same, taking him off the course. This time, after his 30 second time-out, have him lie down and wait for your next turn. Do not give him any attention (no reinforcement) while you wait, but don't be angry—you're simply waiting. When it's your turn again, once more start at a point one or two stations before you lost him, and continue. When he stays focused past the distraction, reinforce with a jackpot. In subsequent sessions, build on this success. Be 100% consistent and watch for any sign of spontaneous recovery. (See page 214.)

If you apply this punishment three times and you don't see any improvement, consider possible reasons.

- You may not have laid sufficient training foundation—your dog needs more practice.
- The distraction may be too much for your dog at this point. You need to do more work around this particular distraction.
- Examine the consequence to determine if it is really punishment.
- Explore anything else that may be relevant.

Having worked through the issue in your training class, when you take your dog to new locations, be prepared to do the same thing. Mark the moment he focuses on something other than you, and remove him for a time-out. If you aren't totally consistent, his "disengaging" behavior will be randomly reinforced. This is true, by the way, with any training method, not just clicker. The importance of consistency crosses methodological lines. Clicker training provides the tools to understand the reasons for our dog's "misbehavior"—and most importantly, to recognize where the responsibility lies.

A universal question: My dog _____ [1] when what I want him to do is _____ [2]. I've tried _____ [3], but it isn't improving. What should I do [4]?

There is a pattern to virtually every training issue. Fill in the blanks, and explore each:

1. Consider why he is engaging in this behavior you don't like.

   • What reinforcement does he get from the behavior itself?

   • What reinforcement does he get immediately following the behavior?

   • Might something you're doing be unintentionally reinforcing this behavior?

   The first step to dealing with any training issue is to *recognize and eliminate unhelpful reinforcement.*

2. The desirable behavior—consider reasons why your dog might not be offering it.

   • Does she really know the behavior—has she had sufficient practice in different contexts?

   • Have you worked through distractions sufficiently?

   • Have you systematically faded any prompts, including weaning from food?

   • What is the reinforcement for the desired behavior? Is it sufficient compensation versus the undesirable behavior?

   Without sufficient foundation, information, and motivation, you're swimming against the current.

3. What have you tried that hasn't worked, and why not?

   • Is the behavior getting worse (being reinforced), getting better (you're on the right track, but may need to up the ante), or staying about the same (the definition of insanity)?

   • Examine your clicker fundamentals. Make sure you're providing clear information to your dog.

   Consider your options. Examine all the bullet points above, and once you've determined where the problem lies, make a plan.

4. What you need to do.
   - Eliminate reinforcement for the wrong behavior.
   - Make sure the dog truly understands the desired behavior.
   - Reinforce the good behavior *before the dog first engages in the other behavior.*
   - Stop reinforcing the good behavior *after having engaged* in the bad behavior.
   - Mark and reinforce the desired behavior at a high ROR and with a high value reward (higher value than the "wrong" behavior offers).
   - If appropriate, give the dog the opportunity to do the "wrong" behavior as a reward.
   - Other considerations. When all criteria are met, consider whether negative punishment might be appropriate. (See Chapter 10.) If so, follow the rules.

There are few training issues that can't be solved with this formula.

Conclusion

Our relationship with our dogs is about so much more than training. It's about creating the best, most communicative, positive, mutually enjoyable, and mutually beneficial relationship possible. We are in this together.

Everything about clicker training enhances this win-win partnership with our dogs— a gratifying, rewarding, joyful relationship between the thoughtful trainer and the thinking dog. Could there be anything better for those of us who are devoted to these four-legged creatures that share our lives, our homes, and our hearts? I think not.

AFTERWORD

"Joy is the simplest form of gratitude."

— Karl Barth

Few dog training books have an afterword, but it feels essential to have one in a crossover clicker training manual. I had this manuscript complete and ready to go to the publisher just before leaving on a two-week lecture tour in England. I asked if I could hold off sending it in, knowing that my two-week immersion in clicker training, talking with British trainers and dog lovers would likely result in new thoughts, new knowledge, and new stories. I was not wrong.

Despite the work Keller Breland did nearly seven decades ago, clicker training is relatively in its infancy. The technology and techniques are fluid and flexible. Even after clicker training for twelve years, I still feel as if every dog I train is an adventure, every experience is an opportunity to learn, every interchange with a client, student, or trainer is a chance to discover something new, not just for my own knowledge, but something that might be helpful to another.

Much as lawyers and doctors "practice" their craft, clicker trainers—even experienced clicker trainers—practice the science, skills, and art of clicker training. The more you train, the better you get. Clicker training never gets dull, old, repetitious or boring. As we humans apply the principles and concepts, "practicing" our craft, we share the adventure with our dogs, in partnership achieving our mutually-beneficial goals.

We humans choose what to train—what behaviors to reward and reinforce, what behaviors are ignorable, and what needs to be discouraged. As a crossover trainer, you have chosen, as well, to open your mind, to consider new learning, and to keep learning. Celebrate the process.

Scientific principles are the foundation of clicker training, but science alone does not encompass the relationship and bond we and our dogs share. While adhering to principles of learning, we act with compassion and integrity, never forgetting this emotional bond. Dogs deserve nothing less.

I hope your crossover journey is as energizing, exciting, and rewarding as mine continues to be. I hope you revel and rejoice in making the wondrous, exhilarating, joyful thinking connection with all the dogs in your life, not just now, but into your futures together.

Appendix A

CORNERSTONES AND CHARTS

Cornerstones

Thorndike's Law (page 16)
Behaviors just prior to a pleasant event are more likely to be repeated; behaviors just prior to unpleasant events are more likely to diminish.

Crossover Cornerstone #1 (page 65)
If the task is available, the trainer must be awake.

Crossover Cornerstone #2 (page 66)
Your dog is your partner—let him know when he's "off the clock."

Crossover Cornerstone #3 (page 75)
If you miss the moment to mark a behavior, don't click late.

Crossover Cornerstone #4 (page 80)
Click progress toward the goal behavior. Avoid clicking the same step more than two or three times in a row.

Crossover Cornerstone #5 (page 130)
"Discovered" behaviors are learned with greater retention than lured or molded behavior.

Crossover Cornerstone #6 (page 155)
The behavior you name is the behavior you get.

Crossover Cornerstone #7 (page 214)
The Rule of Three: If three applications of a consequence do not affect the behavior stop, reexamine, and reevaluate.

Charts and Lists

Clicker Training versus Training with a Clicker (TWAC) .... Page 47

Calming Signals .... Page 72

Observation Checklist (Chart of Behaviors) .... Page   85

Table of Possible Training Goals .... Page 129

Speed Trial Record Sheet .... Page 174

Distraction List .... Page 179

Examples of "Punishers' .... Page 205

When, When, and How to Apply Punishment .... Page 206

Appendix B
DEVELOPING YOUR SKILLS

Websites for building your clicker skills

The following websites help build your clicking reflexes. An Internet search may lead you to others.

Start with this one, a good beginning to timing a click with something you're watching. http://www.happyhub.com/network/reflex/

Another site for developing timing. http://faculty.washington.edu/chudler/java/dottime.html

This one is good fun. It gets you started watching for a behavior—dashing sheep. http://www.bbc.co.uk/science/humanbody/sleep/sheep/reaction_version5.swf

This website is one of my favorites. It more closely resembles what you're going to be doing with your dog—looking for a specific behavior among other actions, improving the bird's behavior by clicking properly, with feedback to chart your success. http://www.uwm.edu/People/johnchay/PL06/OC/OC.html

Video Exercises

It is helpful to video some training sessions to build and improve your skills. All you need is a video camera, a dog, a clicker, lots of treats, and an open mind. Video taping yourself working with your dog can reveal errors or tendencies that are hampering your training efforts. The most common errors are:

- A low rate of reinforcement. Stingy clicking is a turn-off. Clicks are informational—keep information flowing fast and furiously.

- Missed opportunities. Failing to click even tiny increments of behavior.

- Clicking the same step, the same frame in the movie, without progressing.

- Not taking advantage of "accidents." Embrace them as a gift.

- Pessimism and skepticism undermine you. Shaping works. Believe it!

Exercise 1.

Video a five-minute training session shaping a behavior. Choose one that involves several steps such as "settle," ring a bell, or lie down under the table. Train in one-minute segments, stopping after each to give the dog a break. Cue the break and remove the opportunity to perform the behavior. After five minutes of training, stop, and review your video. Remove your dog, or play the sound sufficiently low so it won't impact him.

- The first time you watch you'll need to get past things like, "Look at all the clutter." Or, "Oh, no! Do my hips really look like that?!"
- Watch again, this time objectively assessing the impact of each click.
  - ☐ Was your timing helpful or were your clicks unclear and confusing?
  - ☐ Did the behavior progress or did you click one level too many times?
  - ☐ Did you have a high ROR or did your dog lose interest?
- Watch once more to evaluate treat delivery and luring.
  - ☐ Did you lure with your hand or use a food toss as a lure?
  - ☐ Was luring helpful or harmful? Could your dog perform without the lure?
- Evaluate your position, posture, and movement watching for subtle movements to elicit the behavior. Remember, "helping" is unhelpful.
- Evaluate your skills.
  - ☐ Were you ready to click the moment your dog started offering behaviors? Remember, "If the task is available, the trainer must be awake."
  - ☐ Was your hand in your bait bag? Get it out!
  - ☐ Did you deliver, or move to deliver, the treat simultaneously with the click? Hold still after the click before moving to deliver the treat.
  - ☐ Did you talk or otherwise distract your dog's concentration? Were you "cheerleading," as opposed to giving verbal praise *after the click?*
  - ☐ Were *you* focused 100% on your dog and on what you were doing?
- Finally, count your clicks per minute, noting the shaping step you were on.

Exercise 2.

Train another five-minute session, stop and review the tape, again evaluating the following.

- **Clicking**. Is it sending helpful information?
- **Body posture**. Is it neutral?
- **Movement**. Are you stationary?
- **Rewards**. Is the placement helpful? Are you "luring"?
- **Treat delivery skills**. Get your hand out of your bait bag! Concentrate on click…pause…move to deliver the treat.
- **Track the dog's performance**. Count clicks.

Exercise 3.

Work one more five-minute segment, evaluate, and note what you've learned.

Repeat this exercise for several training sessions until your skills are on track. Be honest—no one else is watching. This evaluation is for you and your growth as a trainer. You cannot fool yourself for long, since your dog's behavior is your ultimate evaluation.

Any time your training isn't going as you think it should be, check yourself with a video. We're all human and it is easy to fall into patterns that are less than helpful.

Appendix C

THEY'RE *ALL* TRICKS TO YOUR DOG

Whether you capture, target or shape, you'll find a wide range of behaviors to click, play with and enjoy.

1. Add x and x (see count)
2. Attention (30 seconds)
3. Attention (1 minute)
4. Back up (4 steps)
5. Back up (10 steps)
6. Back up (20 steps)
7. Bare teeth
8. Beg
9. Bow
10. Bounce
11. Bring—see Find
12. Carry
13. Catch
14. Catch flies (snap)
15. Circle object
16. Climb ladder
17. Close door (with nose)
18. Close door (with feet)
19. Close refrigerator
20. Close suitcase
21. Cock leg
22. Conga line
23. Cough
24. Count
25. Cover eyes (1 forepaw)
26. Cover eyes (2 forepaws)
27. Crawl (10 feet)
28. Creep backwards (5 feet)
29. Dance
30. Dig
31. Distance control (6 behaviors)
32. Down (sit & lower)
33. Down (fold-back)
34. Down (frog)
35. Down (forelegs crossed)
36. Down-relax (on hip)
37. Down—1 minute
38. Down—2 minutes
39. Down—5 minutes
40. Down—3 minutes—out of sight
41. Down—5 minutes—out of sight
42. Ears back
43. Ears forward
44. Endorse with chin

45. Endorse with nose
46. Endorse with 1 paw
47. Endorse with 2 paws
48. Fetch paper
49. Fetch tissue from box (achoo!)
50. Fetch (non-food)
51. Fetch (food item)
52. Fetch beverage can
53. Figure 8 (around objects)
54. Find/bring dish, leash, etc.
55. Find/bring remote control
56. Find/bring the (object)
57. Find/bring the (color)
58. Find/bring the (shape)
59. Find/bring the (larger/smaller)
60. Find/bring the other (e.g., shoe)
61. Finish (go to heel)
62. Flip Finish
63. Free stack (conformation ring)
64. Freeze (hold position)
65. Get the (3 object discrimination)
66. Go 'round (chair)
67. Go-out to (touch w/paw)
68. Go-out to (touch w/chin)
69. Go-out to mark (10 feet)
70. Go-out to mark (30 feet)
71. Growl
72. Grumble
73. Grumble (silent)
74. Happy dog
75. Head down (in sit, down, or stand)
76. Head bob (forward & backward)
77. Head nod (up & down)
78. Head shake (left & right)

79. Head tilt (right or left)
80. Heel backwards (5')
81. Heel forward (100')
82. Heel with turns
83. Heel in Figure 8
84. Hide head (under cushion/blanket)
85. Hold—30 seconds
86. Hold up paw
87. Hold a hoop
88. Howl
89. Hug
90. Hula hoop right (5X)
91. Hula hoop left (5X)
92. Jump in the air
93. Jump into arms
94. Jump over arm
95. Jump over a jump
96. Jump through arms
97. Jump through hoop
98. Kiss
99. Lead by hand or wrist in mouth
100. Lick lips
101. Limp (10 steps)
102. Look away
103. Moon-walk (back up in a bow)
104. No (shake head)
105. Open door—pull with mouth
106. Open door—push with feet
107. Open door—push with nose
108. Open refrigerator (add #51, 52)
109. Open suitcase
110. Pack a bag
111. Pick a card (from deck)
112. Pick up a credit card

113. Pick-pocket
114. Pirouette
115. Play dead (side)
116. Play dead (back)
117. Pounce
118. Pray
119. Pull light switch
120. Pull a cart or wagon
121. Pull (blank) on harness
122. Pull up blanket (or pull off)
123. Push ball with nose
124. Push ball with feet
125. Push (object) with nose
126. Put away (3 object discrimination)
127. Read & do (flash card recognition)
128. Recall
129. Recall with sit in front
130. Retrieve
131. Ride in cart
132. Ride a horse (or other dog)
133. Ring bell with foot
134. Ring bell with nose
135. Ring bell by string
136. Roll over
137. Roll over holding ball with paws
138. Rub back on floor
139. Rub muzzle on floor
140. Rub muzzle with paws
141. Run away
142. Sad dog
143. Salute
144. Say "hello"
145. Scent/search
146. Scent discrimination
147. Scratch body

148. Scratch face
149. Settle on mat
150. Shake body
151. Shake hands (left & right)
152. Shake an object
153. Shame (lower head)
154. Side step left (10 steps)
155. Side step right (10 steps)
156. Sit
157. Sit X# minutes
158. Sit 2 minutes—out of sight
159. Sit 5 minutes—out of sight
160. Sit on chair or couch, feet on floor
161. Sit in chair, paws on table
162. Skateboard (ride 10 feet)
163. Sleep
164. Smile
165. Sneeze
166. Spanish Walk (10 steps)
167. Speak (loud)
168. Spin (counterclockwise)
169. Stand up from sit
170. Stand up from down
171. Stand X# of minutes
172. Stand 1 minute—out of sight
173. Stand 2 minutes—out of sight
174. Stand—stranger exam
175. Stick 'em up
176. Tail up
177. Tail down
178. Tail out straight
179. Tail wag
180. Tap floor
181. Tap dance
182. Take cookie from dog

183. Take cookie (182) & give it back
184. Take money
185. Take to (name)
186. Toss ball
187. Toss object
188. Touch target with paw
189. Touch target with nose
190. Turn away to left / right
191. Turn on/off light switch
192. Turn your back
193. Twirl (clockwise)
194. Twist left
195. Twist right
196. Walk the dog (by leash)
197. Walk on forelegs
198. Walk on hind legs
199. Walk sideways
200. Wave right or left forepaw
201. Wave both front feet
202. Wear clothing & hat
203. Wear sunglasses
204. Weave (legs)
205. Weave (walking)
206. Weave through hoop
207. Whine
208. Whisper
209. Yawn
210. Yes (nod head)

Appendix D

Earn Life: A Program of Polite Living for Thinking Dogs

Earn Life is for all dogs—those in training, "pushy" dogs, bright dogs, bored dogs, and even puppies. It's good for virtually all dogs, but is especially helpful with bright, assertive dogs—the ones that are often incorrectly labeled "dominant."

Earn Life is about teaching and requesting mannered behavior. Not at all difficult to implement, it fits easily into your daily routine. Requesting manners doesn't require any special training time. Use the pleasures and rewards in your dog's everyday life—a meal or a treat, a walk, a game of ball, being stroked and petted, chasing the cat, romping with the kids, going outside, to the beach, for a ride, the list goes on. A dog's daily life is filled with potential fun, tasty, enjoyable, entertaining, and pleasurable things to use as rewards.

Why should a dog earn life? Why not?! We require even young children to earn a cookie by saying "please," but dogs are rarely asked to do anything for their pleasures. We ask nothing at mealtime, for example, we just put down the dog's dish. We ask nothing when we take the dog out for a romp, or play ball, or pet and stroke her. Such generosity has three drawbacks. First, it excuses and even rewards pushy, obnoxious behavior. Second, it misses opportunities to reinforce manners. Finally, it ignores guidelines for and boundaries of polite behavior—as important for dogs as they are for people. Think of Earn Life as you would "earn cookie" for a child. The child says, "please," and figuratively, so does your dog.

Say "Please"
Your dog's default behavior (generally sit or down) is the key to open the hypothetical (or actual) door to what your dog wants. This behavior says, "Please."

Earn my meal
Fix your dog's meal, hold his dish at waist or chest height, and look at your dog. Chances are your dog will sit or lie down. If not, hold the bowl over his head so he looks up, likely causing him to sit. You could, of course, say "sit," but the goal is for your dog to respond *automatically*, so wait for the behavior without a cue.

If your dog jumps up, say your LOM, "too bad" or "oops," and turn away. Then turn back and start again. Repeat this until he offers his default behavior without jumping up. Mark his success with "yes," reward him with his dinner, and walk away.

Build self-control

Repeat this at the next meal. When she sits, praise with "good" and start to put the dish down. As you lower the dish, chances are your dog will get up. The moment she does, say your LOM, lift the dish, and start over. Repeat this until your dog remains in position as you put the dish on the floor. Pause, say "yes" or "okay!" and let her eat. If your dog gets up before you release her, say your LOM and start over.

Over the next few meals, gradually teach your dog to wait after the dish has been down for a few seconds, before you release her to eat. Be consistent picking it up to start over each time your dog moves, and she'll quickly get the message, "I 'earn' dinner by controlling myself until I get permission to eat." No verbal cue is involved, just an expectation of good behavior. Your dog earned it.

Earn petting

Your dog asks for attention or petting, nudging your arm. Rather than automatically petting, here's another opportunity to Earn Life. This time use a cue, "sit" or "down," to earn petting. If your dog doesn't respond, say your LOM and fold your arms. Your posture and the loss of attention are "punishment" for not saying "please."

Wait 10 seconds then repeat your cue in a calm, unemotional voice. If he responds, pet him. If he doesn't, repeat this until he does. Don't raise your voice or give a firmer cue—you want your dog to respond to a calm, quiet tone of voice, even if it takes several tries. Once your dog has responded, the reward is your attention, which your dog earned.

Earn "Go outside" or "Go for a walk"

You want to take your dog for a walk...and your dog wants to go. She's excited and happy at the prospect of a nice romp. You pick up her leash and collar to put them on. She's spinning happily, too excited to sit still. But she can—honest. This is another opportunity to teach self-control. You can either cue "sit" or wait for it. When she does, begin to put on her collar and leash. If she gets up, say your LOM and stand up straight. Repeat this until she sits still to have her equipment put on.

It may take several minutes and many tries the first time you do this, but don't give up. Once she realizes that she gets to go outside by simply sitting still for a few seconds, she'll respond faster with each repetition. Soon you'll have a dog that automatically sits and waits as you put on her jewelry to take her for a walk.

Other ways to Earn Life

A dog's life is full of rewards that can easily be used for teaching manners and self-control. The message is simple—you can have all the fun you want if you ask nicely and behave politely. Here are other suggestions, but don't limit yourself.

- Lie down and wait for a treat.
- Sit or stand still to greet you (or guests).
- Sit and wait for a ball to be thrown.
- Sit and wait for the leash to be removed for a romp in the park.
- Come for a treat.

- Sit and wait at the door to go outside.

- Sit and wait to get into the car.

- Sit and wait to get out of the car. This one is a potential lifesaver.

Use any activity your dog enjoys to which you control access, rewarding your dog for earning it by politely saying "please." Far from minding, the truth is that when your dog earns life rewards, your dog likes it, too. Dogs are happiest having a job to do. They like having rules, boundaries, and functions to perform. The Earn Life program is good for everyone—for you and for your dog. Try it. I know you'll like it…and so will your dog.

Sources and Resources

Resources and Websites

Now that you know the difference between CT and TWAC, be an informed (that is, careful) consumer. A simple Internet search brings up over a million sites. Caveat surfer. To get you started, here arc just a few good ones:

All Dogs Academy™. My school for professional trainers and professional groomers. Licensed by the State of New Hampshire Postsecondary School Commission. www.alldogsacademy.com. (800) TRAINOW (872-4669) or in NH (603) 669-4664.

All Dogs Gym®. My website contains information on a wide variety of dog-related topics. In addition to training and dog care information, a new article is posted weekly, along with a monthly newsletter. www.alldogsgym.com. (800) TRAINOW (872-4669) or in NH (603) 669-4664.

APDT—Association of Pet Dog Trainers. A membership organization for dog trainers and owners interested in learning more about training and behavior. A good resource for networking, educational opportunities, and learning about positive training. www.apdt.com (800) PET-DOGS (738-3647).

Click & Treat®. Gary Wilkes' website is filled with interesting articles on clicker training from getting started through becoming an expert. Loaded with insights and information. www.clickandtreat.com. 480-649-9804.

ClickerTrain.com Learning Center. Corally Burmaster's website. Good articles and a resource for The Clicker Journal Collections—important and helpful articles from the early years of the "birth" of clicker training—even if just from an historic perspective, to see how far we've come. www.clickertrain.com.

Dogwise.com. "The widest variety of current cutting-edge dog books and products for serious dog enthusiasts and trainers." You'll find books, sources, and information on virtually anything you ever thought you wanted to know about dogs. www.dogwise.com. (800) 776-2665.

Karen Pryor's Clicker Training (and Sunshine Books). Karen Pryor's website. A source for digital clickers and the latest clicker-related gadgets. Articles, information, opinions, books, and lots of things to buy. www.clickertraining.com. (800) 47-CLICK (472-5425).

Books

The Resources section in virtually all clicker training books contain "the standards"—*Don't Shoot the Dog!*, *The Culture Clash*, and the like. Check out the "clicker training" (www.dogwise.com/browse/SubCatList.cfm?SubCat=Clicker%20Training) section of dogwise.com for a rundown of what's available—41 items as of this writing! Meaning no disrespect to those not listed below, the following are either my favorites, are rarely mentioned in other dog training books' resource section, and/or are important books to read and own.

Training

Clicker Training for Your Horse. Alexandra Kurland, Sunshine Books. One of the best clicker training books out there. I recommend this book regardless what species you're training.

How to Behave So Your Dog Behaves. Sophia Yin, DVM, TFH Publications. I wish I had thought of this title. Aside from the wonderful title, this book is well-written with clear explanations, filled with good training and common sense.

New Clicker Training Manual Volume I & II. Gail T. Fisher (self-published). These are the class manuals we hand out to our students. Available as a resource for class instructors, or for training at home. Includes the common sense advice about living with a dog that dog training instructors want their students to know.

Positive Perspectives. Love Your Dog, Train Your Dog. Pat B. Miller, Dogwise Publishing. Actually you won't go wrong with any of Pat Miller's books. Her head (and heart) are definitely in the right place.

Learning

Excel-erated Learning. Pamela Reid, James & Kenneth Publishers. Clear-cut explanations about learning theory.

Handbook of Applied Dog Behavior and Training. Volume I, Steven R. Lindsay, Iowa State University Press. Not for the casual trainer, this is a scholarly yet readable text for those who want to take their learning to the next level.

How Dogs Learn. Mary R. Burch, Ph.D. and Jon S. Bailey, PhD, Howell Book House. Clear explanations of the science and principles of learning with (mostly accurate) dog examples. A well-laid-out, easy-to-reference format.

Behavior & relationships

Bones Would Rain from the Sky. Suzanne Clothier, Warner Books. A wonderful book about the unique relationship we share with our dogs, and our responsibility for and to that relationship.

Dog Behaviour, Evolution and Cognition. Ádám Miklósi, Oxford University Press. A compilation of the latest research on the title subjects. Chock full of information!

Dominance: Fact or Fiction? Barry Eaton (self-published). It's short but on-point, dispelling the myths about where the dog wants to be in the human-dog pack.

Oh Behave! Jean Donaldson, Dogwise Publishing. I ordered this new book while I was finishing editing this manuscript. I haven't read it yet, but knowing Jean, this book, as well as her others, is worth having.

On Talking Terms with Dogs, 2nd Edition Turid Rugaas, Dogwise Publishing. It's been called a "nice little book"—little, and jam-packed with important information. Read and study this book for a profound understanding of your dog's subtle communication. In the latest edition, you'll see a photograph of three dogs on a sit-stay looking in different directions. This photo is of my students' dogs trained by my "old" method.

Dogs Bite, But Balloons and Slippers are more Dangerous. Janis Bradley, James & Kenneth Publishers. An important book with a wonderful perspective on the misunderstanding, understanding, and prevention of dog bites. Read it, buy it, give a copy to everyone you know (along with this book, of course!).

Periodicals

The Whole Dog Journal. The "Consumer Reports" of the dog world. A monthly publication that takes no advertising. Each issue has something for everyone, with articles on health, nutrition, training, behavior, reviews of toys, equipment and gadgetry-you name it. Each year they do an annual review of different types of dog food-references every dog owner and consumer should have. www.whole-dog-journal.com. (800) 829-9165.

Your Dog. A monthly newsletter published by Tufts University School of Veterinary Medicine, that includes a variety of topics including medical advances, care of your geriatric dog, health, behavior, and relationship information. www.tufts.edu/vet/publications/yourdog. (800) 829-5116.

The Bark. A quarterly magazine that focuses on relationships between people and dogs. Includes review, interviews, essays, stories, and more. A wonderful gift for you and your dog-loving friends. www.thebark.com. (877) 227-5639.

BIBLIOGRAPHY

The following are referenced in the text. Note: Inclusion does not imply recommendation (see Sources & Resources for recommendations).

Clothier, Suzanne. 2002. *Bones Would Rain from the Sky.* New York, Warner Books.

Dunbar, Ian. 2006. "The State of Training Today." *Town Hall Meeting Teleconference.* http://www.raisingcanine.com.

Koehler, William. 1962. *The Koehler Method of Dog Training.* New York, Howell Book House.

Lindsay, Steven R. 2000. *Handbook of Applied Dog Behavior, Volume I.* Ames, Iowa, Blackwell Publishing Professional.

Lindsley, Ogden R. 1992. "Precision Teaching: Discoveries and Effects." *Journal of Applied Behavior Analysis, Number 1,* http://www.fluency.org/lindsley1992a.pdf. (Spring 1992). See also Binder, Carl, Elizabeth Houghton and Denise Van Eyk. Increasing Endurance by Building Frequency: Precision Teaching Attention Span. http://www.fluency.org/PT_Attention_Span.PDF.

Mott, Maryann. 2006. "Dog Whisperer to Critics: My Techniques are 'Instinctual'." *National Geographic News,* http://news.nationalgeographic.com/news/2006/07/060731-dog-whisperer.html. July 31.

Pryor, Karen. 1975. *Lads Before the Wind.* New York, Harper & Row.

Pryor, Karen. 1999. *Don't Shoot the Dog!* New York, Simon and Schuster.

Pryor, Karen. 1996. *A Dog and a Dolphin 2.0.* Waltham, MA, Sunshine Books.

Volhard, Joachim and Gail T. Fisher. 1983. *Training Your Dog, The Step-by-step Manual.* New York, Howell Book House.

Volhard, Joachim and Gail T. Fisher. 1986. *Teaching Dog Obedience Classes, The Manual for Instructors.* New York, Howell Book House.

INDEX

A

adages 4, 5, 191, 231
agility 112, 119, 128-29, 162, 212, 213, 230, 254
Aha! moment 13, 14, 35, 119, 136, 162
alert noise 264, 267, 268
All Dogs Academy™ 303
All Dogs Gym® vii, 2, 303
alpha 199
alpha roll 10
American Kennel Club (AKC) 8, 270
analogies 50, 53, 144, 145, 175-78
Antecedent-Behavior-Consequence (A-B-C) 45-46, 155
arthritis 256
attitude, trainer's 53, 126-27
attention barking 215
attractions and distractions 142, 240
aversives 192, 195, 196, 198, 202, 203, 205, 209, 212, 215, 217

B

Bailey, Bob and Marion 8, 9
bait bag or container 62, 64, 98, 102-03, 136, 148, 227, 228, 250, 274, 287
barking frustration 95
"be a tree" strategy 23, 263
begging 26, 187
behavior
    adding to learned 235
    and consequence 16
    associations with 135, 136, 138, 142
    building 128-65
    chains 81-82, 84, 91, 230, 234, 236, 248, 250-51, 275
    clusters 223, 249
    core 99, 122
    default 168, 259, 300
    defining the 236, 264
    deterioration of a 124, 164, 173-74
    deviations in 145
    discovered 130
    draught 147
    erratic 95
    extinction 143, 144, 187
    fitful 95
    goal 82, 83, 101, 115, 116, 117, 118, 119, 122, 128-29, 173, 220, 235-36, 255
    high-probability 32
    instinctive 23, 29-30, 32, 187-88
    learned 95, 99, 124
    losing the 150
    low-probability 32
    lured 130
    marker 38, 39, 60, 73, 90-91, 204
    modification 185
    molded 130
    prevention 199
    previously learned 234
    reaching goal 76, 80
    reinforced 31, 32
    re-set 224, 226, 245, 248, 251-52, 255, 258-59
    superstitious 99, 120, 121
    target 191, 196, 236, 270
    what is a 81, 161
        word association for 201
behavior-in-development 150
behavioral effectors 17-23
behaviors
    as tricks 127
    clickable 81, 111
    clicker trained 67
    complex 109, 111
    eliminating 210
    extinguishing 116, 144, 187
    fluent 172-73, 174
    foundation 233-36
    fun 126-27
    incompatible 201
    incremental 81, 82, 83-84, 111
    jumpstarting 89, 130-33, 138, 153
    one-action 82-83
    recurring 209
    self-reinforcing 187
    simple 82-83, 101, 109, 259
    spontaneous 209

trained 59, 99, 108
  to capture, target or shape 296-99
  vs. actions ix, 161
bite inhibition 194
body language 50, 71, 84, 89, 130, 180
  association 162
body signals 67, 71, 72, 249
bolt snap 62
Bones Would Rain from the Sky 71-72, 304
boundaries 195
bowl of treats 98
breaks between repetitions 66
breathing 54
Breland, Keller 9, 10, 290
bribe 45
  vs. reward 25-26
bridging stimulus 9
building distractions, distance, duration 228,
  236, 261, 262
bungee lead 63, 269
Burmaster, Corally viii, 6, 116, 303

C

calming signals 72, 84, 197
"Caninepomorphism" 11
captured behaviors
  predictable 86, 87, 231, 235
  serendipitous 86, 87, 120
  typical-but-unpredictable 86, 87
capturing
  advantages to 87
  how it works 86-87
  pitfalls to 87
  with clicker training 87
cause and effect 16
chipmunk cheeks, association with 98
click
  as "acoustic arrow" 39-40
  delaying the 146
  does not end behavior (CDNEB) 91-92
  ends behavior (CEB) 91, 92, 94, 100, 105,
    260
  equals payoff 102
  is for behavior 102-03
  vs. command 41, 42
  what you choose to 148-49
  withholding a 145, 224
  without treat 151, 153-54

click and treat 12, 13, 45, 54, 90, 95, 101,
  105, 123, 144, 151, 153, 154, 158, 160,
  161, 169, 210, 212, 223, 225, 240, 248,
  252, 255, 256, 260, 264-65, 267
click-a-lot 105, 116
clicker-trained dogs 125, 204, 251
clicker 36-39, 41, 64, 101, 227
  as a teaching tool 40, 41, 42, 252
  as marker 73, 226
  charging the 101
  coordination, developing 77
  do's 101
  don'ts 100
  exercises 77-78
  fundamentals 288
  revolution 42
  timing 73-75, 241
  trainer 42, 54, 55, 75, 90-91, 95, 111,
    130, 145, 167, 250, 290
  training (C-T)
    basics 36-47
    concepts focus 44
    knowledge of 7
    resistance to 42, 55
    rules for 75-77
    tactics 54
    vs. training-with-a-clicker training
(TWAC) 46-47
    diversity of 220
    the power of 219
    using punishment in 198-218
clicker-wise 127
clickers 60-81
clicking
  poor repetitions 164
  vs. connecting 69-73
Clothier, Suzanne 71, 304
collar corrections 90
collars 64
  buckle 62
  choke 63
  citronella 198
  for walking 62
  Martingale limited-choke 62
  shock 198
  slip 63
command-action sequence 45
command-based training categories 49

commands 56, 57, 128
  re-training 161
common questions 55-57
  about four steps to trained behavior 164-65
  about specific training and training sessions 286-89
communication 23, 35, 48, 66, 69, 71-72, 119, 132, 217, 235, 256
  establishing 264
  through touch 70
competition-oriented behaviors 236
completing the process 167-81
compound-cue association 157, 162
compulsion, definition of 51
compulsion-praise (C-P)
  training 7, 8, 16, 19, 20, 48, 49, 51, 86, 196
  trainers 52, 54
  with clicker 55
conditioned association 99
conditioning, operant 3
conformation 113
consequences 17-19, 55, 185, 217, 218, 220, 287
  effectiveness of 208
  as outcomes 192, 193, 194, 195, 196, 197, 199, 200, 201, 202, 210, 212, 213, 214
consistency 287-88
contexts 220-21, 225, 227, 228, 259, 288
  changing 224, 234, 235, 237, 252, 255
continuous reinforcement 116
correction 1, 47
  collar 7, 9, 16, 20, 51, 63, 188, 196-97, 203, 216
  leash 41, 188
corrections 7, 8, 9, 51, 54, 55, 86, 90, 96, 127, 157, 184, 197
counter surfing 206, 210
crate 31, 86, 113, 138, 185, 199, 204, 210
create a "third hand" 62, 268
crossing over
  from compulsion-praise training 51-52
  from lure-reward training 50, 52
crossover 6, 10, 43
  as philosophy 1, 11
  cornerstones 65, 66, 75, 80, 130, 155, 214
  definition of 6

experience vii
journal entries 6, 14, 15, 18-19, 27, 33, 36, 38, 43, 46, 48-49, 56, 57, 58, 60, 64-65, 67, 70, 73, 74, 76, 81, 88, 98, 99, 109-11, 113, 114-15, 119, 120, 121, 122, 123, 124, 135, 136, 138, 141, 154, 162, 163, 166, 184, 186, 187, 191, 192, 194, 205, 209, 212, 214, 223
process 48
shut-down 145
students 4, 76
thinking 1
transition 3
cue
  adding the 154, 156, 158, 233, 235, 240, 245-46, 250, 252, 259, 268, 273
  "all done" 66, 67
  as prompt 154, 155, 156
  after behavior 156
  before behavior 155, 156, 169, 225
  control 168-69
  during behavior 155-56
  for variable behavior (CVB) 160
  unclear 177
  vs. command 44-45, 46
  when to 155, 156
  word/signal 155, 157, 227, 245
    changing 162-63
cue-behavior
  association 155-56, 157, 158
    testing 13
  sequence 158
cues
  adding 162, 233
  as rewards 162
  changing 56, 136, 162-63, 234, 235, 245
  conflicting 177
  teaching 143, 234
  types of 154
  using interim 235, 236, 251, 271, 273, 274, 279
cuing
  predictable behaviors 158
  without reinforcement 173
compulsion-praise training (C-P) 7, 8, 16, 19, 20, 48, 49, 52, 55, 86, 196

D

Dead Man's Rule 81

deaf dogs, markers for 39
delay between "click" and "treat" 95
"delimish" 18-19
delivery-related associations 99
deprivation strategies 34
desensitization 12, 13
desensitizing 101
  to presence of food 181
differential reinforcement 116-17, 234, 250, 255
discipline 15
distance 272
  increasing 146, 224, 228, 233, 234, 235, 236, 237, 239, 244, 245, 250
distractions (see also attractions and distractions) 45-46, 57, 69-70, 131, 132, 140, 142, 165, 225, 228, 240, 247-48, 274, 279, 287, 288
  as rewards 234
  building immunity to 175, 178-80, 263
  building tolerance for 141, 142, 143
  introducing 260
  resistance to 168, 172-73
  sample list of 179, 263
  training with 234, 235, 240, 260, 268
  unpredictable 175
dog proofing 185
Dog Writers Association of America 2
Dogwise.com 2, 303
dominance 31-32, 199
Donaldson, Jean 11, 99, 305
Don't Shoot the Dog! ix, 10, 144, 304
double clicking 256
down 146, 157, 159, 235, 251
  training plan for 253-58
  active 253-54
  capturing 254
  lured 254-55
  relaxed 253-54, 255
Dunbar, Ian 9, 21, 166, 168
Duncan, Lee 8
duration, increasing 252

E

ear pinch 20, 55
energizing the lethargic or non-participating dog 133
engaging your dog 221, 226-27, 228

environment 142
  teachable 190
  distraction-free training 221, 222, 223, 225, 228, 240
environmental aids 236
equipment 64
ethics of using punishment 215-17
exercises 70, 77-78, 85, 105-08, 171, 231, 251
exercise-based approaches 44
experiences 221
  prior to crossover 52-53
  crossover dog's 52
  crossover trainer's 52-53
experimenting with behaviors 145
extinction burst 214-15, 216

F

factors to crossing over 49-54
fade targets 233, 234, 236
  how to 244
fear of clicker, strategies for 101
finish, the (go to heel) 236
  training plan for 274-79
first cue 160
fluency 172-73, 221, 223, 225
food
  as an enticement 49, 250
  in bait bag 98, 102
  in hand 96-97, 102
  in pockets 98, 102, 274
food lures 233, 237, 248-49
  rules for using 89-90
  using and fading 235
food treats
  fading 236, 274, 287
  reducing 181
  reducing frequency of 181
foundation behaviors 233-36
free shaping
  voluntary behaviors 113
  vs. targeting 112
freedom 17, 23, 31, 32, 33, 190
frustration in dog 95
futility in dog 95

G

game, random reinforcement 41, 150-54
games 23, 28-29, 60

generalization as learned response 136
generalizing trained behaviors 134, 143, 158, 259
genetic independence 28
getting started 102-08
go to heel 236
   training plan for 274-79
goal setting 64, 223
goals, defining trainer's 235
grooming 254

H
Hamburger Tree 68, 181
hand signals 8, 38, 39, 49, 171, 234, 245-46, 255
hand target 233-34, 244, 274
   training plan for 237-42
handler-dog relationship 51
handler's location as lure or target 89, 234
harnesses 62, 90, 269
head halters 22, 51, 62, 90, 269
heel 146, 147, 236
   sit at 130, 138, 275
   training plan for 270-74
hierarchies 10, 31
hip dysplasia 256
history
   of dog training 7-10, 221
   of breeds 30
Holmes, John 15, 16
hot dogs as treats 61
housetraining 279
human-dog bond, creating 69

I
improving known behavior 161-62, 164
inappropriate attention-seeking behavior 18, 187, 207
inappropriate barking 190, 207
information 23, 30, 34-35, 37, 38, 39, 42, 43, 46, 91, 92, 105, 116, 119, 139, 192, 198, 200, 201, 202, 210, 212, 216-18, 226, 227, 256, 288
in-training contexts 220-21, 227
incentives 17
incompatible behaviors 201
   teaching 189-91, 200, 203, 210, 237
instinct as distraction 176, 178
instinctive behavior 23, 32

examples of 29-30
   as reward 269
"instructive reprimands" 21
interference 130
interruptions 66
intervention 185, 191-92

J
jackpot 124, 126, 147-48, 153, 173, 222, 227, 228, 229, 241, 247, 287
   appropriate times for a 147
   delivery of a 148
jackpots, over-use of 148
jumping up 191, 206, 209, 210, 213

K
Kerhsaw, Elizabeth 18, 84, 147
Koehler Method, the 1, 8, 157
Koehler, William 8, 9

L
language of peace 72
latency 164
laughter as reward 28
learn, how dogs 16-17, 51
learning 215-17
   axiom of 16
   effect of 64
   laws of 16
   opportunity for 68, 220
   theory 11
leash handling 268
leashes 62, 64
life-and-death decisions 217-18
limited hold 158-61, 225
Lindsay, Steven 216, 304
Lindsley, Ogden 172
listening 170-71, 225, 228, 234, 255
location 142, 224, 255
   changing 237, 239, 240, 244, 274, 279
   in-training 227
loose-leash walking 17, 51, 62, 236, 263-64, 270, 273
   training plan for 264-269
lost opportunity marker (LOM) 158-60, 163, 169, 170, 225, 234, 235, 240, 242, 252, 255, 259, 260-61, 263, 300, 301
lure-reward (L-R)

training 1, 2, 9, 16, 19, 21, 43, 44, 48, 49-50, 52, 54-55, 86, 92, 95, 130, 157, 254, 263
trainers 49-50, 52, 54, 76
with-a-clicker 43, 54
lures
directing 88, 89
for agility 88
hand-held 88, 89, 96
target 88
luring 1, 2, 9, 12, 41, 44, 47, 50, 52, 54, 81, 86, 92, 109, 113, 130, 148, 180, 255, 258-59
advantages of 89
how it works 88
pitfalls of 89
with clicker training 89
with food 89, 130, 248

M

management 185-86, 187, 190, 191, 192, 199, 217
manners
pet 128-29
training 186, 188-89, 191, 203, 254, 300
marker 37, 38, 39, 69, 91, 95, 228
behavior 73, 211
event 38, 47, 95, 184, 209
reinforcement 200
verbal 39, 68, 73, 75, 113, 180-81, 221, 235, 240, 259
vs. praise 73
marker-reward combination 181
markers for deaf dogs 39
marking
behavior 146
wrong behavior 73
marks, how to time 148-49
massage 70-71
method 5, 7, 16, 36, 43, 48, 49, 54, 57, 76, 111, 155, 161, 167, 175
choosing a 11
mechanics and exercise-based 2, 44
motivational 1, 9, 16
"natural" 10, 11
non-clicker 52
"pack mentality" 10
previous training 49, 52, 55

methods, using two 54-55
Millan, Cesar 10
Miller, Pat 11, 304
molding a behavior 86
advantages of 90
how it works 90
pitfalls of 90
with clicker training 90
Most, Konrad 7, 8, 9,
motivation 17, 23, 37, 91, 130, 132, 133, 225, 267
conflicting 33, 177
improving 34
insufficient 288
love as 28
respect as 32

N

new "rules" for training 75-77, 78
nipping 207
no reward marker (NRM) 160
non-compliance
handling 234, 242
reasons for 175-78
nose tease 90, 130-32, 133, 134, 138, 163, 258-59, 286

O

obedience (competition) 112, 125, 126-27, 128-29, 162, 167, 230, 236, 254, 270
observational skills 84-85
older dogs 65
operant conditioning 8-9, 217
operant learning 7, 9, 17
opportunistic training 221
opposition reflex, activating 244
orientation 138-39, 224, 239, 249, 252, 255, 262
outcomes 17
outlet for energies 30
overweight dogs, treating 61

P

pack leader 31
pairing reward with click 41
paradigm 58
Pavlov, Ivan 155-56
Pearsall, Milo and Margaret 9
pestering for attention 187, 193

petting as a reinforcer 151, 154

philosophy 4, 11, 48, 71
  and principles 4, 42
  crossover as a 1
  training 215, 217

physical placement (see molding a behavior)

play 17, 23, 28, 33, 34, 67, 95, 133
  as a break 66

"positive" vs. "permissive" 15, 195

post-performance pause 147, 236

posture and expression 136-38, 141, 223,
  224, 239, 249, 252, 255, 261, 262, 301

praise 17, 26, 27, 37-38, 41, 47, 51, 57, 66,
  68, 69, 145, 151, 156, 159, 160, 170,
  197, 225, 228, 240, 252, 255, 260-61,
  301
  to mark behavior 39, 68, 69, 181
  vs. food 26

precision teaching 172

Premack Principle 30, 32-33, 34, 68, 181,
  263

premise 260
  changing/adjusting 223-24, 234, 249-50

proactive strategy 185

proximity 139-42, 224

Pryor, Karen vii, 6, 9-10, 12, 78, 105, 144,
  231, 303

pulling 23

punishment 7, 8, 9, 17, 18, 19, 23, 66, 92,
  184, 192-218, 224, 241, 287, 301
  considerations before use of 198-217
  history 208
  intermittent 210, 211
  negative 18, 19, 20, 21, 22, 23, 47, 160,
    203-06, 209, 211, 212, 217, 235, 261,
    289
  noncontingent 197
  positive 18, 19, 20, 21, 22, 23, 47, 196-
    98, 203-06, 211-12, 215-18
  application of 196-98
  purpose of 210
  reactive 210
  training session 210
  unintentional 194-95

punishment-assessing principles 196-98

punishment marker (PM) 195, 200, 201,
  202-03, 206-07, 209, 210-12, 213, 215,
  287

Puppy Kindergarten 9

Q

quadrants (see also behavioral effectors) 19,
  192

R

rally-obedience 112, 122, 128-29, 214, 236,
  254, 270, 287

random reinforcement game 150-54

rapid-fire conduct and behavior marking 91

reading the dog 51, 60, 71, 72

real life situation 223, 225, 241, 252, 255,
  263
  planning 210

recall 234, 255
  training plan for 244-28

regression 122, 124, 250

reinforcement
  adding variety to 143
  continuous 116, 117, 143, 144, 153
  crossover trainer 133
  differential 116-17, 224, 250, 255
  environmental 208, 236, 269
  history 208
  life 68
  mixing 286
  negative (R-) 17, 19, 20, 21, 22, 23, 47,
    263
  positive (R+) 3, 9, 17, 19, 20, 21, 22, 23,
    27, 47, 69, 178, 184, 193, 198, 204,
    216
  random 143, 144, 145, 150, 152, 153,
    287
  rate of (ROR) 75-76, 78, 105, 119, 139,
    145, 222, 223, 226, 227, 234, 236, 241,
    250, 267, 268, 271, 286, 289
  unintentional 214, 288
  variable 147, 164, 224, 234

reinforcement schedule 124, 143-46, 151
  continuous 143-44
  intermittent 143, 150, 250
  random 143-44, 171, 181, 242
  variable 143, 145, 151, 224, 233, 240,
    262, 273
  variable duration 146

reinforcing
  bad behavior 215
  behaviors in Speed Trial 173
  undesirable behavior 91

wrong behavior 286, 289
reliability, two aspects of 168
repetitions 65, 92, 96, 121, 126, 134, 143,
    147, 150, 151, 153, 156, 157, 158, 162,
    163, 164, 168, 169, 170, 173, 196, 212,
    222, 223, 225, 227, 240, 249, 250, 259,
    275, 286
reprimand 20, 21, 22, 52
    spontaneous 209
resource guarding 200
retractable leads (flexi-) 63, 269
    dangers of 63
reward 17, 20, 23, 24, 25-26, 28, 29, 30, 31,
    32, 33-34, 35, 37, 39, 40-41, 45, 49, 51,
    58, 68, 75, 84, 91, 92, 144, 147, 301
    associations 96-99, 181
    in place 94
rewards
    delivered in situ 92
    high-value 47, 99, 289
    "life" 268, 273
    motivational value of 34
    ranking 32
    self-reinforcing 209
    six categories of 24-32
    vs. bribe 25-26
ring a bell
    foot targeting 282-85
    objective 237, 279
    targeting with nose 280-82
Rugaas, Turid 71, 72, 264, 305

S

Saunders, Blanche 8
Sdao, Kathy 175, 231
scallop effect 147, 273, 286
scolding as reinforcement 193, 195
selective clicking 12
self-control, dogs learning 51, 301
"separation anxiety" 199
settle 130, 234-35, 248, 254
    training plan for 248-53
shaping (see also free shaping) 109-27, 130,
    147, 148, 160, 233, 235, 236, 248, 250,
    252, 270, 271, 274, 279
    behavior 6, 39, 56, 58, 67, 69, 74, 77,
        78, 79, 80, 82, 83, 84, 88, 86, 90, 108,
        109-27, 130, 134, 237, 248-49

cluster 116, 119, 144
process 136, 161, 256
rules of 115-27, 146, 153, 234, 248
"settle" 112, 118
with a target 112
without a prompt 112
shoulder dysplasia 256
shut-down futility 95
sit
    as simple behavior 259
    at heel (see heel)
    capturing 258
    training plan for 258-59
sit from stand vs. sit-up from down 171
Skinner, B. F. 9, 17
sociability 28
sound sensitivity 53, 101
speed equates with fluency 172, 225
Speed Trials 173-74, 221, 225, 234, 241,
    255
spinal problems 256
Spitz, Carl 7, 8
spontaneous recovery 214-15, 287
sports as shaping activities 113, 128, 270
stay 140, 141, 146, 228, 235, 259-60
    sample training plan for 228
    training plan for 259-63
stimulus control 168-69, 222
stress
    avoiding 146, 222
    recognizing signs of 69
Strickland, Winifred 8
symbols 17

T

take a break 65-66, 69, 132-33, 170, 171,
    223, 224, 228, 229, 249
taking food from child or off table 207
talking to your dog 69-70
target
    stick 89, 99, 221, 236, 243, 274, 275-77
        with butterfly clip 270-73
        with duct tape 270
    the behavior, not the dog 199-200
    touching the 102-05, 141
targeting 112-13, 125, 237
    hand 81, 233-34, 237-42
    with foot or nose 237, 279

targets 43, 95, 103, 112, 138, 139, 141, 234, 242
  fading 233, 244
  hand 245
  visual vs. tactile 63
teaching
  "click" to your dog 100
  good behaviors 188-91
  people vii
  responsiveness ix
  wait for cue 170, 234, 240
temperament 49, 51, 53-54, 221
  crossover dog's 53
  crossover trainer's 54
terminology issues 17
test your dog's preferences 24-25
Thorndike, Edward 16, 17
  Law of Effect 16, 34, 153, 158, 185, 194
time frame 158, 173, 212, 224, 252, 262
  varying 146, 271
time-out 18, 204, 206-07, 208-09, 210, 212, 213, 214, 215, 287
timing 73-75, 77, 79, 84, 88, 95, 99, 101, 121, 200, 226, 241, 250
  critique 79
  PM and punishment 213
  poor 74-75
  the cue 155
  two seconds 95
Tosutti, Hans 7-8
touching your dog 70-71
toys and resources 29
trained behaviors 59
  four steps to 128
trainer issues
  in crossing over from L-R 50
  in crossing over from C-P 52
training 304
  all-positive 175
  animals 9
  behavior-marker 16
  boundary 17
  command-based 44, 49, 128, 143, 157
  correction-based 9, 175
  dominance-oriented 52
  informal 68
  marker 38, 40, 43, 44, 53, 55, 87
  mechanics of 71

methods 2-3, 5, 16, 19, 132, 143, 157
  military 8
  new rules for 75-77, 78
  off-leash 62
  opportunistic 68
  partnership 48, 77, 127, 130
  pet dog 8
  plan 64
  police 7
  positive behaviors 64
  positive-reinforcement 200, 215
  regimens 60
  reward-based vs. dominance-based 31-32
  sequence 221
  service-dog 7, 55, 98, 113, 167
  six steps of 223-26, 227, 259, 274
  target 112, 230, 233, 236, 243-44
  technique criteria 11
  tools 60-63
  "traditional" 1-2, 46, 53, 120
  training-with-a-clicker (TWAC) 46, 92
training factors
  combining 143
  intangibles 142
  when to change 143
"Training Game" 60, 64, 69, 78-79, 99, 108
training session 63-67, 249
  ending the 67, 126, 227, 228
  length of 66
  plan 227, 228, 288-89
  typical 227-29
training sessions
  setting up 191
  with real-life simulations 191, 225
  without food 99
Training Your Dog 2, 7, 157
transitioning 54
  from clicker and food treats 180-81
treat delivery 62, 78-79, 99, 102, 137, 223, 227, 233, 234, 237, 251, 266-67
  after click 95
  options 92-95, 105
  plan 91
  to further behavior 90-96
  to re-set behavior 92-93
treat-related associations, preventing 96-99
treating dogs on special diets 61
treats 62, 64, 66, 227, 228

preparing 61
readily available 62
types of dogs 221-22, 227, 286

U

undesirable behavior 184-94, 196, 197, 200,
    201, 203, 209, 211, 215, 288
unpleasant associations 177, 244
unskilled handler 51

V

variability, playing with 148, 24
verbal cue association 162, 234
video exercises 293-94
voice cue 234, 255
Volhard, Jack vii, 1, 9, 11
voluntary action behavior 157

W

Walker, Helen Whitehouse 8
weaning
    off of clicker and treats 180-81
    off of continuous reinforcement 145
    off of food 288
    off of prompts 288
    off of treats 143
Weatherwax, Rudd 8
Weber, Josef 7-8
whiplash 63
Wilkes, Gary vii, 6, 10, 12, 150, 154, 303
window of opportunity 158-61, 165, 176,
    225, 234, 235, 240, 255, 259
work ethic 219-20, 227

Y

yo-yoing 146, 190, 224, 228, 235, 239, 250,
    252, 260, 267, 271-73, 286

ABOUT THE AUTHOR

With over 30 years professional experience, Gail's background in dogs covers virtually all aspects of the field—breeding, showing, competitive obedience and agility, and training dogs from household pets to behavior problem solving to training specialties such as service and hearing dogs. She bred Mastiffs and Vizslas, handling many dogs of her own breeding to breed championships and obedience titles. She has operated a boarding, grooming and training kennel, worked for a professional handler and as a professional groomer. he founded and is President of All Dogs Gym®, the largest dog activity center in the Northeast and one of the largest all-clicker-training programs in the country.

While Gail's direct involvement with dogs has been the mainstay of her professional life, she has made even more significant contributions to the field as a mentor—the "teacher of teachers" and "trainer of trainers." The list of trainers and internationally-recognized experts who got their start with Gail makes a virtual Who's Who in the dog world.

In 1978, Gail developed the first university program for dog obedience instructors, a two-year certificate course she taught at the University of New Hampshire until 1982. This course formed the foundation of Gail's All Dogs Academy™ for Professional Dog Trainers providing the knowledge and skills of humane training to serious hobbyists and professionals.

Named one of the top five lecturers in the world on dog behavior and training by England's Our Dogs Magazine, Gail's entertaining and educational seminars spread the word of humane dog training and a greater understanding of dog behavior to audiences throughout the United States, Canada and Europe. Her commitment to learning and sharing knowledge benefits dog owners, professionals and the dogs themselves.

Author of two award-winning books, several dog-training manuals, a weekly news-paper column, and a contributor to many magazines and publications, Gail has been featured on numerous national and regional network and cable television broadcasts, and was recently elected to the APDT Board of Directors.

A pioneer in the field of interactive doggie daycare, in 1993 Gail opened one of the first interactive daycares in the U.S. Her business model is being copied by dog professionals throughout the country. The knowledge gained from observing dog interaction in such a "laboratory" has been invaluable to her, her staff, and her audiences.

Most importantly, it is Gail's principles and philosophy that energizes her staff, students, clients and participants at seminars. It is her belief and commitment to her mission that all dogs can reach their highest potential when their owners have an understanding of their dogs, when dogs live in a mentally, physically and emotionally healthy environment, and when they are trained.

Gail and her family (including 2 dogs and 2 cats) live in Manchester, New Hampshire. Her family recently expanded with the adoption of Kochi—a rescue dog she used for some of the photos in this book. After the photo sessions, Kochi had found a home with Gail.